Media, Audience and Social Structure

Media, Audience and Social Structure

Sonia Mahajan

RANDOM PUBLICATIONS
NEW DELHI (INDIA)

Media, Audience and Social Structure

ISBN 978-93-5111-514-4

Published in 2015 in India by

RANDOM PUBLICATIONS

4376-A/4B, Gali Murari Lal, Ansari Road
New Delhi-110 002
Phone : +9111-43580356, 011-23289044, 011-43142548
e-mail: sales@randompublications.com,
info@randompublications.com, randomexports@gmail.com

Reprinted 2024

Type Setting by : Friends Media, Delhi-110089
Digitally Printed at : Replika Press Pvt. Ltd.

Preface

In today's world, media has made a very special place for itself in our lives. There is no denial that media is playing a very significant role in making the world smaller. Through various mediums of media whether it is radio, television, newspaper or internet, we are able to connect with large number of people around us. Internet has truly become the need of every individual both for our work and to connect with our friends and well wishers. Media is like a mirror of the society which reflect each and everything about the society to us.

Media has a huge responsibility of conveying the truth and relevant information to the common man. But somewhere this seems to be taking a back seat for media people as they are focusing more on commercialization. Now a days, hot news which can help in increasing the TRP rates of the channel becomes the priority for them. But there are still some ethical people in media who are struggling to maintain the real purpose of it. But media is not just confine to informing us about the world happenings and serving a means to connect with people, in fact it also affects out thinking patterns as well. The way we think and perceive various issues about the world is also shaped up by media. Today everyone especially youth is growing so aware about his responsibilities towards society is because of media.

The present book is an authoritative attempt which discusses the role media in the changing world. It presents an integrated overview of current sociological research on media, audience and society. Specific questions addressed include the media's role in various social processes; how and why media organizations operate as they do; the relationships between media and audience; how to conceptualize and measure media effects and their impact on public opinion; and how to analyze media content. This book will serve as a useful reference tool for media personnel, social scientists, educationists, research scholars and the general audience.

Author

Contents

1

The Mass Media Today

The mass media are all those media technologies that are intended to reach a large audience by mass communication. Broadcast media transmit their information electronically and comprise television, radio, film, movies, CDs, DVDs, and other devices such as cameras and video consoles. Alternatively, print media use a physical object as a means of sending their information, such as a newspaper, magazines, comics, books, brochures, newsletters, leaflets, and pamphlets. The organizations that control these technologies, such as television stations or publishing companies, are also known as the mass media. Internet media is able to achieve mass media status in its own right, due to the many mass media services it provides, such as email, websites, blogging, Internet and television. For this reason, many mass media outlets have a presence on the web, by such things as having TV ads that link to a website, or having games in their sites to entice gamers to visit their website. In this way, they can utilise the easy accessibility that the Internet has, and the outreach that Internet affords, as information can easily be broadcast to many different regions of the world simultaneously and cost-efficiently.

Outdoor media is a form of mass media that comprises billboards, signs, placards placed inside and outside of commercial buildings and objects like shops and buses, flying billboards (signs in tow of airplanes), blimps, and skywriting. Public speaking and event organising can also be considered as forms of mass media.

History of Mass Media

The history of mass media can be traced back to the days when dramas were performed in various ancient cultures. This was the first time when a form of media was "broadcast" to a wider audience. The first dated printed book known is the "Diamond Sutra", printed in China in 868 AD, although it is clear that books were printed earlier. Movable clay type was invented in 1041 in China. However, due to the slow spread of literacy to the masses in China, and the relatively high cost of paper there, the earliest printed mass-medium was probably European popular prints from about 1400. Although these were produced in huge numbers, very few early examples survive, and even most known to be printed before about 1600 have not survived. The term "mass media" was coined with the creation of print media, which is notable for being the first example of mass media, as we use the term today. This form of media started in Europe in the Middle Ages. Johannes Gutenberg's invention of the printing press allowed the mass production of books to sweep the nation. He printed the first book on a printing press with movable type in 1453.

The Gutenberg Bible, one of the books he published, was translated into many different languages and printed throughout the continent. The invention of the printing press in the late 15th century gave rise to some of the first forms of mass communication, by enabling the publication of books and newspapers on a scale much larger than was previously possible. The invention also transformed the way the world received printed materials, although books remained too expensive really to be called a mass-medium for at least a century after that. Newspapers developed from about 1612, with the first example in English in 1620; but they took until the 19th century to reach a mass-audience directly. The first high-circulation newspapers arose in London in the early 1800s, such as The Times, and were made possible by the invention of high-speed rotary steam printing presses, and railroads which allowed large-scale distribution over wide geographical areas. The increase in circulation, however, led to a decline in feedback and interactivity from the readership, making newspapers a more one-way medium.

The phrase "the media" began to be used in the 1920s. The notion of "mass media" was generally restricted to print media up until the post-Second World War, when radio, television and video were introduced. The audio-visual facilities became very popular, because they provided both information and entertainment, because the colour and sound engaged the viewers/listeners and because it was easier for the general public to passively watch TV or listen to the radio than to actively read. In recent times, the Internet become the latest and most popular mass medium. Information has become readily available through websites, and easily accessible through search engines. One can do many activities at the same time, such as playing games, listening to music, and social networking, irrespective of location. Whilst other forms of mass media are restricted in the type of information they can offer, the internet comprises a large percentage of the sum of human knowledge through such things as Google Books. Modern day mass media consists of the internet, mobile phones, blogs, podcasts and RSS feeds.

During the 20th century, the growth of mass media was driven by technology, including that which allowed much duplication of material. Physical duplication technologies such as printing, record pressing and film duplication allowed the duplication of books, newspapers and movies at low prices to huge audiences. Radio and television allowed the electronic duplication of information for the first time. Mass media had the economics of linear replication: a single work could make money. An example of Riel and Neil's theory. proportional to the number of copies sold, and as volumes went up, unit costs went down, increasing profit margins further. Vast fortunes were to be made in mass media. In a democratic society, the media can serve the electorate about issues regarding government and corporate entities. Some consider the concentration of media ownership to be a threat to democracy.

Classification of Mass Media

Mass media could be classified into eight mass media industries: books, newspapers, magazines, recordings, radio, movies, television and the internet. With the explosion of digital communication technology in the late 20th and early 21st centuries, the question of what forms of media should be classified as "mass media" has become more prominent. For example, it is controversial whether to include cell phones, video games and computer games (such as MMORPGs) in the definition. In the 2000s, a classification called the "seven mass media" became popular. In order of introduction, they are:

1. Print (books, pamphlets, newspapers, magazines, etc.) from the late 15th century
2. Recordings (gramophone records, magnetic tapes, cassettes, cartridges, CDs, DVDs) from the late 19th century
3. Cinema from about 1900
4. Radio from about 1910
5. Television from about 1950
6. Internet from about 1990
7. Mobile phones from about 2000

Each mass media has its own content types, its own creative artists and technicians, and its own business models. For example, the Internet includes web sites, blogs, podcasts, and various other technologies built on top of the general distribution network. The sixth and seventh media, internet and mobile, are often called collectively as digital media; and the fourth and fifth, radio and TV, as broadcast media. Some argue that video games have developed into a distinct mass form of media.

While a telephone is a two way communication device, mass media refers to medium which can communicate a message to a large group, often simultaneously. However, modern cell phones are no longer a single use device. Most cell phones are equipped with internet access and capable of connecting to the web which itself a mass medium. A question arises of whether this makes cell phones a mass medium or simply a device used to access a mass medium (the internet). There is currently a system where marketers and advertisers are able to tap into satellites, and broadcast commercials and advertisements directly to cell phones, unsolicited by the phone's user. This transmission of mass advertising to millions of people is a form of mass communication.

Video games may also be evolving into a mass medium. Video games convey the same messages and ideologies to all their users users. Users sometimes share the experience with each other by playing online. Excluding the internet however, it is questionable whether players of video games are sharing a common experience when they play the game separately. It is possible to discuss in great detail the events of a video game with a friend you have never played with because the experience was identical to you both. The question is if this is then a form of mass communication.

MMORPGS such as Runescape provide a common gaming experience to millions of users throughout the globe. It is arguable that the users are receiving the same message, i.e., the game is mass communicating the same messages to the various players.

Characteristics of Mass Communication

Five characteristics of mass communication have been identified by Cambridge University's John Thompson:

1. "[C]omprises both technical and institutional methods of production and distribution" This is evident throughout the history of the media, from print to the Internet, each suitable for commercial utility.
2. Involves the "commodification of symbolic forms", as the production of materials relies on its ability to manufacture and sell large quantities of the work. Just as radio stations rely on its time sold to advertisements, newspapers rely for the same reasons on its space.
3. "[S]eparate contexts between the production and reception of information"
4. Its "reach to those 'far removed' in time and space, in comparison to the producers".
5. "[I]nformation distribution" - a "one to many" form of communication, whereby products are mass produced and disseminated to a great quantity of audiences.

Mass media is distinguished from local media by the notion that whilst the former aims to reach a very large market such as the entire population of a country, the latter broadcasts to a much smaller population and area, and generally focuses on regional news rather than global events. A third type of media, speciality media, provides for specific demographics, such as specialty channels on TV (sports channels, porn channels, etc.). These definitions are not set in stone, and it is possible for a media outlet to be promoted in status from a local media outlet to a global media outlet. Some lcoal media, which takes an interest in state or provincial news can rise to prominence due to their investigative journalism, and to the local region's preference of updates in national politics rather than regional news. The Guardian, formerly known as the Manchester Guardian is an example of one such media outlet. Once a regional daily newspaper, The Guardian is currently a nationally respected paper.

Forms of Mass Media

Broadcast

The sequencing of content in a broadcast is called a schedule. With all technological endeavours a number of technical terms and slang are developed please see the list of broadcasting terms for a glossary of terms used.

Television and radio programs are distributed through radio broadcasting over frequency bands that are highly regulated by the Federal Communications Commission. Such regulation includes determination of the width of the bands, range, licencing, types of receivers and transmitters used, and acceptable content.

Cable programs are often broadcast simultaneously with radio and television programs, but have a more limited audience. By coding signals and having a cable converter box in homes, cable also enables subscription-based channels and pay-per-view services.

A broadcasting organisation may broadcast several programs at the same time, through several channels (frequencies), for example BBC One and Two. On the other hand, two or more organisations may share a channel and each use it during a fixed part of the day. Digital radio and digital television may also transmit multiplexed programming, with several channels compressed into one ensemble.

When broadcasting is done via the Internet the term webcasting is often used. In 2004 a new phenomenon occurred when a number of technologies combined to produce podcasting. Podcasting is an asynchronous broadcast/ narrowcast medium, with one of the main proponents being Adam Curry and his associates the Podshow.

Film

'Film' encompasses motion pictures as individual projects, as well as the field in general. The name comes from the photographic film (also called filmstock), historically the primary medium for recording and displaying motion pictures. Many other terms exist—motion pictures (or just pictures and "picture"), the silver screen, photoplays, the cinema, picture shows, flicks—and commonly movies.

Films are produced by recording people and objects with cameras, or by creating them using animation techniques and/or special effects. They comprise a series of individual frames, but when these images are shown rapidly in succession, the illusion of motion is given to the viewer. Flickering between frames is not seen due to an effect known as persistence of vision—whereby the eye retains a visual image for a fraction of a second after the source has been removed. Also of relevance is what causes the perception of motion; a psychological effect identified as beta movement.

Film is considered by many to be an important art form; films entertain, educate, enlighten and inspire audiences. Any film can become a worldwide attraction, especially with the addition of dubbing or subtitles that translate the film message. Films are also artifacts created by specific cultures, which reflect those cultures, and, in turn, affect them.

Video Games

A video game is a computer-controlled game where a video display such as a monitor or television is the primary feedback device. The term "computer game" also includes games which display only text (and which can therefore theoretically be played on a teletypewriter) or which use other methods, such as sound or vibration, as their primary feedback device, but there are very few new games in these categories. There always must also be some sort of input device, usually in the form of button/joystick combinations (on arcade games), a keyboard & mouse/trackball combination (computer games), or a controller (console games), or a combination of any of the above. Also, more esoteric devices have been used for input. Usually there are rules and goals, but in more open-ended games the player may be free to do whatever they like within the confines of the virtual universe.

In common usage, a "computer game" or a "PC game" refers to a game that is played on a personal computer. "Console game" refers to one that is played on a device specifically designed for the use of such, while interfacing with a standard television set. "Arcade game" refers to a game designed to be played in an establishment in which patrons pay to play on a per-use basis. "Video game" (or "videogame") has evolved into a catchall phrase that encompasses the aforementioned along with any game made for any other device, including, but not limited to, mobile phones, PDAs, advanced calculators, etc.

Audio Recording and Reproduction

Sound recording and reproduction is the electrical or mechanical re-creation and/or amplification of sound, often as music. This involves the use of audio equipment such as microphones, recording devices and loudspeakers. From early beginnings with the invention of the phonograph using purely mechanical techniques, the field has advanced with the invention of electrical recording, the mass production of the 78 record, the magnetic wire recorder followed by the tape recorder, the vinyl LP record. The invention of the compact cassette in the 1960s, followed by Sony's Walkman, gave a major boost to the mass distribution of music recordings, and the invention of digital recording and the compact disc in 1983 brought massive improvements in ruggedness and quality. The most recent developments have been in digital audio players.

An album is a collection of related audio recordings, released together to the public, usually commercially.

The term record album originated from the fact that 78 RPM Phonograph disc records were kept together in a book resembling a photo album. The first collection of records to be called an "album" was Tchaikovsky's Nutcracker Suite, release in April 1909 as a four-disc set by Odeon records. It retailed for 16 shillings—about £15 in modern currency.

A music video (also promo) is a short film or video that accompanies a complete piece of music, most commonly a song. Modern music videos were primarily made and used as a marketing device intended to promote the sale of music recordings. Although the origins of music videos go back much further, they came into their own in the 1980s, when Music Television's format was based on them. In the 1980s, the term "rock video" was often used to describe this form of entertainment, although the term has fallen into disuse.

Music videos can accommodate all styles of filmmaking, including animation, live action films, documentaries, and non-narrative, abstract film.

Internet

The Internet is a more interactive medium of mass media, and can be briefly described as "a network of networks". Specifically, it is the worldwide, publicly accessible network of interconnected computer networks that transmit data by packet switching using the standard Internet Protocol (IP).

It consists of millions of smaller domestic, academic, business, and governmental networks, which together carry various information and services, such as email, online chat, file transfer, and the interlinked web pages and other documents of the World Wide Web.

Contrary to some common usage, the Internet and the World Wide Web are not synonymous: the Internet is the system of interconnected computer networks, linked by copper wires, fiber-optic cables, wireless connections etc.; the Web is the contents, or the interconnected documents, linked by hyperlinks and URLs. The World Wide Web is accessible through the Internet, along with many other services including e-mail, file sharing and others described below.

Toward the end of the 20th century, the advent of the World Wide Web marked the first era in which most individuals could have a means of exposure on a scale comparable to that of mass media. Anyone with a web site has the potential to address a global audience, although serving to high levels of web traffic is still relatively expensive. It is possible that the rise of peer-to-peer technologies may have begun the process of making the cost of bandwidth manageable. Although a vast amount of information, imagery, and commentary (i.e. "content") has been made available, it is often difficult to determine the authenticity and reliability of information contained in web pages (in many cases, self-published). The invention of the Internet has also allowed breaking news stories to reach around the globe within minutes. This rapid growth of instantaneous, decentralized communication is often deemed likely to change mass media and its relationship to society.

"Cross-media" means the idea of distributing the same message through different media channels. A similar idea is expressed in the news industry as "convergence". Many authors understand cross-media publishing to be the ability to publish in both print and on the web without manual conversion effort. An increasing number of wireless devices with mutually incompatible data and screen formats make it even more difficult to achieve the objective "create once, publish many".

The Internet is quickly becoming the center of mass media. Everything is becoming accessible via the internet. Instead of picking up a newspaper, or watching the 10 o'clock news, people can log onto the internet to get the news they want, when they want it. For example, many workers listen to the radio through the Internet while sitting at their desk.

Even the education system relies on the Internet. Teachers can contact the entire class by sending one e-mail. They may have web pages where students can get another copy of the class outline or assignments. Some classes have class blogs in which students are required to post weekly, with students graded on their contributions.

Blogs

Blogging, too, has become a pervasive form of media. A blog is a website, usually maintained by an individual, with regular entries of commentary, descriptions of events, or interactive media such as images or video. Entries are commonly displayed in reverse chronological order, with most recent posts shown on top. Many blogs provide commentary or news on a particular subject; others function as more personal online diaries. A typical blog combines text, images and other graphics, and links to other blogs, web pages, and related media. The ability for readers to leave comments in an interactive format is an important part of many blogs. Most blogs are primarily textual, although some focus on art (artlog), photographs (photoblog), sketchblog, videos (vlog), music (MP3 blog), audio (podcasting) are part of a wider network of social media. Microblogging is another type of blogging which consists of blogs with very short posts.

RSS Feeds

RSS is a format for syndicating news and the content of news-like sites, including major news sites like Wired, news-oriented community sites like Slashdot, and personal blogs. It is a family of Web feed formats used to publish frequently updated content such as blog entries, news headlines, and podcasts. An RSS document (which is called a "feed" or "web feed" or "channel") contains either a summary of content from an associated web site or the full text. RSS makes it possible for people to keep up with web sites in an automated manner that can be piped into special programs or filtered displays.

Podcast

A podcast is a series of digital-media files which are distributed over the Internet using syndication feeds for playback on portable media players and computers. The term podcast, like broadcast, can refer either to the series of content itself or to the method by which it is syndicated; the latter is also called podcasting. The host or author of a podcast is often called a podcaster.

Mobile

Mobile phones were introduced in Japan in 1979 but became a mass media only in 1998 when the first downloadable ringing tones were introduced in Finland. Soon most forms of media content were introduced on mobile phones, and today the total value of media consumed on mobile towers over that of internet content, and was worth over 31 billion dollars in 2007 (source Informa). The mobile media content includes over 8 billion dollars worth of mobile music (ringing tones, ringback tones, truetones, MP3 files, karaoke, music videos, music streaming services etc.); over 5 billion dollars worth of mobile gaming; and various news, entertainment and advertising services. In Japan mobile phone books are so popular that five of the ten best-selling printed books were originally released as mobile phone books.

Similar to the internet, mobile is also an interactive media, but has far wider reach, with 3.3 billion mobile phone users at the end of 2007 to 1.3 billion internet users (source ITU). Like email on the internet, the top application on mobile is also a personal messaging service, but SMS text messaging is used by over 2.4 billion people. Practically all internet services and applications exist or have similar cousins on mobile, from search to multiplayer games to virtual worlds to blogs. Mobile has several unique benefits which many mobile media pundits claim make mobile a more powerful media than either TV or the internet, starting with mobile being permanently carried and always connected. Mobile has the best audience accuracy and is the only mass media with a built-in payment channel available to every user without any credit cards or PayPal accounts or even an age limit. Mobile is often called the 7th Mass Medium and either the fourth screen or the third screen (counting only TV and PC).

Print media

Book

A book is a collection of sheets of paper, parchment or other material with a piece of text written on them, bound together along one edge within covers. A book is also a literary work or a main division of such a work. A book produced in electronic format is known as an e-book.

Magazine

A magazine is a periodical publication containing a variety of articles, generally financed by advertising and/or purchase by readers.

Magazines are typically published weekly, biweekly, monthly, bimonthly or quarterly, with a date on the cover that is in advance of the date it is actually published. They are often printed in color on coated paper, and are bound with a soft cover.

Magazines fall into two broad categories: consumer magazines and business magazines. In practice, magazines are a subset of periodicals, distinct from those periodicals produced by scientific, artistic, academic or special interest publishers which are subscription-only, more expensive, narrowly limited in circulation, and often have little or no advertising.

Magazines can be classified as:

1. General interest magazines (e.g. Frontline, India Today, The Week, The Sunday Times etc.)
2. Special interest magazines (women's, sports, business, scuba diving, etc.)

Newspaper

A newspaper is a publication containing news and information and advertising, usually printed on low-cost paper called newsprint. It may be general or special interest, most often published daily or weekly. The first printed newspaper was published in 1605, and the form has thrived even in the face of competition from technologies such as radio and television. Recent developments on the Internet are posing major threats to its business model, however. Paid circulation is declining in most countries, and advertising revenue, which makes up the bulk of a newspaper's income, is shifting from print to online; some commentators, nevertheless, point out that historically new media such as radio and television did not entirely supplant existing.

Outdoor Media

Outdoor media is a form of mass media which comprises billboards, signs, placards placed inside and outside of commercial buildings/objects like shops/buses, flying billboards (signs in tow of airplanes), blimps, and skywriting. Many commercial advertisers use this form of mass media when advertising in sports stadiums. Tobacco and alcohol manufacturers used billboards and other outdoor media extensively. However, in 1998, the Master Settlement Agreement between the US and the tobacco industries prohibited the billboard advertising of cigarettes. In a 1994 Chicago-based study, Diana Hackbarth and her colleagues revealed how tobacco- and alcohol-based billboards were concentrated in poor neighbourhoods. In other urban centers, alcohol and tobacco billboards were much more concentrated in African-American neighborhoods than in white neighborhoods.

Purposes of Mass Media

Mass media encompasses much more that just news, although it is sometimes misunderstood in this way. It can be used for various purposes:

1. Advocacy, both for business and social concerns. This can include advertising, marketing, propaganda, public relations, and political communication.
2. Entertainment, traditionally through performances of acting, music, sports, and TV shows along with light reading; since the late 20th century also through video and computer games.
3. Public service announcements and emergency alerts (that can be used as political device to communicate propaganda to the public).

Professions involving Mass Media

Journalism

Journalism is the discipline of collecting, analyzing, verifying and presenting information regarding current events, trends, issues and people. Those who practice journalism are known as journalists.

News-oriented journalism is sometimes described as the "first rough draft of history", because journalists often record important events, producing news articles on short deadlines. While under pressure to be first with their stories, news media organizations usually edit and proofread their reports prior to publication, adhering to each organization's standards of accuracy, quality and style. Many news organizations claim proud traditions of holding government officials and institutions accountable to the public, while media critics have raised questions about holding the press itself accountable.

Public Relations

Public relations is the art and science of managing communication between an organization and its key publics to build, manage and sustain its positive image. Examples include:

Corporations use marketing public relations to convey information about the products they manufacture or services they provide to potential customers to support their direct sales efforts. Typically, they support sales in the short and long term, establishing and burnishing the corporation's branding for a strong, ongoing market.

Corporations also use public relations as a vehicle to reach legislators and other politicians, seeking favorable tax, regulatory, and other treatment, and they may use public relations to portray themselves as enlightened employers, in support of human-resources recruiting programs.

Nonprofit organizations, including schools and universities, hospitals, and human and social service agencies, use public relations in support of awareness programs, fund-raising programs, staff recruiting, and to increase patronage of their services.

Politicians use public relations to attract votes and raise money, and, when successful at the ballot box, to promote and defend their service in office, with an eye to the next election or, at career's end, to their legacy.

Publishing

Publishing is the industry concerned with the production of literature or information – the activity of making information available for public view. In some cases, authors may be their own publishers.

Traditionally, the term refers to the distribution of printed works such as books and newspapers. With the advent of digital information systems and the Internet, the scope of publishing has expanded to include websites, blogs, and the like.

As a business, publishing includes the development, marketing, production, and distribution of newspapers, magazines, books, literary works, musical works, software, other works dealing with information.

Publication is also important as a legal concept; (1) as the process of giving formal notice to the world of a significant intention, for example, to marry or enter bankruptcy, and; (2) as the essential precondition of being able to claim defamation; that is, the alleged libel must have been published.

Software Publishing

A software publisher is a publishing company in the software industry between the developer and the distributor. In some companies, two or all three of these roles may be combined (and indeed, may reside in a single person, especially in the case of shareware).

Software publishers often license software from developers with specific limitations, such as a time limit or geographical region. The terms of licensing vary enormously, and are typically secret.

Developers may use publishers to reach larger or foreign markets, or to avoid focussing on marketing. Or publishers may use developers to create software to meet a market need that the publisher has identified.

Influence of Mass Media

There are 3 theories to describe the influence of mass media. The website CliffNotes explains in detail the theories with examine the role that mass media plays in modern society. The limited-effects theory, which was originally tested in the 1940s and 1950s, states that "because people usually choose what media to interact with based on what they already believe, media exerts a negligible influence". The class-dominant theory states that "the media reflects and projects the view of a minority elite, which controls it". It continues by explaining that the people who own and control the corporations that produce media comprise this elite. The culturalist theory, which was developed in the 1980s and 1990s, combines the other two theories and claims that "people interact with media to create their own meanings out of the images and messages they receive". This theory states that audience members play an active, rather than passive role in relation to mass media.

In an article entitled Mass Media Influence on Society, rayuso argues that the media is dominated by five major companies (Time Warner, VIACOM, Vivendi Universal, Walt Disney and News Corp) which own 95% of all mass media including theme parks, movie studios, television and radio broadcast networks and programing, video news, sports entertainment, telecommunications, wireless phones, video games software, electronic media and music companies. Whilst historically, there was more diversity in companies, they have recently merged to form an elite which have the power to shape the opinion and beliefs of people. People buy after seeing thousands of advertisements by various companies in TV, newspapers or magazines, which are able to affect their purchasing decisions. The definition of what is acceptable by society is dictated by the media. This power can be used for good, for example encouraging children to play sport. However, it can also be used for bad, for example children being influenced by cigars smoked by film stars, their exposure to sex images, their exposure to images of violence and their exposure to junk food ads. The documentary Supersize Me describes how companies like McDonalds have been sued in the past, the plaintiffs claiming that it was the fault of their liminal and subliminal advertising that "forced" them to perchance the product. The Barbie and Ken dolls of the 1950s are sometimes cited as the main cause for the obsession in modern day society for women to be skinny and men to be buff. After the attacks of 9/11, the media gave extensive coveage of the event and exposed Osama's guilt for the attack, information they were told by the authorities. This shaped the public opinion to support the war on terrorism, and later, the war on Iraq. A main concern is that due to this immense power of the mass media (being able to drive the public opinion), media receiving inaccurate information could cause the public opinion to support the wrong cause.

In his book The Commercialization of American Culture, Matthew P. McAllister says that "a well-developed media system, informing and teaching its citizens, helps democracy move toward its ideal state."

In 1997, J. R. Finnegan Jr. and K. Viswanath identified 3 main effects or functions of mass media. The Knowledge Gap: The mass media influences knowledge gaps due to factors including "the extent to which the content is appealing, the degree to which information channels are accessible and desirable, and the amount of social conflict and diversity there is in a community". Agenda Setting: People are influence in how they think about issues due to the selective nature of what media choose for public consumption. After publicly disclosing that he had prostate cancer prior to the 2000 New York senatorial election, Rudolph Giuliani, the mayor of New York City (aided by the media) sparked a huge priority elevation of the cancer in people's consciousness. This was because news media began to report on the risks of prostate cancer, which in turn prompted a greater public awareness about the disease and the need for screening. This ability for the media to be able to change how the public thinks and behaves has occurred on other occasions. In mid-1970s when Betty Ford and Happy Rockefeller, wives of the then-President and then-Vice President respectively, were both diagnosed with breast cancer. J. J. Davis states that "when risks are highlighted in the media, particularly in great detail, the extent of agenda setting is likely to be based on the degree to which a public sense of outrage and threat is provoked". When wanting to set an agenda, framing can be invaluably useful to a mass media organisation. Framing involves "taking a leadership role in the organisation of public discourse about an issue". The media is influenced by the desire for balance in coverage, and the resulting pressures can come from groups with particular political action and advocacy positions. Finnegan and Viswanath say, "groups, institutions, and advocates compete to identify problems, to move them onto the public agenda, and to define the issues symbolically". Cultivation of Perceptions: The extent to which media exposure shapes audience perceptions over time is known as cultivation. Television is a common experience, especially in places like the United States, to the point where it can be described as a "homogenising agent" (S. W. Littlejohn). However, instead of being merely a result of the TV, the effect is often based on socioeconomic factors. Having a prolonged exposure to TV or movie violence might affect a viewer to the extent where they actively think community violence is a problem, or alternatively find it justifiable. The resulting belief is likely to be different depending of where people live however.

Since the 50s, when cinema, radio and TV began to be the primary or the only source of information for a larger and larger percentage of the population, these media began to be considered as central instruments of mass control. Up to the point that it emerged the idea that when a country has reached a high level of industrialization, the country itself "belongs to the person who controls communications."

Mass media play a significant role in shaping public perceptions on a variety of important issues, both through the information that is dispensed through them, and through the interpretations they place upon this information. They also play a large role in shaping modern culture, by selecting and portraying a particular set of beliefs, values, and traditions (an entire way of life), as reality. That is, by portraying a certain interpretation of reality, they shape reality to be more in line with that interpretation.

Mass media has played a large role in the way white Americans perceive African-Americans. The media focus on African-American in the contexts of crime, drug use, gang violence, and other forms of anti-social behaviour has resulted in a distorted and harmful public perception of African-Americans. African-Americans have been subjected to oppression and discrimination for the past few hundred years. According to Stephen Balkaran in his article Mass Media and Racism, "The media has played a key role in perpetuating the effects of this historical oppression and in contributing to African-Americans' continuing status as second-class citizens". This has resulted in an uncertainty among white Americans as to what the genuine nature of African-Americans really is. Despite the resulting racial divide, the fact that these people are undeniably American has "raised doubts about the white man's value system". This means that there is a somewhat "troubling suspicion" among some Americans that their white America is tainted by the black influence.

Lack of local or specific topical focus is a common criticism of mass media. A mass news media outlet is often forced to cover national and international news due to it having to cater for and be relevant for a wide demographic. As such, it has to skip over many interesting or important local stories because they simply do not interest the large majority of their viewers. An example given by the website WiseGeek is that "the residents of a community might view their fight against development as critical, but the story would only attract the attention of the mass media if the fight became controversial or if precedents of some form were set".

The term "mass" suggests that the recipients of media products constitute a vast sea of passive, undifferentiated individuals. This is an image associated with some earlier critiques of "mass culture" and mass society which generally assumed that the development of mass communication has had a largely negative impact on modern social life, creating a kind of bland and homogeneous culture which entertains individuals without challenging them. However, interactive digital media have also been seen to challenge the read-only paradigm of earlier broadcast media.

Whilst some refer to the mass media as "opiate of the masses", others argue that is a vital aspect of human societies. By understanding mass media, one is then able to analyse and find a deeper understanding of one's population and culture. This valuable and powerful ability is one reason why the field of media studies is popular. As WiseGeek says, "watching, reading, and interacting with a nation's mass media can provide clues into how people think, especially if a diverse assortment of mass media sources are perused".

Since the 1950s, in the countries that have reached a high level of industrialization, the mass media of cinema, radio and TV have a key role in political power. Contemporary research demonstrates an increasing level of concentration of media ownership, with many media industries already highly concentrated and dominated by a very small number of firms.

Changing Role of Mass Media

With the evolution of digital technology, the role of mass media has been changing at a quick pace. By definition, mass media is any medium used to transmit mass communication i.e. a message created by a person or a group of people sent through a transmitting device to a large audience or market. Until recently mass media was clearly defined as comprising of eight industries: books, newspapers, magazines, recordings, radio, movies, television and the internet.

The continuing explosion of digital communication technology has raised new questions about the inclusion of cell phones, video and computer games in mass media. Currently, marketers and advertisers are planning to tap into satellites and broadcast commercials and advertisements directly to millions of cell phones, unsolicited by the phone's user. Advertisers are looking into placing advertisements as well as incorporating product placement into the video games as well.

Mass media has the potential to play a key role in developing a culture of peace and non-violence. Unfortunately, it has failed to live up to its potential. To the contrary, it has not only almost completely ignored the culture of peace and non-violence, but also it privileges news of the culture of war and violence. In fact, it appears as if a campaign or propaganda has been promulgated in the mass media in order to justify political policies of militarism. It has been used to increase publicity in recent decades for the myth that war and violence are intrinsic to human nature.

The present situation can be compared to the earlier use of racist myths to justify slavery and colonialism in mid-19th and mid-20th centuries as a last-resort effort by those who had a vested interest in slavery and colonialism. That was their last effort to defend these institutions by appealing to the vulnerable belief systems of individual psychology at a time when they could no longer justify the institutions by economic or political arguments. If this is correct, even for certain sections of the media, the struggle for culture of peace in the mass media needs to receive top priority and careful strategy.

It has been observed in recent past, during a violent incident, the media goes full-fledged reporting and covering it live. However, the same cannot be said about a peaceful but important event. The media has to remember that it influences how their audiences think and behave. In fact, mass media plays a crucial role in forming and reflecting public opinion, connecting the world to individuals and reproducing the self- image of society.

There is a complex interaction between the media and society, with the media on generating information from a network of relations and influences and with the individual interpretations and evaluations of the information provided, as well as generating information outside of media contexts. Thus, the consequences and ramifications of the mass media relate not merely to the way newsworthy events are perceived, but also to a multitude of cultural influences that operate through the media.

The ability of the media to reach a wide audience with a strong and influential message has the potential to have a strong social and cultural impact upon society. Marshall McLuhan uses the phrase "the medium is the message" as a means of explaining how the distribution of a message can often be more important than content of the message itself.

It is through the persuasiveness of influential media such as television, radio and print media that they have been largely responsible for structuring people's daily lives and routines. Television broadcasting has a large amount of control over the content society watches and the times in which it is viewed. The internet creates a space for more diverse political opinions, social and cultural viewpoints and a heightened level of consumer participation.

Studies of various commercials, advertising and voter campaigns prove that media influence behavior. In the 20th century, aggressive media attention and negative coverage of trials involving celebrities like Roscoe Fatty Arbuckle or Michael Jackson influenced the general public's opinion, before the trials effectively started.

Though the media could have an effect on people's behavior, it is not necessarily always the case. Many copycat murders, suicides and other violent acts nearly always happen in abnormal upbringings. Violent, emotionally neglectful or aggressive environments influence behavior more than watching certain programs, films or listening to certain music.

Just because an audience sees acts of violence in media, this does not mean they will actually commit them. Of the millions of people who watch violent films, only a small number have carried out acts of violence as a direct result. People regularly exposed to violent media usually grow up to be completely normal people. If there are any effects from media, they only affect a very small number of people. So, there also develops a case where it is wrong to always blindly blame the media because people are not copycats, instead we should be aware of someone mental state and take other factors into account before making such claims.

There are other social and cultural factors in criminal acts in which the media are not the basic influence. Actually, there is no such thing called violence in the media that either could or could not cause violence. It is the social factors and background that make some people consume media in specific way. There is no connection between exposure to media violence and real life violence, because humans are not copycats and can realize what is wrong and what is right. Although some research claims that heavy exposure to media violence can lead to more aggressive behavior, it has been suggested that exposure alone does not cause a person to commit crimes.

Often, there are demands for the banning of certain songs or the labeling of obscene albums. Such demands are put forward by people with political objectives. The public is bribed with good radio, television and newspapers into an acceptance of the biased, the misleading, and the status quo. The media are, thus, not crude agents of propaganda, but are those who organize public understanding.

However, the overall interpretations they provide in the long run are those most preferred by, and least challenging to, those with economic power. It cannot be denied that the mass media play an agenda-setting function as people tend to share the media's composite definition of what is important.

Although a sizable portion of mass media offerings particularly news, commentaries, documentaries, and other informational programmes deal with highly controversial subjects, the major portion of mass media offerings are designed to serve an entertainment function. These programmes tend to avoid controversial issues and reflect beliefs and values sanctified by mass audience.

Such programmes have the potential to make individuals 'irrational victims of false wants' that are thrust upon them by corporations through both the advertising in the media and through the individualist consumption culture it promulgates. Thus, the modern media train the young for consumption. It would not be wrong to state that 'leisure had ceased to be the opposite of work, and had become a preparation for it.'

Again, there is a threat of media bringing hyper-reality i.e. projecting more than what the reality is. The case of O.J. Simpson is an example. Another threat arises from self-censorship by members of the media in the interests of the owner, or in the interests of their careers. The two-way relationship between mass media and public opinion is now beginning to change, especially after the advent of new technologies such as blogging.

References

Blanchard, Margaret A. (1998). *History of the mass media in the United States: an encyclopedia*. Fitzroy Dearborn.

Fourie, Pieter J. (2008). *Media Studies: Media History, Media and Society*. Juta and Company.

Lorimer, Rowland & Scannell, Patty (1994). *Mass communications: a comparative introduction*. Manchester University Press. pp. 26–27.

Martin, James B. (2002). *Mass Media: a bibliography with indexes*. Nova.

2

Media-Audience Relationship

A media audience may be as small as one person reading a magazine or as large as billions of people around the world watching events, like 9/11, unfold live on television. Audiences have a complex relationship with the products they consume. Media producers intend audiences to read their product in a certain way, but in actual fact everyone 'reads' and enjoys a product differently due to the individual's background and lifestyle.

Media audiences may be consuming different types of media at any one time (such as listening to an iPod, watching TV, chatting on the Internet) and be engaging at different levels – for example, the television may be turned on whilst a family has dinner.

Media consumers are organised into identified groups (based on such things as lifestyle or earning power) by producers, broadcasters, and advertisers who can then target consumers.

The relationship between media and audience is the media the most important operations of a relationship. In the current fierce competition in the media, as the media audience the focal point of, has become a fact beyond reproach.

Media and the Methods of Dissemination

The printed medium (i.e. books, texts, scripts) enables the end user (audience) to use their own imagination and fill in the blanks for themselves. This gives every audience member a completely unique and original experience based on the limits of their own intellect and application of it in the areas of creativity. This can however lead to them feeling disappointed when viewing the same basic story in another medium. When a book is transposed onto the big screen (cinema) the audience member is then finding themselves in the position of having to accept the film director's interpretation of it. The Director, Producer and Script Writer now have control of the project, which in turn, affects how the characters look, the backdrops/settings and locations used. This is also furthered by the choice of lighting and moods portrayed by incidental music and so forth. A screen adaptation of a book or short story can change so much that it is sometimes almost unrecognisable from the original printed version from whence it was derived. The use of existing and new dialogue in the transition from book to film is often one of the key areas that people who are familiar with the original written piece find that they are left feeling cheated. It must be understood though that the two mediums are completely different and have to use different sets of rules in applying the craft to produce a best seller as opposed to a box office hit. It is therefore understandable that fans of the written work may not like the film version of that 'special book'. The film fan however who sees the film prior to reading the book may experience different opinions on the transposition. The enjoyment of the film may then inspire him/her to seek out the book from which the film was based. This in turn gives the audience member a new angle to which they approach the book, as they will now have a mental picture of the characters and sets gained from the viewing of the film. This ultimately limits or controls the amount of personal imagination that can be exercised in their overall interreaction with the printed version.

A book that is transposed to radio can more often than not adhere more closely to the original script. This medium relies on people's imagination nearly as much as the printed word. The use of sound effects and music are used to paint a picture of mood and tempo. This still gives the audience the opportunity to listen and get a feel for what is happening but still enables them the input of their own imagination to give characters faces and make locations seem real to them. A radio play also lends itself to the almost seamless transfer to webcasting.

Webcasting suits both spoken word and musical transmissions and can be accessed at anytime by the audience with the use of computers and/or convergent technologies. This new medium give the audience the opportunity to choose when to listen and also the opportunity to record or even transfer to other technologies for playback at a later time such as use on an iPod. The audience is now also able to discuss the show/play not only with other fans on message boards and discussion groups on the internet but also in many cases with the actors and directors and producers of the show themselves, thus enriching and adding value to the listening experience. Previous generations of listeners may have discussed radio plays and television soap operas with friends and work colleagues as a form of social interaction but never to the extent that we are seeing today. The high adoption rate of convergent technology amongst the younger generation has changed the way film/video/music etc. is accessed and the worlds largest companies and broadcasters are continually looking and reviewing the way that they use these mediums to feed the ever hungry audiences the diet of media they desire.

News items are always in demand from audiences all over the world and the hunger for news will never cease. The audience experience depends on how the news is received, a picture accompanying an article on children starving in Africa will usually not have the same impact as viewing the same child on television with the sound recording of him/her crying in pain from the situation they are in. It could be said that the reporting of news on the television of wars, starving children and shootings desensitises the audience and they become numb to the atrocities of the world. It then follows on that if this is so only the most horrific, gruesome and abhorrent news items now actually shock or make the audience think or react to items. If this is the case it could be said that the effects on audience will eventually lead to the collapse of moral standards. The reporting of graphic images of wounded and dead soldiers during the Vietnam war on television desensitised audiences and ultimately gave Horror film audiences an appetite for gore which film makers served up in the wave of blood and gore Horror films that post dated that period.

News items that were once only broadcast through the news programmes of television and radio stations now make ready use of all the technologies available. People (audiences) are also not only the receivers of news, but they have; through the use of convergent technologies, become news machines themselves. It is now not uncommon for a 'person on the street' to witness a newsworthy event unfolding before their very eyes, this can be recorded on video phones for example and within minutes be uploaded onto internet websites like YouTube. This takes away governments and broadcasters ability to edit or censor items of news. People all over the world are becoming empowered, thus enabling them to broadcast stories that might otherwise be suppressed to a global audience. This use of convergent technology also allows the media to be used in the narrowest of narrowcasting when an item may be sent to just one person.

Audiences will always seek (if not demand) the best possible experience when using the media for information or pleasure. The human brain feeds off 'experience', sight, sound, emotion and a host of intellectual and sensory mores need to be satisfied. This drive and search pushes the boundaries to which the media and entertainment industries constantly try to meet. 'There is no substitute for being there'. At an Ultimate Fighting competition the audience not only experience the buzz of being in the crowd but also the smells of the hotdogs and beer perhaps. The smell of sweat and the sounds of men physically fighting each other. This does not give you the same feeling if viewed on television or on a webcam. This is barbarism and you are experiencing it at first hand - you could almost be at the Coliseum in Rome in another time! Any true sports fan or music fan will tell you the same story, "A live match or concert cannot be beaten". You can shout encouragement at your sporting heroes, abuse the other team and fans or sing along to your favourite band. Yes, you can shout at the TV but it won't respond or react.

In today's world we have the greatest choice of channels of communications to choose from than at any other time in history. It has never been easier for the individual or broadcasting giant to reach its audience. The true challenge still remains the same today, as it did when the first radio message was transmitted and the first book printed; and that is ensuring that the right message is delivered to the right audience and the objectives of the message are received and meet with the audience's expectations. Until that science is perfected the media in all its incarnations will continue to experiment with technologies both old and new to satisfy its audience.

Audience Theory

Audience theory is an element of thinking that developed within academic literary theory and cultural studies.

With a specific focus on rhetoric, some, such as Walter Ong, have suggested that the audience is a construct made up by the rhetoric and the rhetorical situation the text is addressing. Others, such as Ruth Mitchell and

Mary Taylor have said writers and speakers actually can target their communication to address a real audience. Some others like Ede and Lunsford try to mingle these two approaches and create situations where audience is "fictionalized," as Ong would say, but in recognition of some real attributes of the actual audience.

There is also a wide range of media theory and communication studies theories about the audience's role in any kind of mediated communication. A sub-culturally focussed and Marxism-inflected take on the subject arose as the 'New audience theory' or 'Active audience theory' from the Centre for Contemporary Cultural Studies during the 1980s.

Hypodermic Needle Model

The hypodermic needle model (also known as the hypodermic-syringe model, transmission-belt model, or magic bullet theory) is a model of communications suggesting that an intended message is directly received and wholly accepted by the receiver. The model is rooted in 1930s behaviorism and is largely considered obsolete today.

Concept

The "Magic Bullet" or "Hypodermic Needle Theory" of direct influence effects was not as widely accepted by scholars as many books on mass communication indicate. The magic bullet theory was not based on empirical findings from research but rather on assumptions of the time about human nature. People were assumed to be "uniformly controlled by their biologically based 'instincts' and that they react more or less uniformly to whatever 'stimuli' came along". The "Magic Bullet" theory graphically assumes that the media's message is a bullet fired from the "media gun" into the viewer's "head". Similarly, the "Hypodermic Needle Model" uses the same idea of the "shooting" paradigm. It suggests that the media injects its messages straight into the passive audience. This passive audience is immediately affected by these messages. The public essentially cannot escape from the media's influence, and is therefore considered a "sitting duck". Both models suggest that the public is vulnerable to the messages shot at them because of the limited communication tools and the studies of the media's effects on the masses at the time.

Later developments

The phrasing "hypodermic needle" is meant to give a mental image of the direct, strategic, and planned infusion of a message into an individual. But as research methodology became more highly developed, it became apparent that the media had selective influences on people.

The most famous incident often cited as an example for the hypodermic needle model was the 1938 broadcast of The War of the Worlds and the subsequent reaction of widespread panic among its American mass audience. However, this incident actually sparked the research movement, led by Paul Lazarsfeld and Herta Herzog, that would disprove the magic bullet or hypodermic needle theory, as Hadley Cantril managed to show that reactions to the broadcast were, in fact, diverse, and were largely determined by situational and attitudinal attributes of the listeners.

Lazarsfeld disproved the "Magic Bullet" theory and "Hypodermic Needle Model Theory" through elections studies in "The People's Choice". Lazarsfeld and colleagues executed the study by gathering research during the election of Franklin D. Roosevelt in 1940. The study was conducted to determine voting patterns and the relationship between the media and political power. Lazarsfeld discovered that the majority of the public remained unfazed by propaganda surrounding Roosevelt's campaign. Instead, interpersonal outlets proved more influential than the media. Therefore, Lazarsfeld concluded that the effects of the campaign were not all powerful to the point where they completely persuaded "helpless audiences", a claim that the Magic Bullet, Hypodermic Needle Model, and Lasswell asserted. These new findings also suggested that the public can select which messages affect and don't affect them.

Lazarsfeld's debunking of these models of communication provided the way for new ideas regarding the media's effects on the public. Lazarsfeld introduced the idea of the two step flow model of communication in 1944. Elihu Katz contributed to the model in 1955 through studies and publications. The two step flow model assumes that ideas flow from the mass media to opinion leaders and then to the greater public. They believed the message of the media to be transferred to the masses via this opinion leadership. Opinion leaders are categorized as individuals with the best understanding of media content and the most accessibility to the media as well. These leaders essentially take in the media's information, and explain and spread the media's messages to others.

Thus, the two step flow model and other communication theories suggest that the media does not directly have an influence on viewers anymore. Instead, interpersonal connections and even selective exposure play a larger role in influencing the public in the modern age.

Two-step Flow of Communication

The two-step flow of communication or Multistep Flow Model, says that most people form their opinions under the influence of opinion leaders, that in turn are influenced by the mass media. So according to this model, ideas flow from mass media to opinion leaders, and from them to a wider population.

Also known as the Multistep Flow Model is a theory based on a 1940s study on social influence that states that media effects are indirectly established through the personal influence of opinion leaders. The majority of people receive much of their information and are influenced by the media secondhand, through the personal influence of opinion leaders.

Concept

The Multistep Flow Model says that most people form their opinions based on opinion leaders that influence the media. Opinion leaders are those initially exposed to a specific media content, and who interpret it based on their own opinion. They then begin to infiltrate these opinions through the general public who become "opinion followers". These "opinion leaders" gain their influence through more elite media as opposed to mainstream mass media. In this process, social influence is created and adjusted by the ideals and opinions of each specific "elite media" group, and by these media group's opposing ideals and opinions and in combination with popular mass media sources. Therefore, the leading influence in these opinions is primarily a social persuasion.

The two-step flow of communication model hypothesizes that ideas flow from mass media to opinion leaders, and from them to a wider population. It was first introduced by sociologist Paul Lazarsfeld et al. in 1944 and elaborated by Elihu Katz and Lazarsfeld in 1955 and subsequent publications. Lowery and DeFleur argue the book was much more than a simple research report: it was an effort to interpret the authors' research within a framework of conceptual schemes, theoretical issues, and research findings drawn broadly from the scientific study of small groups Unlike the hypodermic needle model, which considers mass media effects to be direct, the two-step flow model stresses human agency.

According to Lazarsfeld and Katz, mass media information is channeled to the "masses" through opinion leadership. The people with most access to media, and having a more literate understanding of media content, explain and diffuse the content to others.

Based on the two-step flow hypothesis, the term "personal influence" came to illustrate the process intervening between the media's direct message and the audience's reaction to that message. Opinion leaders tend to be similar to those they influence—based on personality, interests, demographics, or socio-economic factors. These leaders tend to influence others to change their attitudes and behaviors. The two-step theory refined the ability to predict how media messages influence audience behavior and explains why certain media campaigns do not alter audiences' attitudes. This hypothesis provided a basis for the multi-step flow theory of mass communication.

Paul Lazarsfeld and Elihu Katz are considered to be the founders of functional theory and their book *Personal Influence* is considered to be the handbook to the theory.

One of the first to embark on Communications research, was the first to introduce the difference between 'administrative research' and 'critical research' in regards to the media. Critical research he believed, criticizes the media institutions themselves for the perspective ways they serve dominant social groups. Critical research favors interperspective and inductive methods of inquiry. Lazarsfeld's study of the 1940 presidential election was published as The People's Choice. During the research revealed information about the psychological and social processes that influence voting decisions. The study also uncovered an influence process that Lazarsfeld called "opinion leadership." He concluded that there is a multistep flow of information from the mass media to persons who serve as opinion leaders which then is passed on to the general public. He called this communication process the "two-step flow of communication."

A professor in the School for Communication at the University of Pennsylvania collaborated in 1955 with Lazarsfeld, in research to observe the flow of influence at the intersections of mass and interpersonal communication and wrote their book Personal Influence Katz pursued Lazarfeld's research in a study of the flow of information. This is the basis of Personal Influence. Katz and Lazarsfeld concluded that: ... the traditional image of the mass persuasion process must make room for 'people' as intervening factors between the stimuli of the media and resultant opinions, decisions, and actions."

The presidential election 1940 questioned as to whether President Franklin Roosevelt would seek his third term in office. Funded by grants from the Rockefeller Foundation, Life magazine, and the pollster Elmo Roper, Columbia's Office of Radio Research conducted a new kind of study of voting. It was based on a panel study of 2,400 voters in Erie County, Ohio. Paul Lazarsfeld, Bernard Berelson, and Hazel Gaudet supervised 15 interviewers, who from May–October interviewed the strategically selected 2,400 members of the community several different times in order to document their decision making process during the campaign. They focused on what factors would influence their decisions as the campaign progressed. The People's Choice, a book based on this study presented the theory of "the two-step flow of communications," which later came to be associated with the so-called "limited effects model" of mass media: the idea that ideas often flow from radio and print to local "opinion leaders" who in turn pass them on to those with more limited political knowledge "opinion followers." The conclusion of the research explained that sometimes person to person communication can be more effective than traditional media mediums such as newspaper, TV, radio etc. This idea developed further in the book Personal Influence.

In 1944, Paul Lazarsfeld contacted McFadden Publications in regards to his first book, The People's Choice. The two collaborated forming a mutually beneficial partnership in which Macfadden saw a way to financially profit from advertising to the female population and Lazarsfeld saw a way to gain more information on social influence . Out of this came the study conducted by the Bureau of Applied Social Research in which 800 female residents of Decatur, Illinois, where interviewed through panel interviews to discover what and who primarily influenced their decision making. Lazarsfeld worked with Robert Merton and thus hired C. Wright Mills to head the study. Another part of the research team, Thelma Ehrlich Anderson, trained local Decatur women to administer surveys to targeted women in town. By 1955. the Decatur study was published as part of Elihu Katz and Lazarsfeld's book Personal Influence. The book concluded that ultimately, face to face interaction is more influential than traditional media influence and thus confirmed the two-step flow model of communication.

Criticisms

The original two-step flow hypothesis—that ideas flow from the media to opinion leaders and then to less active sections of the population—has been criticized and negated by myriad consequent studies. Findings from Deutschmann and Danielson assert, "we would urge that the Katz-Lazarsfeld two-stage flow hypothesis, as a description of the initial information process, be applied to mass communication with caution". They find substantial evidence that initial mass media information flows directly to people on the whole and is not relayed by opinion leaders.

Furthermore, the two-step hypothesis does not adequately describe the flow of learning. Everett Rogers' "Diffusion of Innovations" cites one study in which two-thirds of respondents accredited their awareness to the mass media rather than face-to-face communication. Similarly, critics argue that most of Lazarsfeld's findings pertain to learning factors involved with general media habits rather than the learning of particular information. Both findings suggest a greater prevalence of a one-step flow of communication.

However, Lazarsfeld's two-step hypothesis is an adequate description to understand the media's influence on belief and behavior. Troldahl finds that media exposure is a first step to introduce discussion, at which point opinion leaders initiate the second-step flow. These findings also realize opinion leaders decisive role in the balance theory, which suggests that people are motivated to keep consistency among their current beliefs and opinions. If a person is exposed to new observations that are inconsistent with present beliefs, he or she is thrown into imbalance. This person will then seek advice from their opinion leader, to provide them with additional cognitions to bring them back into balance.

Uses and Gratifications Theory

Uses and Gratifications Theory is an approach to understanding why people actively seek out specific media outlets and content for gratification purposes. The theory discusses how users proactively search for media that will not only meet a given need but enhance knowledge, social interactions and diversion .

It assumes that members of the audience are not passive but take an active role in interpreting and integrating media into their own lives. The theory also holds that audiences are responsible for choosing media to meet their needs. The approach suggests that people use the media to fulfill specific gratifications. This theory would then imply that the media compete against other information sources for viewers' gratification.

Stages of the Theory

The Uses and Gratifications Theory was developed from a number of prior communication theories and research conducted by fellow theorists.

Stage 1

In 1944 Herta Herzog began to look at the earliest forms of uses and gratifications with her work classifying the reasons why people chose specific types of media. For her study, Herzog interviewed soap opera fans and was able to identify three types of gratifications. The three gratifications categories, based on why people listened to soap operas, were emotional, wishful thinking, and learning.

In 1970 Abraham Maslow suggested that Uses and Gratifications Theory was an extension of the Needs and Motivation Theory. The basis for his argument was that people actively looked to satisfy their needs based on a hierarchy. The pyramid hierarchy began on the bottom with Biological/ Physical, Security/Safety, Social/Belonging, Ego/Self-Respect and Self-actualization at the top.

In 1954 Wilbur Schramm developed the fraction of selection, a formula for determining which form of mass media an individual would select. The formula helped to decide the amount of gratification an individual would expect to gain from the medium over how much effort they had to make to achieve gratification.

Stage 2

In 1969 Jay Blumler and Denis McQuail began to study why people watched political program on television. The motive they were able to identify helped lay the groundwork for their research in 1972 and eventually the Uses and Gratifications Theory.

In 1972 Denis McQuail, Jay Blumler and Joseph Brown suggested that the uses of different types of media could be grouped into 4 categories. The four categories were: diversion, personal relationships, personal identity and surveillance.

In 1973-74 McQuail, Blumler and Brown were joined by Elihu Katz, Michael Gurevitch and Hadassah Haas, in their media exploration. The collaborative research began to indicate how people saw the mass media.

Stage 3

The most recent interest surrounding Uses and Gratifications Theory is the link between the reason why media is used and the achieved gratification.

Uses and Gratifications Model

According to Katz, Blumler and Gurevitch's research there were 5 components comprising the Uses and Gratifications Model. The components are:

— "The audience is conceived as active."

— "In the mass communication process much initiative in linking gratification and media choice lies with the audience member."

— "The media compete with other sources of satisfaction."

— "Methodologically speaking, many of the goals of mass media use can be derived from data supplied by individual audience members themselves."

— "Value judgments about the cultural significance of mass communication should be suspended while audience orientations are explored on their own terms."

Historical Development

Beginning in the 1940s, researchers began seeing patterns under the perspective of the uses and gratifications theory in radio listeners. Early research was concerned with topics such as children's use of comics and the absence of newspapers during a newspaper strike. An interest in more psychological interpretations emerged during this time period.

In 1948, Lasswell introduced a four-functional interpretation of the media on a macro-sociological level. Media served the functions of surveillance, correlation, entertainment and cultural transmission for both society and individuals

In 1974, Katz, Blumler and Gurevitch realized that many Uses and Gratification studies, to that point in time, were mostly focused on seven areas. The areas were:

1. The social and psychological origins of
2. needs which generate
3. expectations
4. of mass media or other sources, which lead to

5. differential patterns of media exposure (or engagement in other activities), resulting in
6. need gratifications and
7. other consequences, perhaps mostly unintended ones

Therefore, Katz, Blumler and Gurevitch developed the Uses and Gratifications model to better study how and why people were using media for personal satisfaction.

The Active Audience

Jay Blumler presented a number of interesting points, as to why Uses and Gratifications cannot measure an active audience. He stated, "The issue to be considered here is whether what has been thought about Uses and Gratifications Theory has been an article of faith and if it could now be converted into an empirical question such as: How to measure an active audience?". Blumler then offered suggestions about the kinds of activity the audiences were engaging with in the different types of media.

— Utility : "Using the media to accomplish specific tasks"
— Intentionality: "Occurs when people's prior motive determine use of media"
— Selectivity: "Audience members' use of media reflect their existing interests"
— Imperviousness to Influence: "Refers to audience members' constructing their own meaning from media content"

25 years later, in 1972, Blumler, McQuail and Brown extended Lasswell's four groups. These included four primary factors for which one may use the media:

— Diversion: Escape from routine and problems; an emotional release
— Personal Relationships: Social utility of information in conversation; substitution of media for companionship
— Personal Identity or Individual Psychology: Value reinforcement or reassurance; self-understanding, reality exploration
— Surveillance: Information about factors which might affect one or will help one do or accomplish something

Katz, Gurevitch and Haas saw mass media as a means by which individuals connect or disconnect themselves with others. They developed 35 needs taken from the largely speculative literature on the social and psychological functions of the mass media and put them into five categories:

— Cognitive Needs: Acquiring information, knowledge and understanding
— Media Examples: Television (news), video (how-to), movies (documentaries or based on history)
— Affective Needs: Emotion, pleasure, feelings
— Media Examples: Movies, television (soap operas, sitcoms)
— Personal Integrative Needs: Credibility, stability, status
— Media Examples: Video
— Social Integrative Needs: Family and friends
— Media Examples: Internet (e-mail, instant messaging, chat rooms, social media)
— Tension Release Needs: Escape and diversion
— Media Examples: Television, movies, video, radio, internet

Uses and Gratifications of Animated News Viewing

In 2011, a survey was conducted with 312 college students to investigate their viewing of animated news. The use of melodramatic animation in news has been an emerging technique used in news reporting. It is regarded as a news technique that is going mainstream and is going global. The respondents were given 59 statements to rate according to how well each of these statements applies to their viewing of animated news. Factor analysis and hierarchical regression were employed for data analysis.

In the study, seven motives were identified, through factor analysis, for viewing such animated news videos. These motives included companionship, social Interaction, relaxation, information Seeking, interpersonal Learning, entertainment and pass time.

— Social interaction motive: getting information for facilitating discussion with others
— Relaxation motive: watching animated news to release pressure and unwind
— Information-seeking motive: viewing animated news to stay abreast of current events or to search for information
— Entertainment motive: viewing animated news for amusement and enjoyment

— Pastime motive: viewing animated news to occupy time or when individuals have nothing better to do
— Interpersonal learning motive: the desire to understand the minds of friends or significant others by watching the animated news videos that are shared by these individuals
— Companionship motive: to alleviating loneliness

The results of hierarchical regression analysis suggest predictive relationships among personality characteristics (sensation seeking and locus of control), the seven motives, the effects of perceived news credibility and newsworthiness, and the intention to share such animated news videos with others.

New Media Example of Uses and Gratifications Theory

The application of New Media to the Uses and Gratifications Theory has been positive. The introduction of the Internet, social media and technological advances has provided another outlet for people to use and seek gratification through those sources. Based on the models developed by Katz, Blumler, Gurevitch and Lasswell, individuals can choose to seek out media in one outlet, all falling within the proscribed categories of need. The only difference now, is that the audience does not have to go to multiple media outlets to fulfill each of their needs. The Internet has created a digital library, allowing individuals to have access to all content from various mass medium outlets.

In 2007 a study was conducted to examine the Facebook groups users gratifications in relation to their civic participation offline. The Web survey polled 1,715 college students, ranging in age from 18-29, who were members of Facebook groups. The respondents were given 16 statement through an electronic survey and asked "to rate their level of agreement with specific reasons for using Facebook groups, including information acquisition about campus/community, entertainment/recreation, social interaction with friends and family, and peer pressure/self satisfaction." The Likert scale indicated the 1 was strongly agree and 6 was strongly disagree. To ensure those results were not skewed, the respondents were also asked to complete a set of level of agreement questions to properly gauge their level of life satisfaction.

The study ultimately yielded results through principal components factor analysis with varimax rotation. The results showed that there were four needs for using Facebook groups, "socializing, entertainment, self-status seeking, and information."

Gratification Received from Use of Facebook Groups

— Socializing: Students interested in talking and meeting with others to achieve a sense of community and peer support on the particular topic of the group
— Entertainment: Students engaged with the groups to amuse themselves
— Self-Seeking: Students maintain and seek out their personal status, as well as those of their friends, through the online group participation
— Information: Students used the group to receive information about related events going on and off campus

Theory Criticism

The data behind the theory is hard to extrapolate and at times is not found. How each audience, individual and group perceives a given media outlet is extremely difficult to gauge. A main argument lies in how the media, producers and editors want the material to be interpreted. News reports on a rising restaurant could be seen as a threat to local establishments but was intended as a positive note to how well the community is doing. Morley (1992) says that "creators of media content have a preferred reading that they would like the audience to take out of the text. However, the audience might reject it, or negotiate some comprise interpretation between what they think and what they text is saying, or contest what the text says with some alternative interpretation". The biggest issue for the Uses and Gratifications Theory is its being non-theoretical, vague in key concepts, and nothing more than a data-collecting strategy.

Using this sociologically-based theory has little to no link to the benefit of psychology due to its weakness in operational definitions and weak analytical mode. It also is focused too narrowly on the individual and neglects the social structure and place of the media in that structure.

Due to the individualistic nature of Uses and Gratification theory, it is difficult to take the information that is collected in studies. Most research relies on pure recollection of memory rather than data. This makes self-reports complicated and immeasurable.

The Uses and Gratifications theory has been denounced by media hegemony advocates who say it goes too far in claiming that people are free to choose the media and the interpretations they desire. Audiences interpret the media in their own terms and any debate for or against this can be argued, and depending on the circumstances, won by either side. Each individuals' actions and effects on those actions will depend solely on the situation. The Uses and Gratifications theory does not properly account for these natural occurrences but does hold a valid argument that each individual has unique uses to which the media attempts to meet their gratifications.

Theorist Explanation

"The nature of the theory underlying Uses and Gratifications research is not totally clear." This makes the line between gratification and satisfaction blurred, calling into question whether or not we only seek what we desire or actually enjoy it.

"Practitioners of Uses and Gratifications research have been criticized for a formidable array of shortcomings in their outlook — they are taxed for being crassly atheoretical, perversely eclectic, ensnared in the pitfalls of functionalism and for flirting with the positions at odds with their functionalist origins".

Reception Theory

Reception theory is a version of reader response literary theory that emphasizes the reader's reception of a literary text. It is more generally called audience reception in the analysis of communications models. In literary studies, reception theory originated from the work of Hans-Robert Jauss in the late 1960s. It was most influential during the 1970s and early 1980s in Germany and USA, amongst some notable work in Western Europe. A form of reception theory has also been applied to the study of historiography; see Reception history.

Cultural theorist Stuart Hall is one of the main proponents of reception theory, having developed it for media and communication studies from the literary- and history-oriented approaches mentioned above. This approach to textual analysis focuses on the scope for "negotiation" and "opposition" on the part of the audience. This means that a "text"—be it a book, movie, or other creative work—is not simply passively accepted by the audience, but that the reader / viewer interprets the meanings of the text based on their individual cultural background and life experiences. In essence, the meaning of a text is not inherent within the text itself, but is created within the relationship between the text and the reader.Stuart Hall also developed Hall's Theory of encoding and decoding, focusing on the communication processes at play in the televisual form.

Reception theory has since been extended to the spectators of performative events, predominantly theatre. Susan Bennett is often credited with beginning this discourse within theatre. Reception theory has also been applied to the history and analysis of landscapes, through the work of landscape historian John Dixon Hunt, motivated by recognition that the survival of gardens and landscapes is due to their public reception.

A basic acceptance of the meaning of a specific text tends to occur when a group of readers have a shared cultural background and interpret the text in similar ways. It is likely that the less shared heritage a reader has with the artist, the less he/she will be able to recognise the artist's intended meaning, and it follows that if two readers have vastly different cultural and personal experiences, their reading of a text will vary greatly. Umberto Eco coined the term aberrant decoding to describe the case when the reader's interpretation differs from what the artist intended.

Reception theory and landscape architecture

In literature, the interaction between text and reader occurs within a framework that controls and limits the interaction, through genre, tone, structure, and the social conditions of the reader and author, whereas in landscapes the interaction occurs through movement and viewing, framed by typology instead of genre and tone. Instead of an "implied reader," reception theory of landscapes assumes an "implied visitor," who is an abstracted concatenation of responses of many visitors at different times.

The theory recognizes that there is no single reading of a landscape that fulfills its entire potential, and that it is important to examine the motives of visitors and the factors influencing their visits (whether they read guidebooks about the place before visiting, or had strong feelings about the place or the designer, for instance).

One key difference between reception theory in literature and reception theory in landscape architecture is that while literary works are accessible only to the imagination, physical landscapes are accessible to the senses as well as to the imagination. However, purely mythological gardens (such as the Garden of Eden and the gardens of the Hypnerotomachia Poliphili) are accessible only to the imagination, and extant historical gardens form a middle ground, with their reception influenced by sensory experience as well as readings of historical accounts of visits to those gardens.

Reception theoretical analysis of landscapes differs from typical writing on the history and analysis of landscapes, which tends to focus on the intentions of the designers, the conditions leading to the creation of the design, and the building process. Reception theory also tends to de-emphasize commonly used terms of description like 'formal' and 'picturesque,' unless those terms were known to have meaning to landscape visitors themselves.

According to Harold Marcuse, reception history is "the history of the meanings that have been imputed to historical events. It traces the different ways in which participants, observers, historians and other retrospective interpreters have attempted to make sense of events both as they unfolded and over time since then, to make those events meaningful for the present in which they lived and live."

Media Influence in Audeince

Media influence or media effects are used in media studies, psychology, communication theory and sociology to refer to the theories about the ways in which mass media and media culture affect how their audiences think and behave.

Media-influenced Violence

Many studies illustrate that media affects public opinion. However, this is a contentious issue.

To explain the problem of violence in society, researchers should begin with that social violence and seek to explain it with reference, quite obviously, to those who engage in it: their identity, background, character and so on.

Gauntlet goes on to criticize studies that focus on children by stating that they do not as a control group, and that the studies are conducted primarily to further a "barely-concealed conservative ideology." He counters the premise of these studies with the concept that not all depictions of violence are even bad to witness. USC Professor Henry Jenkins, for instance, suggested in his speech to congress that The Basketball Diaries utilizes violence in a form of social commentary that provides clear social benefit.

Gauntlet explains further that objects defined as “violent” or “anti-social” may not be judged as such in the minds of the viewer and tend to be viewed in artificial circumstances. These objects are furthermore based on previous studies with flawed methodology, and are not grounded in theory. Additionally, he claims that the effects model attempts to understand the meanings of media.

Historical criticisms situate the ‘meta-narrative’ of effects theory within a long history of distrust of new forms of media, dating as far back as Socrates’s objections to the deleterious effects due to the written alphabet.

Political criticisms pose an alternative conception of humans as rational, critical subjects who are alert to genre norms and adept at interpreting and critiquing media representations, instead of passively absorbing them.

Supporters of effects theory contend that commercials and advertising prove that media influence behavior. In the 20th century, aggressive media attention and negative coverage of trials involving celebrities like Roscoe Fatty Arbuckle or Michael Jackson have influenced the general public’s opinion, before the trials effectively started. However, these critics do point out that while the media could have an effect on people’s behavior this isn’t necessarily always the case.

Critics of the media effects theory point out that many copycat murders, suicides and other violent acts nearly always happen in abnormal upbringings. Violent, emotionally neglectful or aggressive environments influence behavior more than watching certain programs, films or listening to certain music. Most people who carry out these acts are also mentally unstable to begin with.

Also there are other thinkers who criticize effects based research, such as Terry Flew and Sal Humphrey, Barker and Freedman.,,-Martin Barker (2001) criticised Elizabeth Newson who alleged link between media violence and real life violence in her report in 1994, Brooke (2003–07),for example talks about this in details. The report gained media attention when it claimed the horror film Child’s Play 3 had influenced two 10-year-old boys’ behavior and led to the Murder of James Bulger in Feb. 1993. After examining and assessing Newson’s report, it was apparent that there was no clear link between the film and the crime. Critics pointed out that Newson’s case studies were reliant on press accounts and opinions rather than independent research. However, Newson’s report was influential, and has led to more censorship of videos and more concern from the British Board of Film classification on the psychological effects of media violence. The attention and question become whether they were watching violent media.

But Barker (2001) doesn't agree with Elizabeth Newson. He rejected her claim about the connection between media violence and real life violence, in his argument he justifies his position, he indicates that there was not a scrap of evidence that the boys had seen the movie and Child's Play 3 is a moral film. He also criticized anti media campaigns and described them as ignorant and disguised political campaigns. He states that these claims are represented by media and most of people have no chance to check the credibility of them, he also points out that these films including Child's Play 3 are often attacked because they deal with political issues. Moreover, he lists real cases, for example "a man takes a gun and shoots his entire family after watching the news, arrested and tried, he explains his actions on the basis that the world news was so bad there seemed no point in anyone going on living". Barker suggests that this case for example is no different that other putative cases of media a causing violence, Barker said that we should not always blindly blame the media because people are not copycats, instead we should be aware of someone's mental state and take other factors into account before making such claims. For example, in his case he states that the man's reaction was abnormal. Therefore, his behavior could not be explained by suggesting "the effects of the news". There are other social and cultural factors in criminal acts in which the media are not the basic influence. Barker also suggests 'that we must look beyond a specific film to think about the specific context in which it has been consumed, and the wider social background of the people'.,according to Barker there is no such thing called violence in the media that either could or could not cause violence, we should rather pay attention to how social factors and background make some people consume media in specific way., for instance, even the news also show lots of violence, so people should rather pay attention to how social factors and background make some people consume media in particular way. In addition Barker proposes further research, he suggests that the theory of media violence connection must be tested because identification with particular element in a film is not something can be seen. He also noted problem with campaigners treating delinquents as normal people who become influenced by the media. Therefore, he suggests further research on how these people understand and consume media.

— Critics of effects research see no connection between exposure to media violence and real life violence. Although some research claims that heavy exposure to media violence can lead to more aggressive behavior, it has been suggested that exposure alone does not cause a child to commit crimes.

— Flew and Humphreys said that the assumptions of effects researchers are frequently flawed. According to Flew and Humphreys, Freedman and Goldstein the number of studies on games and violence is small and the research suffers from flawed methodologies which do very little to prove a direct link. Terry Flew and Sal Humphreys also state 'that differing context of consumption will always mean we need to take account of the particularities of players and how and why they play, effects researches often give insufficient account to the relevance of cultural contexts and the way in which media are actually implicated in the circulation of meanings in our cultures'.

— Freedman is another thinker who rejects this idea, in reference to the FCC 'the Federal Communications Commission in US' report that suggests link between media violence and real life violence, Freedman indicates the lack of discussion and states that the FCC does not make a sufficiviolence. For example a recent long-term outcome study of youth found no long-term relationship between watching violent television and youth violence or bullying

Certain groups tend to argue for media effects in an effort to promote a political cause. Demands for the banning of certain songs or the labeling of obscene albums came specifically from conservative political groups in the United States. However, Tipper Gore, the wife of Al Gore, was the founder of the Parents Music Resource Center, and was the main figure in pushing for warning labels on music although she does not fit into the conservative demographic. They argued that such material had simple and identifiable effects on children, and thus should be banned/labelled. Political factions use the media to influence possible members into joining their groups. ent distinction between people's opinions, intuitions and musings on the one hand, and the hard scientific data on the other, and he indicates the lack of discussion of one of the strongest arguments against the idea that media violence causes aggression. According to Freedman the rate of violent crime in the United states increased sharply from 1965 to 1980 and some people blamed that increase on media. The rate of violent crime leveled off until about 1992, since that time, television continued to have violent programs, there was also more scenes and media showing more violence, if exposure to violent media cause real violence one would surely expect the rate of violent crime to have increased sharply, yet, since 1992 there has been a dramatic drop in violent crime, it seems clear that media violence did not cause the earlier increase. Therefore, it is widely accepted that there is no convincing evidence that prove that media violence cause violent crime or any type of real life

Framing

The agenda-setting process is an almost unavoidable part of news gathering by the large organizations which make up much of the mass media. (Just four main news agencies — AP, UPI, Reuters and Agence-France-Presse — claim together to provide 90% of the total news output of the world's press, radio and television.) Stuart Hall points out that because some of the media produce material which often is good, impartial and serious, they are accorded a high degree of respect and authority. However, in practice the ethics of the press and television are closely related to that of the hegemonic establishment, providing vital support to the existing order. Independence (e.g. of the BBC) is not "a mere cover, it is central to the way power and ideology are mediated in societies like ours."

The public is bribed with good radio, television and newspapers into an acceptance of the biased, the misleading, and the status quo. The media are not, according to this approach, crude agents of propaganda. They organize public understanding. However, the overall interpretations they provide in the long run are those most preferred by, and least challenging to, those with economic power. Greg Philo demonstrates this in his 1991 article, "Seeing is Believing", in which he showed that recollections of the 1984 UK miners' strike were strongly correlated with the media presentation of the event, including the perception of the picketing as largely violent when violence was rare, and the use by the public of phrases which had appeared originally in the media.

McCombs and Shaw demonstrate the agenda-setting effect at work in a study conducted in Chapel Hill, North Carolina, USA during the 1968 presidential elections. A representative sample of un-decided voters was asked to outline the key issues of the election as it perceived them. Concurrently, the mass media serving these subjects were collected and their content was analyzed. The results showed a definite correlation between the two accounts of predominant issues. "The evidence in this study that voters tend to share the media's composite definition of what is important strongly suggests an agenda-setting function of the mass media."

New media

Theorists such as Louis Wirth and Talcott Parsons have emphasized the importance of mass media as instruments of social control. In the 21st century, with the rise of the internet, the two-way relationship between mass media and public opinion is beginning to change, with the advent of new technologies such as blogging.

Mander's theory is related to Jean Baudrillard's concept of 'hyperreality'. We can take the 1994 O.J. Simpson trial as an example, where the reality reported on was merely the catalyst for the simulacra (images) created, which defined the trial as a global event and made the trial more than it was. Essentially, hyperreality is the concept that the media are not merely a window on to the world (as if a visiting alien were watching television), but are part of the reality they describe. Hence (although additionally there is the question of navel-gazing) the media's obsession with media-created events.

It is this which led Marshall McLuhan in the 1960s to say that "the medium is the message", and to suggest that mass media are increasingly creating a "global village". For example, there is evidence that Western media influence in Asia is the driving force behind rapid social change: "it is as if the 1960s and the 1990s were compressed together." A notable example is the recent introduction of television to Bhutan, resulting in rapid Westernization. This raises questions of 'cultural imperialism' (Schiller) — the de facto imposition, through economic and political power and through the media, of Western (and in particular US) culture.

An instrument for social control

Social scientists have made efforts to integrate the study of the mass media as an instrument of control into the study of political and economic developments in the Afro-Asian countries. David Lerner has emphasized the general pattern of increase in standard of living, urbanization, literacy and exposure to mass media during the transition from traditional to modern society. According to Lerner, while there is a heavy emphasis on the expansion of mass media in developing societies, the penetration of a central authority into the daily consciousness of the mass has to overcome profound resistance.

Government and Mass Media

They include licensing in advance; censorship of offending material before publication; seizure of offending material; injunctions against publication of a newspaper or book or of specified content; requirement of surety bonds against libel or other offense; compulsory disclosure of ownership and authority; post publication criminal penalties for objectionable matter; post publication collection of damages in a civil action; post publication correction of libel and other misstatements; discrimination in granting access to news source and facilities; discrimination and denial in the use of communications facilities for distribution; taxes; discriminatory subsidies; and interference with buying, reading and listening.

Mass Media in a free enterprise capitalist society

Although a sizable portion of mass media offerings – particularly news, commentaries, documentaries, and other informational programmes – deal with highly controversial subjects, the major portion of mass media offerings are designed to serve an entertainment function. These programmes tend to avoid controversial issues and reflect beliefs and values sanctified by mass audience. This course is followed by Television networks, whose investment and production costs are high. Jerry Mander's work has highlighted this particular outlook. According to him, the atomized individuals of mass society lose their souls to the phantom delights of the film, the soap opera, and the variety show. They fall into a stupor, or apathetic hypnosis, that Lazarsfeld called the 'narcotizing dysfunction' of exposure to mass media.

Individuals become 'irrational victims of false wants' – the wants which corporations have thrust upon them, and continue to thrust upon them, through both the advertising in the media (with its continual exhortation to consume) and through the individualist consumption culture it promulgates. Thus, according to the Frankfurt School, leisure has been industrialized. The production of culture had become standardized and dominated by the profit motive as in other industries. In a mass society leisure is constantly used to induce the appropriate values and motives in the public. The modern media train the young for consumption. 'Leisure had ceased to be the opposite of work, and had become a preparation for it.'

Mass media, mass culture and elite

The relation of the mass media to contemporary popular culture is commonly conceived in terms of dissemination from the elite to the mass. The long-term consequences of this are significant in conjunction with the continuing concentration of ownership and control of the media, leading to accusations of a 'media elite' having a form of 'cultural dictatorship'. Thus the continuing debate about the influence of 'media barons' such as Conrad Black and Rupert Murdoch.

For example, the UK Observer reported the Murdoch-owned HarperCollins' refusal to publish Chris Patten's East and West, because of the former Hong Kong Governor's description of the Chinese leadership as "faceless Stalinists" possibly being damaging to Murdoch's Chinese broadcasting interests. In this case, the author was able to have the book accepted by another publisher, but this type of censorship may point the way to the future. A related, but more insidious, form is that of self-censorship by members of the media in the interests of the owner, in the interests of their careers.

Focus on Audience in Media Studies: Advantages and Limitations

At the most basic level, audiences are vital in communication. It is for the audience that the media are constructing and conveying information, and, if it were not for the audiences, the media would not exist. The exact relationship between the media and their audiences has been the subject of debate since the media were first seriously studied and emphasises the importance of the audience and of their relationship with the media.

The Frankfurt school, set up in 1923, were concerned about the possible effects of mass media. They proposed the "Effects" model, which considered society to be composed of isolated individuals who were susceptible to media messages. The Frankfurt school envisioned the media as a hypodermic syringe, and the contents of the media were injected into the thoughts of the audience, who accepted the attitudes, opinions and beliefs expressed by the medium without question. This model was a response to the German fascists use of film and radio for propaganda uses, and later applied to American capitalist society. The followers of the hypodermic model of Effects adopted a variant of Marxism, emphasising the dangers of the power of capitalism, which owned and controlled new forms of media. Researchers in the fifties also supported the Effects model when exploring the potential of the new medium of television. Researchers were particularly concerned over increases in the representation of violent acts on television, which correlated with increases in violent acts in society. In the nineties, there was considerable concern over what were called "video nasties". The tabloid papers created a moral panic over whether particular violet films could influence child behaviour – and whether *Childs Play 3* influenced the child killers of Jamie Bulger.

However, theorists since have thought that media could not have such direct effects on the audiences they serve, and consider the media as a comparatively weak influence in moulding individual beliefs, opinions and attitudes. Other factors present in society, such as personal contact and religion, are more likely to influence people. The Effects model is considered to be an inadequate representation of the communication between media and the public, as it does not take into account the audience as individuals with their own beliefs, opinions, ideals and attitudes:

> Audiences are not blank sheets of paper on which media messages can be written; members of an audience will have prior attitudes and beliefs which will determine how effective media messages are. (Abercrombie 1996, 140)

Supporters of the Effects model assume the audience is passive in the receiving and interpretation of media texts. Great emphasis is placed on the text itself and its power to directly influence the audience. Meanings in the text are readily available and easy to find. The impossibility to measure media effects is as a result of not being able to isolate the media from all the other potential influences at work in society. This leads to the Effects model generally being disregarded when considering the audiences response to the media.

A new approach to the dynamics of audience/text relationship was suggested in the Uses and Gratification model. In this model, theorists were not asking how the media effects audiences, but how were the audiences using the media. They suggested that audiences had specific needs and actively turned to the media to consume various texts to a satisfaction of these needs. The audience in Uses and Gratifications were seen as active, as opposed to passive audience in the Effects model. Uses and Gratifications acknowledged that the audience had a choice of texts from which to chose from and satisfy their needs. Blumler and Katz suggested that there were four main needs of television audiences that are satisfied by television. These included – Diversion (a form of escaping from the pressures of every day), Personal Relationships (where the viewer gains companionship, either with the television characters, or through conversations with others about television), Personal Identity (where the viewer is able to compare their life with the lives of characters and situations on television, to explore, re-affirm or question their personal identity) and Surveillance (where the media are looked upon for a supply of information about what is happening in the world).

While acknowledging that the audience are active and chose what to watch, the Uses and Gratifications model as a model for understanding audiences also has its limitations. The model still implies that messages are packages of information that all the audience will read as the same. It does not consider how the messages are interpreted or any other factors affecting the audience's interpretation.

> Another criticism is that of the tendency to concentrate solely on why audiences consume the media rather than extending the investigation to discover what meanings and interpretations are produced and in what circumstances, i.e. how the media are received. (O'Sullivan, Dutton & Rayner 1994, 131)

The Uses and Gratification model assumes that the audience's wish for satisfaction results in a media output to fulfil their desire, rather than acknowledging that audiences have to enjoy whatever is produced by the media.

Both the Effects and the Uses and Gratifications model ignore to some extent the audience and their social backgrounds, how they form their interpretations of the media messages and their specific relationship with the media text. In the 70s, the academic journal *Screen*suggested that audiences were positioned by the media text. Theorists started to take an approach influenced by semiotics and structuralism, to discover what meanings were made from texts and how this meaning was achieved. Great emphasis was placed on the text, particularly film. *Screen* thought that the position of the viewer of Hollywood film was determined for them through the use of camera shots. For example, the shot/reverse shot commonly used during dialogue enabled the viewer to position themselves as one of the characters. Another example is a close up of somebody who then looks offscreen. The next shot of the object that the character is looking at is shown, again placing the viewer in the position of the character. Writers, such as Laura Mulvey considered the "gaze" in Hollywood film to be a masculine gaze, where the camera shots adopt the male gaze and constructing the female as the object of that gaze.

Screen theory suggested that all media texts have a "mode of address" – a term used by semioticians which proposes that media texts address its intended audience in a particular way, establishing a relationship between the producer of the text and the media's audience. The mode of address is dependant on the particular medium. For instance, cinema rarely addresses the audience directly. Films are usually shot to suggest the film is reality. In comedy characters occasionally look into the camera. Recently there has be a trend in which films have become self-reflexive, drawing on and manipulating the conventions of the audience's expectations of the medium. The "Scream" films are a good example of this. Television differs from cinema, as the audience are not expected to pay the attention which cinema demands, so television has to work to attain and maintain the audience's attention. The medium employs a wide range of techniques to address its intended audience. Youth programmes constantly have unusual camera angles and short shots to capture and keep children's attention. Quiz shows often address the audience ("who are playing along at home."). It is assumed that television viewing is done in family groups in a domestic setting. The scheduling highlights this view of the television audience; as the television output is regulated so that there is minimal "adult" material, such as strong language, sex scenes and violence, before the 9o'clock watershed. Whenever sport is on television and the national team is participating, such as the World Cup, the usual objective and neutral commentary changes to a more patriarchal and emotive mode of address. Newspapers clearly have a particular mode of address, reflected in the headlines and phrasing of the article. Broadsheet papers like *The Times* and *The Guardian* have a more impersonal and formal mode of address when compared with the tabloids *The Sun* and *The Mirror,* which are more emotional and often xenophobic.

The limitations of focusing on audience in media studies can clearly be seen in the mode of address made by the media. Different audiences use different media; both the audience that is assumed to be using the media and the particular type of media that is being consumed determines the mode of address.

The mode of address will be vital in constructing audiences' thoughts about an issue raised in media. However, previous models of audience reception do not take into account what actual audiences are going to do to the media texts. *Screen* theory, Uses and Gratifications and Effects models suggest that meaning is embedded within the text, which audiences can access easily and accept without questioning these meanings. Just because producers of media texts have a certain opinion and meaning does not mean that this meaning is obvious in the text, that, in turn, does not mean that the audience will read these meanings or agree with them.

The Centre for Contemporary Cultural Studies at Birmingham during the 70s again used a semiotic approach to understanding an audience response to media texts. David Morley studied audiences of an early evening news programme and argued in his paper *The Nationwide work* that audiences actively decode meanings from a media text. The Centre for Contemporary Cultural Studies, working under Stuart Hall, expanded on Morley's hypothesis and suggested that meanings were encoded by the producer into the media text and the audiences decodes the meaning from the text. This theory acknowledges that there is a preferred meaning in the text – the meaning made by the producer. This meaning is encoded by the codes and conventions of the particular medium to hide the texts own ideological construction. The audience then read, listen or watch the media text and interpret the message. The audience's interpretation is dependant on a number of frameworks outside the text. These include socio/economic frameworks such as class, gender, age education and ethnicity. They include the individual's past experiences and also include previous knowledge and experience of the medium.

This current theory on audience reception in media studies takes into account the individual members of the audience. It realises there is a preferred meaning in the text, but also places emphasis on the audience in the process of constructing a meaning. Hall's encoding/decoding model draws upon two extreme ends of a spectrum, what Abercrombie refers to as the dominant text view and the dominant audience view. Researchers who give the text priority support the dominant text view, wherein the text is monolithic, there is a well marked preferred meaning and is difficult for other meanings to be read. The audience is seen as passive and heavily influenced by the text. Hall and his colleagues took the dominant audience view, which acknowledges the presence of a strong preferred meaning, but also saw texts as polysemic – they have a number of possible meanings, and that is up to the audience to analyse and interpret the text.

The advantage of the Encoding/decoding model is that it realises that the meaning made by the audience is affected by various other factors – including socio/economic frameworks and past experiences, but also involving the context in which the media message is consumed. Meanings constructed by the individual watching televisual news at home with two distracting siblings will be different to meanings constructed while concentrating on the television alone. These meanings will be different to those formed when the individual is reading news articles in the newspaper in a quiet room.

The Centre for Contemporary Cultural Studies also proposed a model for the types of audience decoding. The audience member assumes the dominant hegemonic position when they recognise and agree with the full-preferred meaning offered by the media text. Theoppositional hegemonic position is established when the audience member understands the preferred meaning, but disagrees with it due to their own set of attitudes and beliefs. The negotiated hegemonic position is established when the audience member opposes or has to adapt the preferred meaning. The forth type of audience response is referred to as aberrant decoding. This is where the audience member reads the text in an unpredicted way, producing a deviant meaning. There are still a number of limitations to this model of audience reception, as David Morley notes:

> The extent to which the model tries to conceive of language merely as a conveyor belt for preconstituted meanings or messages; the way in which it tends to confuse textual meaning with the conscious intentions of broadcasters; and the tendency to blur together under the heading of "decoding" what are probably best thought of as separate prosesses along the axes of comprehension/incomprehension, as opposed to agreement/disagreement with the prepositional content of messages. Furthermore, the concept of the preferred meaning, which is of course central to the encoding/decoding model has a number of criticisms. (Seiter 1989, 18.)

The preferred meaning is a difficult concept to understand, and is simpler to identify in factual texts, such as newspaper reports, television news and documentaries. In fiction-based texts there are more likely to be different readings of he preferred texts. Additionally, it is unclear whether the preferred meanings are embedded in the text, or whether it is something agreed on by the majority of the texts audience. By considering the audience in the interpretation of the media text, it is clear to see that the process of media communication is not a simple concept. Meaning is considered to be what the audience make of the text, taking away most of the power of the producer and the text.

Abercrombie emphasises the importance of the producer, text and audience and reiterates Hall's opinion that all three, and the relationship between them, are vital in the process of media communication. By reviewing the past theories on the way audiences receive and interpret media messages, we can see that there are various ways in which the audience can be viewed. The emphasis on audience in the encoding/decoding model is advantageous for a number of reasons. As Andrew Hart states "...the meaning is not in the text, but in the *reading*". This illustrates the possibilities of the media. Emphasising audiences in this way insists that the media are not as manipulative as they were thought to be. By understanding how the audience construct meaning and make sense of texts, producers can change their texts so that audiences will read whatever meanings the producers want. Ultimately, it is the audience that controls the output of the media, and thus the content of popular culture:

> The audience, regardless of the medium, has not been historically passive or inconsequential in shaping its participation in, or the content of, popular media. (Rokeach & Cantor 1986, 200.)

The producers of media texts often work with an image of the audience and what it wants. Therefore, a focus on audience is advantageous, as the media must work to satisfy the audience. Assuming that meaning is only constructed by the reading of the text by the audience highlights the polysemic nature of texts and ambiguity of meaning. One sequence of pictures on the television will mean a number of meanings, depending on the individual in the audience. The phrasing of a newspaper could connote any number of meanings considering the experiences and background of the reader. The focus on audience in media studies illuminates the richness and potentials available in the media. As the audience construct meaning from a media text using frameworks already present in culture, it is

> ...only by understanding the meanings constructed by the audiences that we can understand how that (cultural) form functions within the larger culture. (Cruz & Lewis 1994, 20.)

By understanding how audiences read meanings in the text, we are also able to gain a closer understanding of the culture to which that audience belongs.

The main limitation of a focus in audience has been highlighted by the various ways in which past theorists have thought audiences receive media messages. There are many different ways to conceptualise the audience and the way in which they work with media, but there appears to be no "right" way. This is complicated by the very nature of actual audiences. There are many different audiences for many different media. Newspaper readers and radio listeners are two types of audience, but some newspaper readers will also be part of the radio audience. People who watch one type of programme on television will also watch another type of programme, and will be part of another audience. There is a tendency to think of audiences as masses, but a Williams observed, there are no such things as "the masses", only ways of imagining people as masses. Audiences are "unstructured groups...with…no social organisation…merely an aggregate of demographic characteristics." Different media will attract audiences which will consist of a mix of people who formed audiences of other media.

There are no effective ways to measure audiences, or to measure all the individual's responses to the media. The existing ways of measuring audiences seem inadequate. For example the equipment that monitors a sample television audience notes which channels are being watched. This method is ineffective as it does not take into consideration how audiences are watching the television, for example, if they are carrying out other activities while watching they will pay less attention compared to when they tune in especially to watch a programme dealing with issues close to their hearts.

> The realisation that audience is not adequately explained by researching either the people of the audience or the texts they like, but that audience is distinctively inflected by the nature and cultural significance of the interaction between audience activities and textual character (understood in the widest possible sense) causes a reconsideration of the very nature of audience. (Nightingale 1996)

The existing methods of studying audience do not measure how and why the audiences differ in their viewing. For instance the audience watching one episode of a serial will not necessarily watch the following episode or, indeed, any of the other episodes. Additionally, the existing methods do not consider what meanings the actual audience is constructing. Questionnaires are limited by the questions that they ask and audiences will be trying to answer what they think the researcher is trying to find. There is no exact or easy way to study or compile accurate details of the particular aspects of the audience. Hart notes the difficulty in judging and representing audiences when he asks:

> How can we study audiences without relying at one extreme on personal anecdotes or, at the other, on masses of indigestible figures? (Hart 1991, 30)

It is impossible to set up controlled or laboratory experiments with the media and their audience, as if you change the way in which the media is usually received you will undoubtedly change the interpretations made by the audience of the media text. The key issue about media is that exists as a comment and as a part of our culture and cannot be examined easily due to this.

The methods used for audience research (including ethnography, survey, experiment, text analysis or social commentary) result in class groups or "life style" groups – in which all the members of the audience of one media text are categorised together. This type of classification seems inadequate as the categories can be broad and there seems no benefit in categorising people in this way. The main limitation of a focus on audience in media studies is that the research and techniques used to research the audience are not effective.

A focus on audience is important in media studies. There have been many different theories on how audiences respond to and interact with the media. This shows clearly the complexities of focusing on the audience and the ways in which audiences can be visualised. By giving a focus on audience researchers are able to see the complex process of the construction of meaning made by the audience as a response to media text. No audience member will interpret the media message in the same way. This alerts uses of the various media to the ambiguity of meaning and the richness inherent in the medium, aspects that producers need to be aware of in the construction of their texts. The limitations of a focus on audience derive from the impossibility of investigating and measuring audiences and their responses. Existing methods of audience research are inappropriate, as they do not consider how the medium is being used and what the various responses are of audiences to the specific texts.

REFERENCES

Abercrombie, Nicholas (1996): *Television and Society*. Cambridge: Polity Press

Cruz, J. & Justin Lewis (1994): *Viewing, Reading, Listening: Audiences and Cultural Reception.* Boulder, CO: Westview

Hart, Andrew (1991): *Understanding the Media: A Practical Guide.* London: Routledge

Nightingale, Virginia (1996): *Studying Audiences: The Shock of the Real.* London: Routledge

O'Sullivan, Tim, Brian Dutton & Philip Rayner (1994): *Studying the Media.* London: Edward Arnold

Seiter, Ellen *et al.* (Eds.) (1989): *Remote Control.* London: Routledge

3

Changing Landscape of the Mass Media

Modern mass media consumption habits are changing—and fast! Today, environmental law and policy advocates must appreciate the changing landscape of mass media to successfully harness its power. For more than a decade, the audiences for most traditional news sources have steadily declined, as the number of people getting news online has surged. However, today it is not a choice between traditional sources and the Internet for the core elements of today's news audiences.

Over the past few years, distinctions between the traditional categories of mass media—including print and broadcast news—have blurred. With the proliferation of the Internet, numerous media organizations produce news in a variety of platforms. While this is impacting mainstream media, it is also happening in the trade press.

Imagine a 35 year old newspaper reporter whose experience includes more than a decade at newspapers. The reporter has never spent a day working in television news, but in minutes, s/he is about to "go live." In other words, the newspaper reporter's job has changed, so it is no longer just covering news for the newspaper, but now may include reporting on television and/or radio, and perhaps turning the results into a multi-media story for the news outlet's website. It could include a Twitter post and a tag on a social media site.

In the twenty-first century, a wide range of news outlets, news operations, and venues provide information about the rapidly changing world. Cable television has opened hundreds of channels for news, entertainment, and information, and the Internet provides many thousands of sites. Yet audiences are becoming fragmented while news media ownership is becoming more concentrated. At the same time, the audience is becoming more involved in all aspects of the news.

Media Convergence

Though convergence as a concept is here to stay, how things will ultimately play out in the new world of media is unclear. In the convergent media universe, various modes and platforms of communication and information are continually reforming. This means that journalists, environmental advocates, and lawyers must be ready to adapt to the ever-changing demands of technologies.

The Internet is going broadband and television is going interactive. What is seen on, and how the television is used are similar to how the desktop computer is used. With convergence of media new types of use evolve. The users are now able to use media by controlling the stream of information and they have the opportunity to interact with not only the media, but also with the provider of the content and with other users. Technical achievements have resulted in sophisticated and affordable media production equipment available off the shelf.

Today, it is probably easier to set up a worldwide accessible radio or television channel on the Internet than it is to get employment at a traditional broadcasting company. This means that the control of the media production is diverging and that novel, sometimes less traditional content providers, enter the media industry.

Powerful computers, broadband and ubiquitous computing increase the opportunities for the content providers to reach an audience, as well as create possibilities for people to select, change and interact. We are approaching media and media convergence from a mobile informatics field. From this perspective ubiquitous computing is a reality, as the Internet is accessible from a cellular phone or hand-held terminals, as well as terminals in cars and airplanes. The fundamentals of media convergence, mobile informatics and mobile information technology are discussed and related to when proposing mobile media convergence as the next phase in the evolution of the media industry.

Research on convergence of media commonly approaches three interrelated aspects. First, convergence of different types of media businesses and of media itself. Second, on the aspects of regulation and control. Third, the research has been on different forms of interactivity and user participation in the media, and with the media.

Different perspectives of media convergence have been put forward in the literature. The perspectives range from mergers of different organizations such as the Time Warner and America On Line (AOL), and Disney and ABC, to convergence of different types of technology such as the desktop computer and the television, or the desktop computer and the newspaper. The convergence of organizations is a result of how business models change when people's demands and expectations change.

Time Warner merged with AOL to bring movies, music and journals to people over AOLs online web-distribution system. Television broadcast over the Internet started in mid 1990s but has only lately become a reality to Internet users. Almost the same progress has the area of video-on-demand and interactive television.

As this applies to high bandwidth applications such as streamed video, it does naturally also apply to audio: radio broadcast, music distribution and telephony, the later being one of many major subjects in the convergence research. Newspaper on the Internet started out as a way to reuse already edited and published material. This has changed. It is now a way to compete for market shares by keeping contact, interacting and involving the readers.

New types material is published on the web continuously. Opinion polls, email to journalists and chat areas urges the reader to interact. Still, it is sometimes argued that this is solely a remediation and refashioning of old media. Scandinavia which has a strong tradition of public broadcasting service (PBS) and consequently a large number of public television viewers.

New actors are entering the market and the current legislation is trying to accommodate them. The Swedish PBS television demand that computers at home with broadband connections should be considered as television sets, i.e., the owners should pay the television license fee. Media and especially the Internet content regulation and protection of children have received extensive interest.

Interactivity promotes new ways of watching television. Quiz shows have web-sites where the viewer can view and answer the same information as the contestant see in the television studio. Many television programs invites the viewers to participate through telephone and more recently through electronic mail or chat.

Viewers expect more opportunities to interact with the broadcasted program rather then being a passive consumer. In the research on domestic computing and the interactions between children and parents in their homes the findings show that the computer has a symbolic value as both a toy and a tool. As new media is emerging it is important to recognize the interaction the user has with other users, the media itself and the providers of content.

The computer-human Interaction (CHI) research field is concerned with these forms of interaction and interactivity. Recently, the conception of Informatics research as a "design oriented study of information technology use with the intention to contribute to the development of both the use and the technology itself" has influenced much of the conducted research the the Informatics community. The central interest of Informatics research is to intervene and contribute to the process of change rather than to just observe and describe the process.

Information technology changes people's work and it should be emphazised that the informatics interest is to augment people's proficiency rather than to replace them with information technology. The information technology studied has primarily been of a stationary nature, e.g. desktop computers, but as mobile information technology becomes a part of our daily life, both vocational and mundane, a new field of research has emerged, referred to as mobile informatics.

Mobility can be understood as a person in a mobile situation, which is defined by the environmental, physical and social settings surrounding the individual and how these aspects affect her possibilities to perform a certain activity. In some sense all people are mobile for parts of their day. Professional use of information technology in organizations as well as more mundane use of information technology is changing towards increased mobile use.

This change applies to work related cooperation, the way we travel to and from our workspaces, and to leisure time habits. Part of this is due to the development of wireless networks and handheld terminals. The understanding of the development and the technology in a mobile context has been described as "nomadic computing". Nomadicity is defined as: "... the system support needed to provide a rich set of capabilities and services to the nomad as he moves from place to place in a transparent and convenient form".

Mobility is believed to be a key factor in the future and this implies that a new perspective of information technology reltaed research is needed. Hence, mobile informatics is the research field concerned with the development of innovative and useful services for the mobile person in a mobile society.

Mobile Information Technology Cellular phones, personal digital assistants (PDAs) and laptops computers are what we usually refer to as mobile information technology. Cellular phones have been globally adapted and although the network standards differ between the continents it is possible to keep in touch with co-workers, friends and the rest of the world regardless of where you are.

Both via voice and via SMS (short text messages up to 160 characters). PDAs have been widely accepted ever since the handwriting recognition technique and other input techniques proved sufficient. Handheld devices are increasingly powerful and equipped with color screens, speakers, microphones and networking capabilities.

Laptops continue to lose weight and the interface is sufficient with large screens and full size keyboards. They are close to as powerful as stationary computers, and they are mobile. The comparison between the developments of mobile devices is as rapid as it is interesting. PDAs are converging with cellular phones and now host phone functionallity. Phones are equipped with e-mail, calendars and word-processing much like laptop computers and PDAs.

Laptops get more sophisticated communication functionality, e.g. wireless local networks (WLAN) and different types of modems. Obviously different handheld technologies inherit features from each other to represent different appliances in one multi functionallty and multi channel device. The main challenge in the mobile information technology area is no longer to develop handheld devices with potent data processing power and low battery consumption.

There are other challenges since there are many different innovations, ideas and ways of interacting with technology when we are on the move. For instance, not being able to rest the laptop computer on a stable surface, or connect to the company intranet. The feature that allows us to perform desktop tasks in a mobile setting is the possibility to connect to the Internet using cellular and wireless technology.

Although the bandwidth is (still) relatively low it is possible to handle e-mail and web access. Wireless application protocol (WAP) A step towards an "anywhere, anytime" culture concerning information technology. The future holds the introduction of the third generation (3G) of wireless communications (UMTS).

The expected high bandwidth renders possibilities to explore high quality multimedia services on mobile devices, such as videoconferencing, voice chat and fast Internet access. The release and adoption of 3G is expected to to be a first step towards convergence between media, the Internet and mobile people.

Convergence of new media and the evolution of the media industry is fruitful to be explored from a mobile informatics perspective. Mobile informatics is a powerful research field to explore the convergence of media and evolution of the media industry.

This claim is illustrated with three examples, which comprise large groups of media consumers in a temporary mobile context, that is, events of various sorts. The participants have chosen to be mobile since they share a common interest for an event, i.e. their main interest does not lie in the media, but in the event itself.

Media brings additional information that enhances the event experience. WAP makes it possible to request, or pull, information over a GSM telecommunication network. In addition, SMS was used so that the service provider could push information to the users. The cases show examples of mobile IT converging of media.

In short, traditional media have set the standards for the level of information quality and accuracy. A mobile audience is as much information demanding as a stationary or even more so. The demand for qualitative media support and the increasing mobility clearly affect the convergence between the media and mobile information technology.

With media convergence, new forms of media use have emerged: users can enhance a media encounter by controlling the streams of information and have the ability to interact with not only the media itself, but also the content provider and other users. Technical developments have also resulted in affordable off-the-shelf production equipment.

Today it is probably easier to set up a worldwide accessible radio station on the internet than it is to get employment in a traditional radio station. Hence control over media production is diverging and new, sometimes less traditional, content providers are entering the media industries. However, research on media convergence has mostly addressed stationary settings.

But with the growing phenomenon of mobile information technology (IT), it is becoming increasingly important to consider mobility as a dimension of media convergence and mobile media as a new research field. Informatics is the design oriented study of information technology use with the intention of contributing to the development of both that use and the technology itself.

The central interest of informatics is to intervene and contribute to the process of change rather than to merely observe and describe it. The IT studied to date has, however, been primarily of a stationary nature - such as desktop computing- but as mobile IT increasingly becomes a part of our daily life, mobile informatics has started to emerge as research field.

Mobility can be understood as a mobile situation defined by the environmental, physical and social aspects surrounding the individual and how these affect the possibility of performing certain activities. In some sense everybody is mobile, and the professional use of IT in organisations as well as more everyday and mundane use is changing towards increased mobility.

The change is largely due to the shift towards a service society and in organisations there is a trend of performing various tasks as projects requiring cooperation and high levels of mobility among employees. Modern communications technology, the rapid development of wireless networks and handheld terminals have also helped increase society's mobility.

Mobile informatics is consequently defined as a research field concerned with the development of innovative and useful services for the mobile society. Mobile information technology Mobile information technology is currently dominated by cellular phones, personal digital assistants (PDAs) and laptops, although different handheld technologies inherit features from each other so that different appliances are actually incorporated into one device.

The main challenge in mobile technology design is no longer how to develop handheld devices with the necessary data processing power, but rather the many different and innovative ways of using and interacting with technology when we are on the move. The feature that really allows users to perform desktop tasks in a mobile setting is the possibility of connecting to the internet using wireless technology.

This is the first step towards an information technology culture of 'anywhere, anytime'. In the not too distant future we will see the release of the third generation telecommunications technology, 3G. The high bandwidth of this technology renders possible high-quality multimedia services on mobile devices, such as videoconferencing, voice chat and smooth internet access.

Using mobile media gives them additional information and the possibility of retrieving information on demand to enhance the experience of the event. In all three cases multi-channel platforms were implemented for event visitors. Users equipped with Wireless Application Protocol (WAP) or Short Message System (SMS) enabled cellular phones could take advantage of the mobile media channels provided.

WAP makes it possible to request information over a telecommunications network, while SMS enables the service provider to push information to users. The media coverage available to spectators was either provided at the site or accessed through mobile IT carried by the user. It is the need for useage in a mobile context that determines which media technology is used.

The purpose of going to an event is to participate and experience the atmosphere, and the use of any type of media is only a way of retrieving event-related information. This puts challenging demands on mobile media. For those participating in such events, the need for up-to-date accurate information takes precedence over any preference for a particular technology and when necessary will move from one channel to another to obtain that information.

The convergence between media coverage and mobile communications is consequently the result of the users' mobile behaviour. The use of mobile media takes place, however, in extremely diverse conditions and this impacts on how successful it is at delivering the required information to users. Initially the mobile media worked, but became ineffective when the organisers were unable to deal promptly with the tragic situation and continue to provide up-to-date content.

Furthermore, the mobile technology proved to be neither dynamic nor robust enough when thousands of people attempted to phone home simultaneously. Handheld devices, mobile communications and conventional media are converging. Traditional media such as newspapers, radio and television have set the standards for information quality, accuracy and delivery.

And it appears that mobile IT users expect accurate, timely and high quality information delivered through reliable channels. People's interest in sporting or entertainment events tend to make them familiarise themselves with the different media channels (radio, TV, the internet etc) through which they can obtain relevant information.

Interest in a particular aspect and/or personal preference may influence the choice of media channel, but fast retrieval of up-to-date information is usually more important. As soon as a media channel proves to be either inaccurate or fragile, the consumer will abandon it for a more reliable alternative. The rapidly increasing penetration of sophisticated mobile IT into society, and the demands users make on that technology, indicates that a new research area of 'mobile media' is emerging.

Economics and the New Media

Economic realities are playing a role in the drive to new technologies. Audience declines coupled with worldwide economic realities have left many news organizations facing financial crises. In fact, the state of the American news media in 2008 is more troubled than ever before, according to a study by the Pew Research Center. The main problem is not the changing media landscape—rather, it is money. As outlets shift, advertising revenue is not migrating in lockstep-fashion online, and income for most media providers is thus dropping.

Changes in the media landscape coupled with economic shifts are forcing many journalists to reinvent their profession and outlets their business models. This situation has led to some transformation in the way journalists cover news. For example, in 2008 WUSA TV became "the first station in Washington to replace its crews with one-person 'multimedia journalists' who will shoot and edit news stories single-handedly." Under this approach, television reporters will be shooting and editing their own stories, and those who have traditionally been the ones behind the camera will be doing the work of reporters, occasionally appearing on TV or in video clips on the stations' Web site. In the print arena, some "daily" newspapers are only publishing six (or fewer) days a week. Conferences on achieving convergence, such as one hosted by the American Press Institute in 2005 entitled, "Cross-Platform Media Teams: Strategic Thinking for a Multi-Platform World," or another hosted by Newsplex at the College of Mass Communications and Information Studies at the University of South Carolina in 2008, entitled "Teaching and Research in Convergent Media," are becoming common.

Such convergence has the most direct impact on those working in the media. For example, one journalist described his experience with simultaneous multi-media reporting of the 2007 Consumer Electronics Show for CNN, as "getting a very personal look at how technology is changing journalism and the consumption of news." He talked about his multi-platform journalism by saying that "[n]ot only was I providing traditional live reports for CNN, Headline News and CNN International, I was also blogging for CNN.com, uploading digital photos . . . for the tech section of the Web site, and, thanks to a flash memory-based microphone, I was providing audio podcast interviews that ended up on Apple's iTunes. A CNN.com camera crew following me around the Convention Center floor produced streaming video reports for the network Web site."

Thus, journalism as a profession is changing. As one reporter wrote in his blog, "[o]ur challenge in this painful, historic time is to invent journalistic forms and alliances that citizens will support to get the facts they need to govern themselves. One journalist told me it will not be a silver bullet, one-size-fits-all answer, but a media cocktail where modern news consumers choose what they want. . . . There will not be one answer, but many."

Many in the media are hoping convergence will offer a long term answer to their problems. However, it is worth noting that stations in Nashville and San Francisco who used multimedia journalists on an experimental basis backed away because of "falling quality" and declining ratings. Just as the first move for convergence for many media outlets has been incorporating a Web presence into their traditional media platform, the environmental lawyer will need to leverage this new media (as well as traditional media) to be successful in the Internet era.

Those seeking coverage must therefore remain aware that journalists are doing plenty and being asked to do even more these days. Journalists are, at the same time, worried about their profession. The President of the

Society of Professional Journalists admitted in 2008 that "it is difficult to be cheery and optimistic about the news business at this time, especially newspapers. We are all susceptible to the possibility of layoffs in our newsroom. . . ." Furthermore, he wrote, "[t]he news business continues to struggle with a bleak economy and an industry evolution that is seeing people's advertising and news consumption habits shift at a pace that has us struggling to keep up." Nevertheless, he concluded that "[d]espite the rough economic news and trends, there is some belief that things will settle and the reshaping and restructuring that has shaken our faith will pay dividends. The role journalists play in democracy is far too important to give up on it."

There is no doubt, however, that convergence has refocused journalism to its core mission—informing the public. Today, that means a multi-layered media approach, involving news from newspapers, television, radio and the Internet. So what does this mean for journalists and the future of journalism? For reporters, this new media is a new way to tell news stories. For the journalism profession, "the most promising element heading into 2008 may be innovation. The news industry now appears to be taking to new technology in earnest." For the environmental law and policy advocate, it means that attracting appropriate news coverage may involve even more effort.

Audience-Centric Reporting

Recent advances in technology have transformed consumers from a passive "audience" to active participants in the creation, analysis, and distribution of mass media content. As a leading media textbook by John Vivian points out, "major media companies also are trying to establish a future for themselves in reaching audiences in new digital ways." That text goes on to explain that "[t]raditional origination points for communication, like a book publisher or a radio station, suddenly have been joined by millions of additional origination points, all interconnected."

The mass media audience has moved front and center as journalism has entered the twenty-first century. Dan Gillmor, a journalism scholar devoted to studying new media trends, describes media that come from the audience as part of "a global conversation that is growing in strength, complexity and power. When people can express themselves, they will. When they can do so with powerful yet inexpensive tools, they take to the new-media realm quickly. When they can reach a potentially global audience, they can change the world." As stated similarly by legal scholar Jerome Barron: "[Forty years ago], the media world in the United States was very different than it is today. The major television networks and the daily newspapers had an influence on and a dominance over the opinion process that they do not have today. These television networks and newspaper chains once operated as the gatekeepers to the opinion process. They are still powerful and influential, but the rise of the Internet has shrunk their domain."

In other words, news has become audience-centric. We adopt the term audience-centric, which is not original to us, as representing the concept we (and other scholars) have observed in recent years. To us, the term audience-centric reporting means journalism that embraces the audience in shaping (including originating, gathering, disseminating, commenting on, etc.) news, both in real time and in reflective or investigative efforts. Terms that others have used to capture this concept include grassroots journalism, networked journalism, open source journalism, citizen media, participatory journalism, hyperlocal journalism, bottom-up journalism, distributed journalism, and others. Regardless of the term used, the concept of audience-centric reporting is not only a "hot topic," it is an essential consideration for those who wish to work with the mass media in this day and time.

Freelance journalist Mark Glaser has summarized the audience-centric phenomenon as follows: "When a traditional media outlet covers a story, the editor usually assigns the story to a reporter, the reporter does the work and turns in a story that gets edited and published. But in the case of ad hoc citizen journalism, a blogger or observer might see something happening that's newsworthy and bring it to the attention of the blogosphere or the online public. As more people uncover facts and work together, the story can snowball without a guiding editor and can produce interesting results—leading to the mainstream media finally covering it and giving it wider exposure." The audience is in the middle of reporting…and often at the beginning or the end as well.

As one considers this new reality, it is important to keep in mind that the transition from the traditional media has not only changed how content is created but *what* content is created. While traditional media had typically involved watching TV news and reading the newspaper to hear stories that reflect general news values, other factors can come into play today. In fact, as the transition to audience-centric media accelerated—when mobile devices such as cell phones became prevalent and connectivity to the Internet became mainstream—the nature of news has changed on many levels. *"Journalism of the future will involve all sorts of media: old and new, niche and mass, the personal and the global. It will involve storytelling in every combination of words, picture, and sound. And it will be propelled not just by journalists but by news audiences. That is already apparent today."*

What does this mean in an environmental law and policy context? Whether it's an update on water quality in a local stream or a disappointed taxpayer voicing objection to a building ordinance proposal, Internet and other technologies have shifted power and made the job of many journalists more participatory. It simultaneously increased the responsibility of environmental advocates to leverage the mass media when appropriate to their causes.

Today, content for the new mass media is often captured, processed, and transmitted through mobile devices, passed along social network sites, and in some cases becomes the headline story for traditional media. The audience is often in the thick of things.

Some audience-centric reporting is purely user-generated. Yet in an attempt to harness the "journalist at large" evolution, traditional media outlets have also incorporated increased audience-defined content into online venues for the media outlet. For example, CNN incorporates user video through iReporter segments, Fox News does the same through the use of UReport, and Reuters has You Witness News to allow the public at large to comment, share, or report on ongoing events of interest. In preparing for coverage of the 2008 Democratic and Republican conventions, Reuters openly embraced the new breed of citizen journalism in its request for mobile journalists to participate in the convention coverage. In so doing, Reuters acknowledged that ". . . because of new technology and online distribution, entire elections can now hinge on moments captured not by traditional journalists, but by ordinary citizens and those closest to the action."

Some journalists are struggling to keep up with these developments. As one commentator put it, "[a]sk any journalist today how the Internet has changed journalism, and the most likely reply will be, 'how hasn't it?'" Professional journalists are being told to "incorporate the freedom to tell the story inherent in citizen journalism without losing traditional principles." This may be easier said than done.

What does this mean for the environmental advocate? The proliferation of readily-accessible and easy-to-use technology can allow even small groups to disseminate information to a wide audience. Of course, a centralized website can continue to ensure consistency of a message and accommodate the audience's schedule. Although website development is not the topic of this book, environmental stakeholders must be prepared to compliment their marketing strategy with an enticing presence on the Internet. Just as national interest groups like Sierra Club, the National Association of Homebuilders, and national environmental law organizations like the Pacific Legal Foundation and Earthjustice, rely on Internet sites to support distribution of information, smaller citizen groups such as the Colusa County Citizens for Safe Water, the South Carolina-based Citizens for Sound Conservation, and the South Carolina Lowcountry-focused Friends of the Rivers are using the Internet to present a message and attract interest in their work.

Good websites are, however, no longer enough. Facebook and Linked-In pages, Twitter Tweets, RSS feeds, blogs and other evolving tools are becoming the common tools used even by lawyers. As will be further explored below, audience-centric media is evolving quickly. In fact, portions of this book will be old news by its publication, in terms of the details of all the options available in this arena. New media expert Amy Gahran has explained that "[o]nline communication and publishing technology isn't just one-way — it's all ways, all the time." The role of the audience in this new world is crucial, and it is shifting.

Beyond the introduction of the Internet, it is the audience-centric aspects of the web that have most impacted the work of journalists. Emily Bell, Editor-in-Chief of *Guardian*, commented in May 2008 on the changing world of news, pointing not to the Internet per se when reflecting on the rapid shifts, but "much more what's happened with various programming protocols since, what you would know as Web 2.0, which is the ability to allow the uploading of information by the local generation. Flickr, blogs, etc. have completely changed the game, because it means all matter of information is exposed and is available to be manipulated, uploaded, reported on, etc. by a whole set of people who are no longer in control of a distribution bottleneck."

Below, we briefly explore some of these new audience-centric media outlets, including blogs, podcasts, RSS, Wiki, Widget and Social Networks. This section of the book is not meant to be a complete list or a definitive exploration of these areas, but rather an introduction to some "new" concepts available in an audience-centric journalism world. Direct links and further exploration of these areas are available on the book website at [INSERT].

Blogs

A blog (a contraction of the term "web log") is an Internet site with regular entries of commentary, descriptions of events, or other material such as graphics or video. There are many approaches to blogging. In light of "the level of activity and creativity, the negative image of blogging in the mainstream media seems to be fading away as blogging becomes more popular."

Blogs by their nature are audience-centric, even though there are many forms of blogs. Many individuals and organizations have their own blogs. There are a plethora of more general blogs dedicated to various environmental topics. Likewise, mainstream media are increasingly relying on blogs in the environmental arena. Individual journalists keep blogs about the journalism industry and related topics. The world of blogs has even expanded to video blogs which are sometimes referred to as VLOGs.

Podcasts

Podcasts are recorded audio programs posted on the Internet. As one podcasting website describes it, "'[a] podcast' is a buzzword to describe a very simple concept: an audio or video file available on the Internet for you to listen to and/or watch." Lawyers use podcasting all the time. As the *ABA Law Practice* magazine explained in 2008, "[p]odcasts are great marketing vehicles for letting a wide market know how knowledgeable you are in your chosen area of expertise. And because they are voice-based, podcasts typically provide your audience with a more personal, engaging view of you, since you can use inflections and tone, inject humor and the like in ways that the written word does not allow."

If you want to use a podcast, first and foremost you must record it. There are various podcasting software applications you can purchase or download for free from the web. Most people use their own computer, but often invest in a good microphone even if one is built into the system. You also can use services to record podcasts by phone. Once you have it recorded, you can use websites dedicated to sharing podcasts, such as Podcast.com, and Podcast Alley, for dissemination. Of course, you also can post your podcast on your organization's website.The important thing to keep in mind about podcasting is that the podcaster can create content and broadcast it via the Internet without any professional media involvement. If you don't want to get in the podcasting business, you might connect with existing environmental podcasting efforts. For example, Public Radio International's weekly "Living on Earth" has a podcast version. The podcast is made available following the weekly broadcast of the show on some 300 public radio stations, which airs in 9 of the 10 top radio markets and reaches 80% of the United States. There are numerous other podcast sites about energy, alternative fuels, the wilderness and wildlife. The options for creative use of podcasts by environmental law and policy professionals are considerable.

RSS

RSS, Rich Site Summary or real simply syndication, "alerts users to new material posted to their favorite blogs or news websites." "Instead of trying to keep up with all the websites you enjoy, or need to read, RSS will push the latest information to you. It's news on demand based on your needs." Most newspapers, magazine and television websites now offer RSS feeds.

RSS creates basically a list of hyperlinks. When you subscribe to RSS feeds, you effectively are creating a wire service tailored to your personal interests. As one expert described it, "RSS will save you time and make your Web surfing much more efficient. Rather than tediously checking dozens of Web sites for new information, RSS enables you to go to one place and find all the latest content from each of those sites. RSS makes it easy to read lots of sites—from weblogs to major media—in very little time."

Where does one get feeds? The Radio Television News Directors' Association delivers RSS feeds that provide updated information on everything from news research to issues regarding Freedom of Information. The American Bar Association offers feeds from the section of Environment, Energy and Resources including highlights from the section on current topics. Countless other RSS feeds are available to the lawyer and others interested in the environment. In addition to subscribing, RSS is also a tool environmental lawyers and advocates can use to share podcasts, website updates, and other current information.

Wiki

The wiki format is another form of audience-centric journalism. Open online forums, called wikis, allow anyone to post and edit information. Wikis are basically collaborative writing projects. The original idea behind wikis was to create encyclopedias collecting knowledge from anyone and everyone, like Wikipedia, which describes itself as "a multilingual, Web-based, free-content encyclopedia project. The name 'Wikipedia' is a portmanteau . . . of the words wiki (a type of collaborative Web site) and encyclopedia. Wikipedia's articles provide links to guide the user to related pages with additional information. Wikipedia is written collaboratively by volunteers from all around the world; anyone can edit it." Wikis have developed into a participatory journalism platform. For example, in response to Hurricane Katrina, wikis proved to be a valuable resource. One site, for example, posted constantly-updated information such as facts about housing, help needed, volunteers, and jobs. There are wikis dedicated to many subjects, including the environment. Participating in drafting or posting links to wikis may be of benefit to environmental lawyers and advocates.

Widget

A web widget is a portable application that you can install on your website, blog, social networking page or computer desktop. For example, CBS News widgets allow you to embed free breaking news and entertainment content on your personal site. Once the widget is installed, it updates itself automatically with fresh stories, photos or video. Widgets can be time savers and important tools for environmental lawyers and advocates.

Social Networks

Twitter, LinkedIN, Facebook, MySpace and FriendFeed are all social networking sites. Scholars who study this phenomenon have defined "social network sites as web-based services that allow individuals to (1) construct a public or semi-public profile within a bounded system, (2) articulate a list of other users with whom they share a connection, and (3) view and traverse their list of connections and those made by others within the system. The nature and nomenclature of these connections may vary from site to site." Because "there is little empirical research that addresses whether members use [social networking sites] to maintain existing ties or to form new ones, the social capital implications of these services are unknown." But they are hugely popular. Knowing this, many mainstream media are active in these social networks.

Twitter: describes itself as "a service for friends, family, and co-workers to communicate and stay connected through the exchange of quick, frequent answers to one simple question: What are you doing?" When you send a message on Twitter, you are "tweeting." Like other social networking tools, Twitter is increasingly being used by media professionals and quickly is working its way into the reporter's toolkit. "In recent months, the Twittering crowd at CNN has exploded from 25 people to about 150." CNN anchors are tweeting while they're on air. According to Victor Hernandez, director of coverage for CNN, "[t]oday it's a part of everyone's lives, and not just the geeks." Twitter has been likewise touted as a tool for legal marketing.

Environmental news is breaking and developing on Twitter. For example, when the Tennessee Valley Authority's coal ash disaster occurred on December 23, 2008, environmental journalist Amy Gahran posted the first of what would become hundreds of tweets about the breach, days before the mainstream media even carried the story. Since then, hundreds of tweets have been shared on Twitter, including many from major outlets.

LinkedIn: is yet another online social networking site. LinkedIn is "an online network of more than 30 million experienced professionals from around the world representing 150 industries." As one lawyer put it, "LinkedIn provides an online method to network. Simply register for a FREE account, enter a few facts about yourself (occupation, employers, education—as much or as little as you want), and you can instantly connect with people like yourself." The American Bar Association's Section on Energy Environment and Resources has many LinkedIn members. Journalists are active on LinkedIn as well, using it for both personal career reasons, as well as finding sources, topics and trends.

The future of social networking is unclear, yet there clearly are opportunities for the environmental lawyer and advocate to use these facile tools.

Video Sharing Sites

There also are websites where anyone with an Internet connection can watch and share original videos worldwide. Perhaps the most well-known of these sites, YouTube, allows people to easily upload and share videos across the Internet through websites, mobile devices, blogs, and email. YouTube even has a citizen journalism section called Citizen News. Recognizing its power, many major broadcast news outlets have feeds on YouTube. At the same time, regardless of viewpoint, many advocates frequently use YouTube on an individual level for environmental matters. Environmental advocates should monitor, and perhaps consider using, this increasingly powerful medium.

In closing, this section shows that much of the news audience can and has moved front and center in terms of the way they interact with news. Be aware that, in light of this audience-centric world, direct communications between individuals (including reporters and sources) have become multi-faceted. No longer is it just a phone call or an in-person interview. Reporters communicate frequently via email. As one reporter described it, "in addition to standard face-to-face interviews and brief questions and fact checking done via email, Instant Messaging (IM) is finding a place of its own across newsrooms across the country as a way to streamline the reporting process. Offering reporters the ability to speak with sources in real time, IM has quickly replaced the wait reporters had to endure for a response to email or phone messages" Other platforms also are becoming increasingly prevalent, including Twittering, and others. Likewise, another journalist has written that Facebook pages "are particularly useful for stories where events are still unfolding because they will often carry eyewitness accounts and background material." Thus even if an environmental lawyer or advocate is not engaged in creating content or active through LinkedIn, Twitter, or YouTube, the reporter covering the story may be getting information and contacting other sources through these audience-centric frameworks. This is an area to watch closely in the coming decade.

Predicting the Future Media Landscape

Predicting the future of media with specificity is, of course, impossible. But using concepts of what is available today, and reflecting on what historically has developed, can help. As some convergence scholars have remarked, dissecting the functions being performed by news media may assist in planning for a broader world. So though the core lessons set forth in earlier chapters apply, times are changing! Nevertheless, a vital role remains for journalism professionals to play in deciding what to report. As veteran journalist Walter Cronkite put it, journalists "make the judgment as to whether something is important or not. That's how things get in the newspaper. That's how things get on the evening news broadcast. What they think is important, it may not be what we judge to be important. When we judge it, we're not judging it from on high, but through the journalism standards, on what interests most of the people at any given moment in time, and that which is important to most of the people get on the air." So being comfortable with traditional journalistic concepts will serve environmental law and policy advocates well. For example, consumers still may want to know that print journalists are investigating and writing big stories, even though they may not read them. Likewise, although network news is not going to disappear, audiences are shifting and, in some demographics, declining. Internet audiences are not stable.

Nevertheless, the increasing role of news as entertainment is real. As the former anchor of Nightline, Ted Koppel, remarked, "[t]o the extent that we're now judging journalism by the same standards that we apply to entertainment –in other words, give the public what it wants, not necessarily what it ought to hear, what it ought to see, what it needs, but what it wants—that may prove to be one of the greatest tragedies in the history of American journalism." Yet it is probably too late to alter the way news delivery choice has moved to the consumer—as one scholar has remarked, "[e]ven if a consensus emerged to reduce media choice for the public good, it would still be technically impossible, even temporarily, to put the genie back in the bottle." Being aware of audience desires and how they may influence media professionals may, however, help the environmental law and policy advocate in achieving effective media coverage.

There is no doubt, as has been discussed throughout this book, that the Internet has changed journalism. The decade-old Online News Association notes "[a]s digital delivery systems become the primary source of news for a growing segment of the world's population, it presents complex challenges and opportunities for journalists as well as the news audience." The American Society of Newspaper Editors has proposed the removal of the word "paper" to reflect plans that will expand its membership to include editors of online-only news Web. Further, "[e]yetracking research" is being used to strengthen news websites. And as one scholar has noted, "[f]rom a media perspective, the emergence of citizen journalism has blurred the line separating mainstream media from online new media." Journalism is transforming. Therefore, environmental advocates must be ready for whatever comes, and responsive to what they see as emerging needs.One must be both responsive, nimble, and focused to maximize effective press coverage of environmental issues.

Media in Globalised Era

The term "globalization" is often portrayed as a positive force which is unifying widely different societies, integrating them into a "global village", and enriching all in the process. It is variously described as an inevitable by-product of human evolution and progress, as if it were an organic process, governed by the laws of nature. However, globalization is not necessarily a natural progression emerging out of the ordinary communication and interaction of people and cultures around the world.

Rather, it results from deliberate human choice by a powerful group of nations, transnational corporations (TNCs) and international organizations which have stakes in the process. The new communications and information technologies have provided methods for large corporations to maximize profits by entering foreign markets.

They have also given nation-states reason to re-examine the strategic implications of globalization for their national economic and political development. Globalization is a complex phenomenon, marked by two opposing forces. On the one hand, it is characterized by massive economic expansion and technological innovation. On the other hand, there is increased inequality, cultural and social tumult, and individual alienation.

Globalization of mass media is an integral part of this phenomenon and is propelled by the same ideologies, organizations and forces. In turn, the digital revolution and the introduction of new communications technologies are redefining our notions of politics and the structures of power in society. Increasingly, power resides in the hands of those who can produce, control and disseminate information most effectively.

Human communication is increasing exponentially in amount and variety and is covering greater distances in shorter time. This proliferation of communications technologies and the increased global interdependence it creates are often erroneously viewed as directly contributing to global understanding, equality and harmony.

However, as many scholars have pointed out, an increase in electronic communication does not necessarily mean an increase in human communication and cooperation. In fact, many suggest that it leads to the replacement of traditional structures such as the family, religion and the community with ones supposedly more relevant to the modern world: the mass media, the nation-state, and the global economy.

As these new systems emerge, they in turn reinforce the globalization process and provide channels for governments, transnational corporations and media distributors to communicate and expand their power and resource base. Thus, globalization is both a prerequisite for and a cause of the development of communications industries.

This shift from the "local" to the "global" is being portrayed as an innocuous effect of human progress and beneficial to all involved. For example, the 1993 U.S. Department of Commerce Report on the Globalization of the Mass Media states that liberalization and internationalization of media markets is improving "the economic welfare of all countries". Interestingly, both the North and the South see globalization as commercial enterprises increasing their activities across national boundaries, providing opportunities for international trade, and simultaneously spreading their cultural and societal values. This description is accurate, but it does not explore any of the larger societal and cultural implications for countries in the South, nor the implications for equity and democracy within the industrialized world.

The assumption is that such international trade will eventually "trickle down" to individuals. It has also been suggested that the new communications technologies and media are spreading the existing structures and values which are dominant globally and emphasize the free-market economy and a capitalist liberal democracy.

In this perspective, the climate of privatization, deregulation and commercialization which exists in the United States is actively being replicated across the world, in order to facilitate international commercial ventures. The marked increase in transportation technologies in recent decades has brought increased travel and opportunities for trade.

The spread of direct broadcast satellite (DBS) and mass media has also served to break down barriers to communications and international commerce, and to make it more difficult for governments and regulatory bodies to protect their cultures and societies. What we are observing as a process of globalization may find its roots in the early development projects and theories which emerged at the end of World War II under such international aid programmes as the Marshall Plan.

These programmes promoted the process of development which came to be known as modernization. Modernization theory sees communications and mass media as a necessary precursor to economic growth and social change. This theory also emphasizes the connection between media expansion and institution-building, political stability, and economic growth.

Thus, it has helped to perpetuate the widespread assumption that broadcast television and radio helps nations "leapfrog" into the information age. According to this dominant view of nation-building, the mass media are a major component in fostering economic, political and social development.

They are cited as methods for helping to spread democratic ideals, increase political participation, create feelings of community, build national unity and loyalty, facilitate informed self-government, and enable participation in the new information society. This assumed connection between media and development is still governing the development process today, and is now being influenced heavily by the aggressive corporate culture of transnationals.

The philosophies, goals and economic approaches of these new commercial enterprises are often entering development agencies and strongly influencing the development process. The new, powerful satellite technology has hastened this process. It gives TNCs the means to bypass national regulations and boundaries and get foreign programming and information into countries which had previously tried to limit foreign messages.

As these commercial enterprises expand their market shares internationally, they are gaining power and influence over governments worldwide, as well as over international regulatory bodies like the ITU, GATT and UN agencies. Since the 1996 Telecommunications Act was passed in the United States, signifying a huge change in U.S. communications policy, there has been an explosion of transnational mergers and acquisitions.

Companies like Disney, Viacom and Time-Warner have diversified their media holdings, bought television networks, movie production houses, cable channels and other media enterprises. Thus, they own both the means of production and distribution, further concentrating the media outlets and the information we receive via the mass media.

Tunstall describes the phenomenon of "Hollyweb". In this process, Hollywood production companies are acquiring television networks, cable channels, and TV stations and are branching out into such areas as theme parks, music production and publishing. The magic word in the U.S. media now is "vertical", where production and distribution companies are allowed to own these various types of networks, channels and television stations.

Globalization of the mass media should also be viewed in the context of its demographic constituencies-an aspect often left to the sidelines in our discourse. Within the next few decades, the populations of China and India combined will constitute almost half of humanity. This demographic shift no doubt will be an important factor in determining the geographical and economic basis of the market, as well as the major conglomerates involved in the mass media.

The rapid expansion of the mass media is based on the assumption that information is inherently neutral. This idea has been greatly magnified by organizations and companies which have a stake in the globalization process, and it ignores the important role that cultural and social values play in shaping information.

The choices made every day by government officials, network executives and media producers and distributors determine what topics are covered, what information is selected and the way it is portrayed. The simple choice of one story over another is as much a political choice as it is economic and professional. It determines what becomes part of our national consciousness and what values and ideas take precedence in the general public.

The choices made by the media and their producers are always a function of their own individual beliefs, but, more important, they reflect cultural, societal and national values and identity. Overwhelmingly, the mass media promise that globalization will bring friendship, harmony and international cooperation.

The mass media are viewed as a means to increase diversity, democracy and empower the individual. However, beneath the overly optimistic image of global cooperation and sharing lies a side of globalization which is generally ignored by the media. There are many unintended and unpredicted side-effects of the information revolution and the spread of mass media.

Few if any of the early modernization theorists predicted the political apathy, increased alienation and dissolution of community and family life which have been widely noted in the industrialized world. Still, the media are often cited as contributing to increased government transparency and democratic participation by playing the role of a "watchdog", pressuring politicians and other leaders into being accountable to their fellow citizens.

Despite this continuing faith in the positive impact of the media, many people are becoming cynical and apathetic about the impact of media and their role in society. The press appears to be losing credibility, and is often criticized as overly preoccupied with appearances, celebrity and wealth, as well as generating new media factions, such as the tabloid press, or the "stalkarazzi".

More important, there is concern emerging over the freedom of the press, and many believe it to be subject to manipulation by government, advertising, and other powerful institutions in society. And yet, globalization is often portrayed as a way to increase the diversity and the richness of our culture by adding to the variety of information circulating in the media outlets.

However, this idea is grossly exaggerated at best, as the global media are often dominated by western products and Hollywood values. The information transmitted through American television and movies is mostly "infotainment" and advertising. The promises that the mass media transmit information necessary for improved political participation and socio-economic development are increasingly seen with skepticism.

In the United States, many people complain of a startling lack of diversity on television and in the print media. In fact, the proliferation of television and cable channels which was supposed to generate variety and consumer choice has churned out an astounding number of programmes on a surprisingly small range of topics. The media portray a very limited and excessively violent view of the world.

There is a type of "silent censorship", where centralization has limited the information able to penetrate through the media gatekeepers. This concentration of media control has also allowed for very few criticisms of the establishment in the media. Criticizing the dominant view of globalization and rapid commercial and technological expansion, or suggesting alternatives, is portrayed as reactionary or "un-business".

In fact, communications scholars have found that in the industrialized world, there is a growing dependence on media which is proving to be quite harmful. There seems to be an almost blind faith in "the new", "the modern" and technological solutions to problems, and a subsequent devaluing of traditional values and structures, no matter how valuable they have proved to be over centuries. People are surprisingly quick to reject their indigenous traditions and cultural values as reactionary, static and irrelevant to their lives.

The most prevalent assumption underlying the process of globalization is that an unfettered free market, fierce competition between companies, and a free flow of information will deliver the greatest good for the greatest number of people. Adam Smith's "invisible hand" is supposed to determine the flow of information and the future path of the world economy.

However, this idea has been transformed to mean the free flow of commercial information and expression. Today, businesses, government structures and international agencies have become so large that they are no longer directly responsive and accountable to the needs and desires of the people they are supposed to serve.

As the media continue to centralize, while simultaneously serving a wider audience, it becomes more difficult for the individual to influence the substance and the systems through which information is produced and distributed. Thus, Korten warns, individuals have less ability to impact the policies, goals and directions of their social, economic and political institutions.

Changing Media Policies

According to the 1993 U.S. Department of Commerce report on the globalization of the mass media, the United States has a marked advantage in this process, and is having a remarkable impact in the liberalization of markets internationally. Ironically, however, communications policies in the United States are surprisingly protectionist, considering the vehement advocacy in the U.S. for an unfettered global free market. Less than 2 per cent of American television is foreign.

Exports of American television, film and video products are $2.1 billion dollars greater than U.S. imports of foreign cultural products. Communication policies are stringent regarding foreign penetration into the domestic market. The communications acts of 1912 and 1927 installed strict regulations on foreign ownership of broadcast and other communications industries in order to protect American national integrity and security.

The new world information and communications order today is being "liberalized" at an unprecedented rate in the U.S. and in the South. Since

1988, there has been an explosion of transnational mergers and acquisitions. In 1996, a new communication act was passed in the U.S. government. It relaxed regulations so as to encourage the convergence of the telecommunication, computer, and television industries, creating the so-called National Information Infrastructure (NII) or "information superhighway".

This was followed by the Global Information Infrastructure (GII) of the European Union, which in great part replicated the framework of NII. This convergence of technologies and alliances means that the prevailing information infrastructure is designed mainly by a small number of sources-and this process of vertical integration is a central part of globalization. The globalization of international markets and the power of U.S. communication industries are generating increased concern around the world about issues of cultural sovereignty and the right to self-determination.

An example from the realm of cultural industries, publishing, illustrates the nature of the phenomenon of globalization. While book production has increased 40 per cent worldwide from 1983 to 1994, there is still a severe shortage of educational and scholarly texts in much of the world. For example, due to this inequality, countries of the South import much of their materials from the industrialized nations.

Diversity is lacking in published works because the large conglomerates controlling the industry do not have competition. To further complicate the issue, chain bookstores have the market power to dictate the nonscholarly texts available, giving them influence over the publishing houses. Similarly, television and film distribution are managed by large con-glomerates which create marketable, not necessarily quality, material.

Many countries in the North, including France and Canada, as well as nations of the South such as Indonesia and Singapore, are looking for communications policies which will ensure the national integrity and unity of their nations. For example, Canada's communications policies have been concerned with issues of cultural, linguistic and national identity and diversity for decades because its population is very multicultural and spread over a large geographic area. The government has participated directly in the media since broadcasting began in the early 1920s, on the premise that political sovereignty and unity are directly linked to communication and culture.

The Canadian Broadcasting Corporation (CBC) was founded to promote Canadian identity and community, despite cultural and linguistic differences. Unlike the American "melting pot" concept, Canadian policies were designed not only to promote national unity, but also to strengthen and validate the myriad cultural backgrounds present in Canada. There has been continued government support and funding for the mass media and cultural production.

All media are expected to have at least 64 per cent "Canadian" content, and there are policies to make the media more representative of Canada's diverse population, including women, Francophones, indige-nous people and other minorities. However, the multicultural policies have been nearly impossible to enforce and had negligible impact on mainstream media.

Creating separate French and English communications industries has not built bilingual national identity, but two separate identities. Flourishing Quebec media and cultural industries have strengthened Quebec culture, nationalism and identity, but also deepened Anglophone/Francophone divisions, perhaps contributing to the dramatic referendum in 1996.

Canada is not alone in its response to globalization and its search for self-determination. Time has proven that commercial mass media rarely meet the needs of all people, especially minorities. Laws and policies governing communication must allow the creation of a space for those not represented in mainstream media.

The United Nations World Television Forum in November 1997 warned that mainstream programming must take into account the constantly changing demographics of our world and address both majority and minority interests. Because commercial media take mass appeal and economic incentives as main determinants of what they programme, they will rarely reflect the far more complex and diverse needs of smaller groups and individuals.

The European Union's audiovisual policy issued in 1989 was another instance of reaction to globalization. The policy included three steps-to promote national and regional broadcasting, foster European communications capabilities, and serve as guarding principles against the onslaught of the American media.

Following the EC directives, France acted to aid the French movie industry with subsidies, protect it from the American influence, and impose quotas on American audiovisual products. French officials claimed they were, in essence, preserving and protecting French culture.

Against the new backdrop of globalization and development of mass media, the South faces both opportunities and challenges. These may best be examined by tracing the four trends of (1) ethnicization of mass media, (2) development of alternative media, (3) design of comprehensive policies, and (4) internationalization of the mass media within the South.

Many countries in the South are concerned with bolstering their national identity and strengthening their role in the globalization of media and technology. They recognize that information and communications are increasingly the source of power in our world today, and those who cannot compete effectively in the communications and information sectors will suffer both economically and culturally.

Indonesia, which launched its own communications satellite in the 1960s, is a case in point. The Indonesian government not only desired to use satellite technology for its telecommunications infrastructure, but wanted to minimize as much as possible the impact of foreign, particularly western, broadcast television on its population.

In response to global economic pressures, the Indonesian government began to privatize communications industries, seemingly to improve communication contents and infrastructure. However, these steps did not necessarily improve democratic participation, as demonstrated by the events of the early part of 1998. Indonesian television and radio industries came to be run by the government, and thus came to serve as a means of reinforcing the *status quo*.

The process of globalization is also leading to change in the very nature of communication in societies where traditional media were the sole means of communication. In a small Kazakh village, social relationships were built on the giving and receiving of gifts (such as camels, sheep, cars) and attendance at feasts. These displays of generosity, often in excess, were part of the social structure based upon reciprocality, and contributed to strong family ties, social networks and communication.

The collapse of the Soviet Union and the advent of privatization and capitalism brought a sharp drop in village living standards, a decline in traditional gift-giving, simultaneous straining of older social networks, and a breakdown of traditional communication channels. As a result, the Kazakhs as described above, as well as a plethora of other ethnic groups across the globe, are having to adapt and create new modes of communication as globalization continues to lessen cultural isolation.

The systems governing communications today, though varied, are mainly those seeking to maximize profits, leading to increased dependence on consumer products. At the same time, there is an increased call by individuals to foster community, cultural integrity and human cooperation and understanding.

International bodies and institutions, such as ITU and WTO, which govern communications and information industries and shape the future of the information society, are increasingly pressured by corporations and trade lobbies. At the same time, the new Global Information Infrastructure, which is being designed and promoted by industrialized countries, has not taken into account the particular needs of countries in the South.

Indeed, many nations in the South are discouraged that they are not being consulted on such far-reaching decisions at the global level. The response of the South to the process of media globalization is varied. The historical experience, level of communication infrastructure, and political and cultural system of each country have an important influence on how it might react and adapt to globalization of the media.

Over the last several years, a number of trends have emerged within the South which may profoundly impact the way the South responds to this worldwide phenomenon. These emerging themes, which result from individual reactions and the responses of private and governmental sectors to globalization, may be summarized as follows:

With immigration and international travel now a recognized facet in the social landscape of many industrialized nations, communication and media flows are exhibiting new patterns as compared to a few decades ago. Immigrant workers in the North had typically stayed together in certain geographical regions of their host countries.

However, socio-political and cultural factors in their host countries have led immigrant communities to become more dispersed. Thus, meeting their cultural needs is increasingly a task for television and radio broadcasting, among other methods, with technology and market economics aiding the phenomenon.

In fact, advances in technology coupled with globalization are now even making it possible for broadcasters from outside the host country to reach these specific audience segments. A good example of this phenomenon of ethnicized media is given in a study on the rise of Turkish media culture in Germany.

Since the early 1990s, the Turkish state-run station, TRT-International, has provided a flow of programming into Germany, targeted to approximately 2 million Turkish migrants in the country. This was facilitated by satellite and as part of German cable TV systems. As a result, TRT is the most watched service among immigrants in Germany, and research shows that fewer and fewer Turkish migrant viewers switch over to German TV stations.

In Australia, many immigrant populations are using community programming as a way of reinforcing their cultural identities, maintaining their ties to their homeland, and constantly renegotiating their role in Australian society. These include significant groups of Chinese, Thai, Vietnamese and Indian people. Since mainstream media and communications policy in Australia do not cater to the diverse needs and interests of this multicultural population, such communities are using small-scale production to produce and disseminate their own programs.

In addition, they rely on pay and satellite television to access programming from their native countries. India boasts the largest film industry in the world and exports its films and cultural products to many of its nationals living abroad, including those in Australia and Fiji. In both countries, Indian communities have created an "ecology of communications", using film and other Indian cultural products as a center for community life and daily activities.

Film stars are invited to appear, and community activities and events are organized around Indian films and videos. Reaching language minorities inside a developing country also takes special effort and leads to ethnicization of media. In India, broadcasting through the Indian National Satellite (INSAT) has achieved a multilingual mix in the programming carried by networks.

These programmes reach linguistic minorities within India's own population, large numbers of immigrants residing in the country, and even speakers of those same languages who live in neighbouring countries. In South Africa, with the rapid growth of broadcasting services since 1995, a number of broadcasters are purchasing imported news from abroad to cater to language minorities.

As a counter to the spread and over-arching reach of global media corroborations over the past few decades, some countries are promoting and making increased investments in local, indigenous programming. "Alternative media" and community programming have developed and grown. This counter-trend is particularly evident in Latin American countries in response to the rise in imported broadcast programmes.

Many countries, including Bolivia, Columbia, Ecuador and Venezuela, are imposing restrictions on imports and requiring television stations to carry a certain percentage of domestic programming, ranging from 20 to 60 per cent of total programming. Alternative media, especially community radio and television, provide grass roots communication outlets which trace their origins back to the link between radio and education.

During the 1970s and 1980s, local and university stations gave impetus to community radio and TV movements. Particularly notable about the community stations in Latin America is that they are being developed by non-profit and civic organizations and are promoting the notion of civil society. With their success and acceptance in the socio-cultural context, community media have begun demanding and obtaining legislative action to give them legal status. This groundswell has come mainly from radio-based media, and in the near future the same standing could be extended to television.

For example, in Columbia, community radio transmitters of up to 500 watts are permitted, and their programmes may carry advertising but not political propaganda. Chile also allows community radio stations, though only up to 1 kilowatt of maximum power, but no advertising. In Ecuador, the maximum permitted wattage is 150 watts for FM, 250 watts for AM. In Bolivia, radio transmitters and inexpensive community-bought radios serve the needs of the poor in an urban slum.

Mexico, Brazil, Argentina, Uruguay and other countries are also framing legislation that would recognize the role of community media. Some consider that Mexico's initiative for setting up "citizen radio and television" is one of the most promising initiatives in the field. As compared to the community media approach in Latin America countries, the battle for audience attention is also being waged on a commercial and market economy basis in many countries of the South. In India, for example, the state-run television organization, Doordarshan, is competing with the private channels for viewers whose number has swollen from 17 million to over 300 million in less than 15 years. The private channels, such as Star TV and Zee TV, are all based outside India since Indian law does not allow private broadcasting from an Indian base.

In short, the rise of alternative media signals the empowerment of the communities of South in expressing their opinions and needs by using modern technologies to obtain their participation in the public sphere. The globalization of communications and media is spurring a new recognition by countries of the South. They are facing issues and concerns similar to those expressed in the 1970s and 1980s debate on a New World Information and Communications Order (NWICO). But these questions are arising in a much more complex manner than they could have been imagined back then.

The pace, style and technology of globalization is forcing Southern countries to take a hard look at their media and communication policies and a more comprehensive approach to their formulation, seeking to move faster in trying to match the aspirations of their peoples. The Islamic Republic of Iran is one nation which has taken a holistic view of communication policy ever since the NWICO era and its national revolution.

Its policy emphasizes self- reliance and an unwillingness to submit to the supply-demand formula of the international market. This policy is carried through by organizational, investment and programming measures. The importance of television is enshrined in the 1979 constitution, which gave it an independent organization outside any single ministry. Particular attention goes to public broadcasting, and there is extensive investment in the expansion of locally produced programs.

The national television system, Islamic Republic of Iran Broadcasting (IRIB), was reorganized in 1979 and now has four major national channels which cover an audience of 30 million out of a population of 60 million. There has been a vast increase in domestic programming and a considerable reduction in dependency on foreign materials. In 1991, 85 per cent of all television programs were produced domestically. News information and documentaries are prepared within the Islamic community framework, thus ensuring a comprehensive approach to communication.

India has been designing policies to empower and strengthen the indigenous communication and media sectors. A Broadcasting Bill in 1997 established an independent Broadcasting Authority of India to facilitate and regulate broadcast services. Also, the Prasar Bharati (Broadcasting Corporation of India) Act, 1990, which came into force in 1997, shows that "...at last the Indian electronic media are truly moving towards the creation of an autonomous, independent and responsible broadcasting structure to meet the information needs and entertainment expectations of television viewers in a democratic country".

India's communication plans are extensive, and its advances in satellite technology have helped expand television rapidly. The NWICO years saw India developing satellite capacities. By 1982, the Indian National Satellite (INSAT) system was becoming fully operational, and colour transmissions were introduced. The expansion of the Indian TV network started with the "install one transmitter a day" philosophy, and about 1,000 terrestrial transmitters are in operation today.

With TV placing primary focus on development, the prime advertising spots (apart from commercials) are taken by public information services which provide development messages related to agriculture, health, education, and other initiatives by the government. National and regional services broadcast primary, secondary and post-secondary learning programmes.

An elaborate infrastructure of production facilities has been created in various states, and within the university system for producing higher education programmes. Television is also being used by over half-a-dozen open universities with their own production facilities. India has successfully maintained control of its national communication policy and planning in technology areas by mandating computer-related technologies and supporting the development of national technological industries.

The South particularly views its dependence on foreign firms and transnational actors as evidence that the important basis for national decision-making is now located outside its national boundaries. To remedy this situation and depending on the resources and infrastructures available within the South, a number of countries in Latin America and the Middle East have succeeded in developing and extending their mass media systems, in particular television, beyond their national boundaries into areas with shared language and cultural characteristics. This phenomenon is occurring within the trend toward commercialization and privatization of public communication in the two regions.

In Latin America, for example, a number of major changes have occurred in the traditional organizations of the mass media industries. The television industry in Latin America is becoming more complex, more diversified and more transnational. The changes are most significant in countries with the largest private media conglomerates, principally Mexico and Brazil. However, on a smaller scale, similar patterns of diversification, growth, and internationalization can be found in other countries of the region.

In Mexico, Televisa is now a complex and diversified transnational company. Its holdings include four television channels, cable companies, and a number of smaller production and distribution firms. It produces and disseminates the largest amount of Spanish language television programs around the world. Its soap-opera series reach as far as Russia, where they are dubbed into local languages.

In Brazil, Globo Television covers virtually all of Brazil's regions, as well as a vast international market network throughout Latin America as well as in Portuguese-speaking countries in Africa and Europe.

In Venezuela, Radio Caracas Television is a major supplier of programming throughout Latin America. It has entered the United States market through Univision, and has its own programming sales company in Miami.

Transnational activities of the media can also be observed in the Arab region of the Middle East. Countries with high oil revenues in the Arab world have absorbed many new communication technologies, satellite infrastructures and other telecommunications innovations. The collective resources of the region have enabled it to invest in such systems as Arabsat and Arab League regional satellite systems. Arabsat offers a range of services, with a footprint reaching from the Atlantic coast of west Africa right across to the Indian Ocean.

During the last decade, a number of Arab-owned conglomerates, often with headquarters in European countries, have used these facilities to launch major television broadcasting and newspaper enterprises. During the last 20 years, London has become the major center of Arab newspaper and magazine publishing, with distribution to Arab countries and the world market. Internationalization of media in the Arab world includes the production of paper, radio and television receivers, printing inks and related equipment, telephone instruments, antennas, and numerous other products. For example,

Egyptian film and cinema production has historically been in the forefront of media development in the Arab world and has received considerable support during the last several years. The Arab League Educational, Cultural and Scientific Organization (ALECSO) considers these industries to be a foundation of what it calls the region's cultural security.

References

Blackman, C. (1998) Convergence between telecommunications and other media: how should regulation adapt? *Telecommunication Policy*, 22:3, 163-170.

Gate, A. (2000). Convergence and competition: Technological change, industry concentration and competition policy in the telecommunications sector. University of Toronto Faculty of Law Review, 58:2, 83-117.

Jenkins, H. *Convergence Culture: Where Old and New Media Collide*. New York: New York UP, 2006. Print.

Menon, Siddhartha. "Policy Initiative Dilemmas On Media Convergence: A Cross National Perspective." Conference Papers — International Communication Association (2006): 1-35. *Communication & Mass Media Complete.* Web. 20 Nov. 2011.

Mueller, M.(1999). Digital Convergence and its consequences. *Javnost/The Public*. 6:3 11-27.

Shin, Dong Hee, Won - Yong Kim, and Dong-Hoon Lee. "Convergence Technologies and the Layered Policy Model: Implication for Regulating Future Communications." Conference Papers — International Communication Association (2006): 1-19. Communication & Mass Media Complete. EBSCO. Web. 26 Oct. 2011.

4

Media and Social Responsibility

The role of media in a democratic system has been widely debated. In recent times media has been subject to a lot of criticism for the manner in which they have disregarded their obligation to social responsibility. Dangerous business practices in the field of media have affected the fabric of Indian democracy. Big industrial conglomerates in the business of media have threatened the existence of pluralistic viewpoints. Post liberalisation, transnational media organisations have spread their wings in the Indian market with their own global interests. This has happened at the cost of an Indian media which was initially thought to be an agent of ushering in social change through developmental programs directed at the non privileged and marginalised sections of the society. Though media has at times successfully played the role of a watchdog of the government functionaries and has also aided in participatory communication, a lot still needs to be done.

Democracy in general terms is understood to be a form of government which is subject to popular sovereignty. It is essentially a rule by the people which is in contrast to monarchies or aristocracies. One of the crowing glories of the democratic system is the freedom of expression and the space that is provided to views from different sections of the society. A democratic system can run to its utmost potential when there is wide participation on the part the general mass which is not possible without people getting informed about various issues. Reliable information resources are an important constituent of any democratic society. This is where media steps in..

Mass media in its different forms have influenced human life in the present century. They have primarily provided information and entertainment to people across countries. Print media, being the leader over a considerable period of time has now got competition from Television, which is reshaping many of the social responses. Radio apart from providing news and views has also developed a flair for entertainment, thereby getting a lot of acceptance. There is also the new media with internet being its flag bearer. Internet has indeed made it possible to disseminate information and ideas in real time across the globe. However, among all these developments there is a cause of concern. Is media really fulfilling its social responsibility? Is a booming global mass media posing threats to the democratic way of thinking? In it posing challenges to a country like India where media has a greater role to play rather than merely providing information and entertainment?

The normative view of the press argues that the conduct of the media has to take into account public interests. The main public interest criterions that the media need to consider include freedom of publication, plurality in media ownership, diversity in information, culture and opinion, support for the democratic political system, support for public order and security of the state, universal reach, quality of information and culture disseminated to the public, respect for human rights and avoiding harm to individuals and the society. The social responsibilities expected from media in the public sphere were deeply grounded with the acceptance of media as the fourth estate, a term coined by Edmund Burke in England. With the formation of the 1947 Commission on the Freedom of the Press the social responsibility of media became a strong debating point. It was formed in the wake of rampant commercialization and sensationalism in the American press and its dangerous trend towards monopolistic practices. The report of the Hutchins Commission, as it was called, was path breaking on its take on social responsibility and the expected journalistic standards on the part of the press. The theory of social responsibility which came out of this commission was backed by certain principles which included media ownership is a public trust and media has certain obligations to society; news media should be fair, objective, relevant and truthful; there should be freedom of the press but there is also a need for self regulation; it should adhere to the professional code of conduct and ethics and government may have a role to play if under certain circumstances public interest is hampered.

Democracy, Media and the Public Sphere

Informing the citizens about the developments in the society and helping them to make informed choices, media make democracy to function in its true spirit. It also keeps the elected representatives accountable to those who elected them by highlighting whether they have fulfilled their wishes for which they were elected and whether they have stuck to their oaths of office. Media to operate in an ideal democratic framework needs to be free from governmental and private control. It needs to have complete editorial independence to pursue public interests. There is also the necessity to create platforms for diverse mediums and credible voices for democracy to thrive. It has already been discussed that media has been regarded as the fourth estate in democracy. Democracy provides the space for alternative ideas to debate and arrive at conclusions for the betterment of society. The publicly agreed norms are weighed over that of actions on the part of economic organizations and political institutions. This is close in essence to the concept of public sphere where rational public debate and discourse is given importance. Individuals can freely discuss issues of common concern. Media plays one of the crucial roles behind the formation of public sphere. However, Barnett is of the opinion that in modern times the true sense of public sphere is getting eroded with the media of public debate getting transformed to mediums for expressing particular interests rather than general interests which are universally accepted. This signifies that public sphere which is essential for a vibrant democracy can actually be channelized to serve vested interests rather than public good.

The political system in India is close in spirit to the model of liberal democracy. In the constitution of India the power of the legislature, executive and judiciary have been thoroughly demarcated. The party system in operation is a competitive one with flexibility of roles of government and opposition. There is also freedom of the press, of criticism and of assembly. Indian democracy has always attracted attention worldwide and has made scholars to ponder over the secret of its success amidst considerable odds. In India diversity is almost everywhere and it is not a developed nation. The problems of poverty and inequality in distribution of income have been constant irritants. Nevertheless, till today democracy has survived in the country. The role of media in India, the largest democracy of the world is different from merely disseminating information and entertainment. Educating the masses for their social upliftment needs to be in its ambit as well. In a country where there is large scale poverty, unemployment and underdevelopment media has a responsibility towards developmental journalism. It has a role to play behind formation of public opinion which can force the political parties to address the core issues haunting the country's progress. However, public opinion can be manipulated by vested interests to serve their own goals. Media can conceal facts and project doctored ideas to influence the electorate and thereby the voting outcome. Values like objectivity and truthfulness in presentation of news and ideas can be totally done away with.

In India public service broadcasting was given much importance after independence. It was used as a weapon of social change. AIR (All India Radio) and Doordarshan, the public service broadcasters in the country had the responsibility of providing educational programs apart from information and entertainment. However, it needs to be taken note of that the public service broadcasting system in the country was closely identified with the state. A monopolistic media structure under state control has the threat of becoming the mouthpiece of the ruling elite. The scenario was bound to change with the opening up of Indian economy in a bid to integrate with the global system. It signalled the emergence of a competitive market in the field of media with public service broadcasters getting challenges from private entities. This, however, had the seeds of a new problem of ownership.

Ownership pattern of media across the globe and in India is a cause for concern. There are big corporate houses who own newspapers and television networks. A higher concentration of ownership increases the risk of captured media. Media independence in such a scenario gives way to safeguarding the interest of the owners who may not serve social responsibilities. The space for plurality of ideas is eroded sending ominous signals for democracy. Bogart opines that in many democratic countries media ownership has reached dangerous levels of concentration. He has cited the examples of News Corporation's (owned by Rupert Murdoch) 37 % share in United Kingdom's national newspaper circulation and Silvio Berlusconi's ownership of top three commercial television channels, three pay TV channels and various newspapers and magazine in Italy which act as his political mouthpieces. Transnational powerful media organizations are in operation in India post liberalisation. These are big multinational corporations who own a chunk of the mass media market ranging from newspapers, television, radio, book publishing to music industry. Five of world's largest media conglomerates include General Electric, Walt Disney, News Corporation, Time Warner, Viacom and CBS. In India there are big players like the Times Group and ABP who rule the roost in the media arena. In a bid to open up the Indian market 26% foreign direct investment has been allowed in news publication and 74% has been allowed in non news segments by the Government. 100% foreign direct investment is available in the film industry. 100% FDI is also allowed in television software production subject to certain government norms. Cable networks and FM Radio networks have FDI limits of 49% and 20% respectively (FICCI and PwC, 2006).Research undertaken by PricewaterhouseCoopers has shown the FDI investment trend across mass media in India. Virgin Media Asia has a holding in HT media's foray into FM radio. Financial Times (Pearson Group) has an arrangement with Business Standard; AmericorpVentures, Mauritius has a stake in Nimbus Communications which deal in television and films and Reuters UK has equity sharing with Times Global Broadcasting, the Indian entity.

Therefore, across mass media options have opened up for availability of transnational homogeneous content. The growth of media conglomerates and their powerful presence has raised fears of manipulation of ideas by a powerful few detrimental to the democratic fabric. The corporate giants have also engaged in severe competition among themselves dishing out news and content which is primarily dominated by sensationalization, sleaze and glitz to capture wider markets. The disturbing trend that has emerged in the present media scenario is the use of media in the battle between rival political groups. In fact, this new phenomenon is in operation in India with newspapers and news channels taking sides while presenting facts. The same event can be presented in two contrasting manners in two newspapers or two television channels. Coronel argues that promotion of hate speech in place of constructive debate and creating an atmosphere of suspicion rather than social trust has the danger of making people cynic about the democratic setup leading to its breakdown.

While discussing the dangers associated with the developments in media it needs to be said that media in India has also undertaken roles which have strengthened democracy. The media as a watchdog of the democratic system has unearthed its various shortcomings. Investigative reporting in print and television media has helped in exposing large scale corruptions which have robbed the nation. The Commonwealth Games Scam, the Adarsh

Housing Society Scam, Cash for Vote Scam and the Bofors Scam are the highpoints of the Indian media. Across newspapers and television channels voices have been raised when the bureaucracy, judiciary or other public functionary have crossed the laxman rekha. There have also been initiatives to promote community media for the citizens to air their concerns. This is a significant leap towards alternative media usage which is distant from the dominant structure. Here the importance lies more in participatory communication right from the grassroots rather than communication which flows top down. Various television channels have also given the space for ordinary citizens to air their views in the form of citizen journalists thereby promoting democratic participation. Newspapers have educated the masses by informing them of the developments in the field of science and technology. They have also expressed strong views against prejudices which harm the society. Much developmental news has also been aired through the medium of radio. Its comparative low cost and wide acceptance among poorer sections have made it a potent tool for expressing ideas beneficial to the public.

Internet, a relatively newer entrant in the field of mass media, has proved to be more democratic than newspaper and television. Internet has provided the opportunity for citizens who are conversant with the medium to express their views about a number of issues. In many cases groups have been formed by likeminded people who discuss and debate over a number of decisions on the part of the government and seek new ideas for way ahead. The power of the internet can be easily judged from the developments in Egypt in recent times. Social networking sites like Facebook and Twitter were used to garner support against the regime of President Hosni Mubarak. Internet has been used by various public service organizations and N.G.Os to inform people about their objectives and also to make them aware of various initiatives on the part of the government as well as non government organisations for social upliftment. In internet the barrier to communication is minimal which helps in the formation of a participative environment. There is also greater empowerment of the users through higher level of interactivity and flexibility in choice of media outlets. The potential of the medium lies in its ability to be more personalized by offering user-created content. Nevertheless, there is the threat of advertising revenues influencing media outputs. Those who control considerable wealth have the opportunity to sway public opinion in their favour with the help of mass media. In the

2G scam the Radia Tapes controversy brought in focus the journalist, politician and industrial conglomerate nexus. Developments like these are a threat to democracy and undermine the media fraternity. Advertisements in newspapers, television, radio and at times the internet have become a part of the present election campaigns. Candidates with better funds have the edge over others in being voted to office because they can buy newspaper space and considerable air time.

Concept of Media Responsibility

The concept of media responsibility is commonly used in relation to media content as well as to its function in society. A single, coherent theory of the media's social responsibility simply does not exist. Social responsibility of the media can be interpreted in terms of both 'responsibility,' referring to the media's responsibility with regards to society, and 'responsiveness,' relating to the manner in which the media listen to and take the public into consideration.

The concept of the media's 'social responsibility' shows remarkable similarities to the German concept of 'Öffentlichkeit' ['public sphere'] that took shape in the 1960s, to become popular again in academic circles during the 1990s. One striking difference is that the main exponent of this theory, Jürgen Habermas, placed more emphasis on the community's so-called 'communicative competence,' in contrast to the more individualistic approach that appeared in the Anglo-American system.

Advocates of 'responsible' media usually originate from the media practice; when urgent problems arise, calls for reflection and action both from within and outside the media profession emerge. An early and important initiative in this respect came into existence after the Second World War. Media owners have an important role in society; "An overall social responsibility for the quality of press service to the citizen cannot be escaped; the community cannot wholly delegate to any other agency the ultimate responsibility for a function in which its own existence as a free society may be at stake". The press both as a commercial product and a 'public trustee'. In the 1940s this was a quite daring vision, since the traditional combination of the freedom of the press and market freedom had always been the firm basis for non-interference in the press sector.

Media responsibility as the 'obligations and expectations' that society has regarding the media. There are four types of responsibility: assigned, contracted, self-assigned and denied responsibilities. 'Assigned responsibilities' are obligations established by law, which the media must meet. In democratic societies this regulation, in pursuance of the above-mentioned tradition of the freedom of expression, is kept to a minimum. 'Contracted responsibilities' arise from self-regulated agreements between the press or broadcasters on the one hand and society or politicians on the other in regard to the desired conduct of the media. 'Self-assigned responsibilities' indicate voluntary professional commitments to maintaining ethical standards and public goals. Denied responsibilities, in order to refute accusations of irresponsibility that are thought to be undeserved or inapplicable.

Responsibility refers to the question: 'What social needs should we expect media and journalists to respond to?' Accountability offers an answer to the question: 'How might society call on media and journalists to account for their fulfillment of the responsibility given to them?' Responsibility thus has to do with defining proper conduct; accountability with compelling it. Pritchard defines media accountability as "the process by which media organizations may be expected or obliged to render an account of their activities to their constituents". Thus media accountability is a 'process' that basically consist of "naming, blaming and claiming".

McQuail indicates that the term social responsibility not only has different meanings, but also implies "differences of location of a given responsibility within the whole institutional complex". Media responsibility can thus be located on different levels; the media institution as a whole, the ownership, the organization and its management, the professional employee and the individual author or performer.

In the last decade, we have seen a clear shift amongst communications specialists from more general and abstract thinking about media responsibility to a more practical and concrete interpretation of these concepts (from responsibility to accountability), in which the emphasis has furthermore shifted from a negative approach to a positive one, from liability to answerability. The liability model of accountability is, according to McQuail "mainly invoked in cases where the media are believed to be capable of causing real harm to individuals, certain categories of people or society as a whole".

Answerability on the other hand implies "responsiveness to the views of all with a legitimate interest in what is published, whether as individuals affected or on behalf of the society. It includes a willingness to explain, defend, and justify actions of publication or omission". At the same time, it must be said that new conceptualisations of media responsibility and accountability primarily come from within academic and policymaking circles, and that the debate has so far reached media professionals only recently and to a limited extent.

Media as a Watchdog

Some media experts argue that the media's influence on foreign policy decisions has an inverse relationship to how clearly a policy is defined and maintained. A strongly articulated and firmly-held policy is less susceptible to being changed due to critical media coverage. The media can play a strong role in setting the agenda of national debate, and in compressing the time available in which decisionmakers must make policy decisions. This is especially the case in situations of war or crisis.

There are additionally several trends visible today in the US and other developed countries that have led some observers to question the effectiveness of the oversight function of the media. The most immediate trend is the climate of securitisation that has followed the 11 September 2001 terrorist attacks on the US. The impact on the media and journalism has been direct, as witnessed by the recent policy of embedding journalists with allied forces for coverage of the 2003 invasion of Iraq, the renewed emphasis on government secrecy, the move to reduce the amount of publicly-available state information on subjects deemed sensitive, the denouncing of leaks by senior officials of the Bush administration, ostracism of outspoken opponents of US policy and retaliation against White House correspondents who ask hard questions of the administration, with a strong possibility that a 'chilling effect' is being produced in the United States.

A second long-term trend has been the increasing emphasis on entertainment at the expense of substantive and informational political news content, sometimes referred to as the 'dumbing-down' of news, in particular, the decline in serious public affairs journalism. In television broadcasting especially, there has been a noticeable shift away from addressing public policy issues and towards entertainment. The trend in many Western democracies towards 'infotainment' style of political coverage portrays election campaigns as horse-race types of contests, paying little attention to important issues and too much attention to gaffes made by candidates.

When less substantive information is communicated, citizens' ability to assess the societal consequences of the electoral choices before them is diminished, and democracy is degraded.

Moreover, for the majority of people in the United States and numerous other developed countries, television has become the primary source of news. This has imposed particular constraints in the reporting of complex security- and foreign policy-related issues, such as war and participation in peace support operations, since the standard television news item comprises about three minutes of air time. One consequence of the shift towards television as a source of news is that there is less discussion of the context and background of news items. A third trend which is thought to have implications on the watchdog role of the media is the establishment of large corporate conglomerates, which include media outlets, and that potentially hold to abuse their control of the press such as through deliberate political bias. Such conglomerates contribute to the creation of monopolies of media ownership, reduce diversity in media perspectives, and link corporate interests to the media, and in the process often form close ties with certain political elites.

There is a perception in many Western countries that mainstream media has become increasingly linked to centres of economic and political power through such conglomerates, constraining independent and critical journalism and reducing the spectrum of perspectives that are aired, especially on vital public issues. The present era of media mergers tends to result in huge, forprofit conglomerates, which often co-operate even while they compete in other domains. As a consequence, enormous political clout is wielded by the conglomerates.

Two of the main questions that arise concerning the media's watchdog role in the broader context of media conglomerates is whether such conglomerates stifle competition, and whether citizens are given access to the news they require. The growth in media conglomerates has raised serious issues of accountability, media diversity and independence, leading one media expert to comment that '[n]ow more than before, perhaps, the great potential private power over the public agenda, hidden behind a mask of objectivity, is imperilling political democracy'.

The issue of objectivity in journalism is now deeply contested within the field of mass communications. Long established with impartiality and balance as one of the fundamental principles of professional journalism, particularly in the Anglo-American tradition, objectivity has been criticised for making journalists 'passive recipients of news, rather than aggressive analysers and explainers of it'. What is 'objective' varies according to who is speaking. In recognition of the problematic nature of 'objectivity', it was dropped from the journalists' code of ethics in 1996. Moreover, the quest for objectivity in reporting, it has been argued, reinforces the tendency of journalists to rely primarily on official sources. The truth that is conveyed is consequently the 'official' truth — the view of state actors and officials.

The news culture that pertains in a particular country may also privilege official news, making it less likely that alternative perspectives to that of the government or state actors will be presented. Similarly, old habits of self-censorship may remain from an earlier time when authoritarian methods were employed to repress criticism from the media and society. The reliance on official sources is especially prominent in reporting on security related issues. This was most vividly demonstrated by the practice of 'embedding' journalists with allied forces in the US-British war in Iraq, but is also visible in regular reporting on defence and security affairs throughout the West.

One of the consequences of over-reliance on official sources is that it becomes more difficult to present alternative perspectives or critiques. If critical reporting on the decisions or policy of a president, minister, police chief or chief of general staff is perceived as 'political bias', the journalist may jeopardise his or her access to the official source. This was vividly demonstrated during the Iraq war via the exclusion of critical journalists during question and answer sessions with Bush government spokespeople.

Furthermore, the dependence on official sources makes editors and journalists more reluctant to raise issues that are not raised officially, and thus reduces the media's capacity to influence the public agenda. Over-reliance on official sources also increases the chances that journalists will uncritically accept 'spin' — that is, the carefully manufactured and managed official statements that constitute the government's position on an issue. In other words, journalists are more likely in such circumstances to 'cover the story not as it is occurring but as it is presented, which is to say it is manufactured'. A major study recently criticised US media coverage of the issue of weapons of mass destruction (WMD), which not only failed to distinguish between the various types of WMD and programmes, but uncritically accepted the Bush administration's equating international terrorism with the acquisition of WMD.

'Many stories stenographically reported the incumbent administration's perspectives on WMD, giving too little critical examination of the way officials framed the events, issues, threats and policy options... The tendency of the US media to lead with the most "important" information and the most "important" players gave greater weight to the incumbent administration's point of view on WMD issues, at the expense of alternative perspectives'. The example underscores that media has not only a duty to inform, but a responsibility to educate, particularly in areas that are in the public interest but which may be too esoteric or specialised for widespread familiarity with the issue to exist.

In North America, there is growing criticism of the bias apparent in much political journalism. Reporters, anchors and media 'commentators' do not merely report facts, but interpret them and predict their impact and implications. The presentation of highly opinionated and speculative commentary in the context of newscasts is also seen as part of the move towards a more entertainment-focused television, including the development of widely-recognised celebrity journalists. Another obstacle to media performing a watchdog role is the indirect consequence of the phenomenon of 'judicial deference'.

Specific legislation to protect media freedom, access to information regimes, and narrow definitions of national security help to protect the scope of media independence. In view of national security exemptions, however, the courts may ultimately determine whether national security or public order claims are justified in law as grounds for restricting media freedom in specific cases. In many states, however, the judiciary tend to perceive themselves as partners of the executive, rather than a separate and autonomous branch of government. Courts also tend to show defence to the executive in matters concerning national security.

In states where judicial deference is common, the courts are unlikely to assertively protect media independence against government claims of national security. Finally, it has been argued that journalists now tend to focus on individuals rather than policies. Personalising issues and conflicts contributes to an increasingly adversarial relationship between the media and its subjects, especially when what is at stake is something broader and more systemic than an individual's decisions and actions, more fundamentally it is about an institutional culture and relations.

Media Accountability

There are many different reasons why the concept of social responsibility of the media has gained new relevance. In putting social responsibility into practice there are different procedures, frames or mechanisms to hold media accountable for their performance vis-a'-vis society. The realization of social responsibility of television results from the interplay between several factors: constitution and law; supervision and control; condition of the television market, journalistic responsibility and self-regulation. Bertrand indicates that there are three approaches to improve the quality of the media: 1) the law and courts; 2) the market, and 3) media ethics and accountability systems.

McQuail defines four accountability frames: law and regulation; the market; public, and professional responsibility. Along the same lines, Bardoel slightly 'remolds' that typology into the following four media accountability mechanisms:

— political accountability, which refers to formal regulation stipulating how broadcasting companies and newspapers will be structured and how they function;

— market accountability or the system of supply and demand, in which the free choices of the public are given free reign and considerations of efficiency also play a role;

— public accountability, which is linked to the media's assignment of maintaining more direct relationships with citizens, in addition to their relationship with the market and the state; and

— professional accountability, which is linked to ethical codes and performance standards used within the media that should help counterbalancing every excessive dependence upon politics and the market.

There seems to be a growing consensus that increasing 'power' or, better, 'influence' of the media has to be counterbalanced by greater media transparency and accountability. However, there is no consensus on how the latter should be achieved. Governments are often considered as the classic guarantee for a sound media system, but they have proven to be quite ineffective in preventing media monopolies in the press or broadcasting industries and in stimulating the plurality of media content. They experience also problems with the organization of public broadcasting 'at arms length'.

More in general, media regulation proves to be rather ineffective in the management of content.

In recent decades, media markets were seen as a new panacea for the problems of public and/or government-controlled media: inefficiency, inflexibility and bureaucratization, paternalism and lack of interest for popular taste and culture, lack of innovation, and so forth. More recently, the dark side of marketdriven media is getting more attention; its mainstream orientation, its interest in consumers (not citizens), the influence of advertisers and sponsors, et cetera. The trend of 'less government' and 'more market' also sheds new light on the position of the media professionals; they have become the 'guardians' of the quality of media output, while at the same time the public spirit of and the public space for professional journalists and other creative people tend to diminish.

Media professionals want to work 'for the people,' but often see accountability to the public and to society as no less threatening than the forces of the market or the state. More than ever in the past, the citizen is becoming an active part of the (mass) communication process, due to the potential of new technologies, more competition between media and, last but not least, a more self-conscious and better educated citizenry. Involvement of citizens and civil society can also provide a 'fourth' way to organize social responsibility in the media, next to the primacy of either the market, the state and/or the professional.

In other words, there is a growing awareness that an adequate media and communications 'ecology' can best be organized, not by exclusively relying on one of these parties or mechanisms, but by way of interrelated and multileveled 'governance' arrangements in the media system. This also corresponds with new approaches in the reflection on public policies and business strategies.

Political Accountability

Political accountability is dominant in public broadcasting, the single most prominent provision to foster the public interest in the media. This system includes the legal framework for regulating the structure and functioning of broadcasting through national political and administrative institutions. However, as of 1989, European policy-making has taken over the primacy from national politics when it comes to broadcasting e. g., European content;

although national regulation continues to be the most extensive, the latter has to remain within the framework of the European legislation.

Generally this shift in governance is felt as threatening for public broadcasting, since a European economic and 'open market' approach overrules national cultural policies. Recognition of the public service as a cornerstone of democracy, as a service of general economic interest, essential to improve the quality of life of all citizens and to conquer social exclusion and isolation

The Commission sees its competence limited to questions whether the chosen financing method is adequate and proportionate to the task imposed, and how state aid is being used or misused in competing, secondary markets such as publicity. A Communication on the application of state aid rules to public service broadcasting was published, but an effort to clarify the EU's stance on PSB was rejected by member states, which leaves the Commission to adopt an 'ad hoc' approach. The real danger is then that the primary role of the nation state in the future of the public service is lost altogether.

Meanwhile, a new communication on services of general interest and the amended 'Transparency Directive' were adopted. Both clarify questions related to the financing of services of general economic interest, among which PSB. These improvements made possible in the Transparency Directive aim at discerning between public service and commercial activities of a public service; transparency needs to be made visible in a clear-cut separation - including separate book-keeping - between the public and non-public activities of the public service. It seems very unlikely that the Commission is going to follow the Directorate of Information, Communication, Culture and Audiovisual Media in wanting to make a program-based distinction between public and commercial broadcasting. One of the reasons being the difficulty of defining public service by means of a mere set of essential institutional and contentrelated characteristics, inspired by normative notions of quality. Article 86(2) has proven very useful and flexible enough to enshrine a wide variety of public service models.

Public Service Broadcasting Models

The public broadcasting service will be assessed according to its power to discriminate its programs from those of the commercial sector, its internal pluralism, its contribution to a production climate, which gives room to innovation. In her search for workable alternatives for the public broadcast service to keep its distinctiveness, Jeanette Steemers warns for the hybridization between public and private broadcasters carrying both the benefits and the disadvantages of each model:

> "Moreover, with the current difficulties faced by commercial television, the questioning of public service broadcasting's 'distinctive' role is quite likely to increase. At the same time, greater thought needs to be given to alternative and complementary forms of public provision which may be better suited at meeting changes in communications needs, content, and delivery forms than the large-scale, public institutions framework."

It is up to the member states and the broadcasting services themselves to come to the Commission with a commitment to the principles of the public service and with an exact declaration of what those principles are. Ironically enough, it proves all but easy to define the current and future role of PSB in the audiovisual landscape of the nation states. Jakubowicz describes this problematic two-tier accountability system as follows:

> "PSB organizations in EU member states are accountable to public authorities, and the member states themselves are accountable to the European Commission for the way they confer, define, organize and finance the public service remit, as well as institute and operate program and financial accountability systems for PSB broadcasters. That would seem to offer hope that an accountability system could be developed on this basis, providing clear criteria at least as to what constitutes the public service remit of PSB broadcasters in EU countries and how to distinguish it from other programming".

As said, this is unfortunately not the case, given that the various bodies of the European Union have not come much further in defining PSB than what had already resulted in the Prague Declaration, signed at the fourth Minister Conference of the Council of Europe in 1994. This resolution dealt with four main aspects of public service: the responsibility of public services in terms of information diffusion; financial requirements; political independence and the duty to public accountability; access to new technologies.

All in all, it is recognized that PSB is directly related to democratic, social and cultural needs seeking to reach a wide audience, willing to invest in innovation. Jakubowicz pleads in favor of a rigorous accountability system that would encompass questions such as accounting for what, to whom, and how. Ingredients for measuring performance would certainly need to include, alongside mission statements, financial accountability on the basis of economic performance measures, audience performance based upon audience shares and reach.

Notwithstanding, numerous problems remain; due to convergence of broadcasting and telecommunication, and the switch from analog to digital communication it has become all the more difficult to define the concept of public service. The decision to create separate regimes for transportation and content calls for the question how to keep these sectors separate. Public broadcasters will want to make use of new communication technologies and after digitization lies the possibility of broadband transmission. In Europe no standard has been chosen yet, therefore penetration is still minimal. Hence public broadcasters set up interactive websites as the easiest solution to keep in touch with their audiences. Protests from the commercial sector against this new strand of activity were vehement.

The European Union demands a clear-cut definition of the mission of public broadcasters and also a clear distinction between public and commercial broadcasting services. This means that the days that national broadcasting policy formation took shape as a strategic ritual between intimate partners are gone, and that more open and transparent relations between regulators and broadcasters will need to emerge. In fact, more explicit legitimization in terms of social responsibility and concrete accountability mechanisms has already become a strategic asset for public broadcasters over the last ten years, as Bardoel and Brants explain for the Dutch case. Next to this more explicit political accountability towards national and European governments, public broadcasters also try to organize more direct interaction and feedback with the public.

Market Accountability

"The objective of the marketplace model", Merrill writes, "is to permit the maximum of individual and independent editorial determinism in what ideally will be a very pluralistic market system. Media that people accept and support will survive and thrive; media that people dislike or reject will suffer and die. This is ultimate accountability. And it is the kind of accountability in harmony with the spirit of individualism, democracy, and freedom."

Market accountability is, only rarely considered an adequate, let alone ideal mechanism of social responsibility. Yet the market undoubtedly is the oldest vehicle for freedom of expression and communication in society. Although it seems at present quite uncommon to associate the market mechanism with communication freedom, in past centuries it has proven to be a liberating power against the vested interests of the church and the state. Also in the present day, the system of demand, supply and competition offers a good, simple and unprejudiced indication of consumer tastes, and the market mechanism does not involve compulsion.

Phenomena like pop music and other forms of popular culture would never have penetrated our culture so rapidly without the freedom of the market. At the same time, this model tends to favor majority preferences over quality of content or critical and minority voices. For public broadcasters this model may function as a useful antidote against the traditional 'supply side' paternalism and as a stimulus towards more efficient behavior and the recent development of a quasi 'internal market'. For them this mechanism is especially relevant to the extent that advertising is a substantial source of income; thus 'market shares,' or in fact 'audience shares,' become an important parameter.

In such a context, marketability may be confused with accountability. Nevertheless, in relation to market accountability we do not, in the first place, think of broadcasting, but of traditionally commercial media sectors such as the press and of newly developed private media practices in the field of commercial broadcasting and new media such as the Internet. The press sector has always been based upon a delicate combination of private enterprise and public responsibility. Most newspapers originally emerged from political and civil movements, but in the meantime they have merged into a small number of media conglomerates with a decreasing number of titles and the concentration of various editorial tasks. Because of similar trends in most countries, the traditional position of the daily press in the Western world as the mouthpiece of societal groups and political movements and as the breeding ground for independent journalism has become ever more vulnerable.

Commercial broadcasters appeared on the scene only very recently in most European countries, and they initially positioned themselves as being so different from the traditional public broadcasters that 'social responsibility' notions were not 'top of mind' thus far. Not surprisingly, Bardoel and Brants conclude that notions of responsibility and accountability are still an almost unknown phenomenon within commercial broadcasting, as the Dutch case shows. Commercial broadcasters want to please their advertisers and shareholders first and foremost, but also prefer to avoid problems with politics that would trigger further regulation.

In terms of the 'liability' or 'answerability' model of accountability proposed by McQuail, commercial broadcasters still seem to prefer a quite defensive 'liability' model. Active accountability by engaging in a dialogue with critics in society has only recently begun to develop. The number of assigned responsibilities, imposed by society and the law, remains, in both the Dutch and European regulation, rather poor. Contracted responsibilities, such as voluntary promises to the audience, are almost absent.

Relatively extensive are the self-assigned responsibilities in order to guarantee a professional and independent information provision by editorial statutes (although imposed by Dutch law) and codes of conduct, but little is known about its implications. At the same time some commercial broadcasters still deny their social responsibility, by referring to the 'realistic' nature of their programming or, ultimately, by pointing at freedom of the viewer to switch the program.

Professional Accountability

Professional responsibility refers to the performance criteria and ethical codes of media professionals that are often supposed to complement to, or better, compensate for the political or market dependency of media organizations. The development of professional responsibility and indeed of professionalization of media occupations has in past decades often been seen as a progressive force vis-a'-vis the traditional influences of the political or the market system.

According to McQuail this professional framework is likely to work because it is voluntary, self-regulatory, non-coercive and in the self-interest of media and professionals. But it has in his view also serious limitations, since professionalism is in most cases not strongly developed within the media and as a result media professionals have relatively little autonomy from media management and ownership.

Media professionals have steadily improved their position within media organizations over the last forty years, thanks to a better professional training and strong negotiations that have led to professional privileges as 'editorial statutes' in every newspaper and broadcasting organization. At the same time it remains to be seen if this collective, informal professional culture and its privileges will survive the current processes of commercialization and globalization. Practice has shown, however, that editorial statutes only seldom protect newsrooms against press concentration and media mergers.

The press sector has, given its well-known aversion against externally imposed regulation and codes of conduct, always relied on mechanisms of internal criticism and self-regulation. In the past, Dutch newspapers that originated from a political or social movement could count on the loyalty and commitment of citizens who belonged to the same movement. These classical forms of participation have eroded though, and are replaced by a (quasi) commercial, consumerist relationship.

As a result, the relation of newspapers with their respective readerships has become looser, and since most newspapers have recently lost circulation, some of them have tried to revitalize the relationship with the reader. This results in new initiatives such as reader's pages, ombudsmen and so on.

More recently, there is much more debate and introspection within the journalistic profession itself. This debate was triggered by external criticism on reporting on issues such as the Scebrenica massacre and the murder of Pim Fortuyn. Media were accused of being partly 'guilty' in these cases, since most media unanimously took position in favor of a Dutch military intervention in Bosnia or against the populist politician Fortuyn. Elsewhere in Europe there were similar debates on the role of the press in relation to the rise of right-wing extremism.

The media and media professionals were also accused of operating too close to the inner circle of vested politics and culture, which are recruited from the same social middle class as most journalists, and too distant from the problems and needs of ordinary citizens. Concentrating on the journalistic position in light of the Internet, we notice that publishers, broadcasters and Internet service providers (ISP's) each provide about 30 percent of the almost 200 news sites currently available in The Netherlands.

Most of the news supplied on the Internet still is of a 'parasitic' kind, usually referred to as 'shovelware'. Internet journalism finds itself still close to traditional formats of news distribution, as recent research showed time and again. Within the terms of this modest practice, it is not surprising that - according to research findings - newspaper sites prove to be better in using the interactive potential of the Internet, such as discussion groups, feedback via e-mail and access to archives. Television news sites on the other hand make a better use of the multimedia features of the Internet and also offer more hyperlinks.

Internet journalism is thus a mere affiliate of its big brothers, and the potential of the new medium is often not fully used in order to avoid cannibalization of the traditional medium. Given the high potential but still poor performance of the Internet as a journalistic medium and the lack of research and development in this respect by newspaper publishers, The Netherlands Press Fund has decided to fund research on and offer financial support for journalistic content production on the Internet.

Public Accountability

Finally, public accountability has gained considerable popularity over the last decade. Although the concept and the very name of 'public broadcasting' already suggest a strong emphasis on public responsibility, the reality was and is that public broadcasters rely heavily on their (exclusive) relationship with politics. In trying to define 'public responsibility,' McQuail indicates that the general idea behind this is that the media ought to serve public purposes and be socially responsible; the theory of social responsibility of the media and the idea of media as a 'public trustee' are relevant here again.

These ideas find both support, according to McQuail, from within the media that choose an active role in society and wish to contribute to the public good and, outside the media, with individuals and groups as constituents of civil society and operating in the public sphere. All things considered, these many voluntary action groups are part of the informal 'mechanisms' by which media are constrained to meet certain standards of performance in society. Alongside these feedback mechanisms with informal but still collectively organized institutions, the relationship with the audience also becomes an ever more important part of public responsibility.

Already conscious citizens hold the media accountable for their performance through a process of naming, blaming and claiming. With individualization being a formidable social trend, public broadcasters can no longer rely on their relationship with formal and informal groups and collectivities; they have to establish a relationship with the individual, 'unorganized' public. The problem with this kind of accountability procedures is, however, that they are voluntary most of the time; it is often hard to see the difference between real feedback procedures and ritual PR strategies.

The increasing consideration for the citizen's position is also noticeable from the growing support for 'public' or 'civic' journalism wanting to focus on, instead of political or media priorities, the 'agenda of the citi-zen' and trying to stimulate public discourse and civic participation. Some academics point out the fact that the relationship between citizens and media has changed considerably, and as a result want to do away with the classical distinction between politics, journalism and the public sphere on the one hand and popular culture, entertainment and the private sphere on the other.

This implies that, looking at responsibility and accountability of the media, we should not exclusively refer to the institutional aspects and traditional forms of participation, but instead also include the actual media use of citizens (entertainment and hybrid formats - 'infotainment' - having acquired a prominent status in their daily media menus).

Practices of Media Accountability

In sharp contrast with the traditional, somewhat stubborn journalistic attitude grounded in a 'common sense' approach, a new, cautious attitude seems to emerge among media professionals who do want to be held accountable for the ways in which they shape their responsibility, based upon verifiable criteria, such as a transparent editorial statute and an internal professional codex. To what extent media ethics indeed do offer solace remains questionable.

Traditionally, relations between journalism and ethics are somewhat strained; journalism pretends to register, to report facts, while ethics refer to so-called 'preferred visions'. Moreover, ethics-related issues predominantly tend to get the attention in times of crisis reporting only. In a lot of countries in the Western world, discussions on media ethics have become fashionable, but this does not mean, however, that some concrete initiatives have not yet been taken.

For years, so-called Media Accountability Systems were settled as undesirable, imposed shackles that would constitute impediments for journalistic freedom, even human rights and the exercise of democracy. The following paragraphs will assess a number of concrete appearances of accountability mechanisms that can be considered best practices in different geographical contexts. What are the main characteristics of these accountability mechanisms?

A public accountability system is to be seen as a set of interconnecting elements, of which the main ingredients should be: (1) enhancing the involvement of media professionals in organizational policy-making; (2) greater interplay between social scientific researchers and media makers; (3) greater involve-ment of social groups in debates of broadcasting policy; (4) greater involvement of, and attention to, radio and television criticisms in the media; (5) greater role for citizens' organizations in broadcasting accountability in order not to limit the discourse among the 'elite' alone; (6) periodic appointment of bodies at the national and regional levels in an effort to 'stuff' the broadcasting policy debate with all these different strands of opinion.

Jakubowicz realistically remarks that unfortunately not much has survived from these idealistic proposals, since "(...) 'upward' lines of largely formalized accountability (reports, audits, execution of license obligations, etc.) continue to prevail". In an attempt to grasp the variety of concrete accountability mechanisms1, both internal and external, according to the above-mentioned political, professional, and public 'frames' of media accountability (the market rarely being an adequate mechanism of social responsibility), a contract between the government and the public broadcaster refers to the political accountability frame. Such a contract sets out some sort of legal framework for regulating the functioning of broadcasting.

Conditions for the management contract to work are, among others: a solid, legal basis; stable financing; a good definition of output; preferably a long-term contract; a relationship based upon mutual trust; necessary monitoring tools. A combination of external formal regulation through a supervisory body and some kind of internal, self-regulatory mechanism is the British new Office of Communications (Ofcom), operational as of December 29, 2003, which merged the functions of five formerly existing regulatory bodies: the Independent Television Commission (RTC), the Broadcasting Standards Commission (BSC), the Office of Telecommunications (Oftel), the Radio Authority (RAu) and the Radiocommunications Agency (RA) in an effort to regulate the full realm of the electronic communications sector.

The professional accountability frame refers to identification of media practitioners with the standards of their own profession. CBC/Radio Canada has an ombudsman with authority over all information programs offered by public broadcasting (radio, television and Internet). Appointed for five years, the ombudsman operates entirely independently of CBC staff, reports directly to the chairperson of the CBC about complaints regarding lack of accuracy, balance or integrity in the reporting. Another example of internal accountability mechanisms are forms of self-regulation within the media organization, such as the Deutscher Presserat in Germany. Readers may address themselves directly to this Presserat without having to go through an intermediary. The impact of this form of self-regulation is limited, however.

A similar self-regulation instrument, the Deutscher Werberat, exists for advertising. This council is composed entirely of professionals from the advertising world, but it is not known for having a consistently critical attitude with respect to its own professional practice. The BBC's Producer Guidelines act as a code of professional conduct and the broadcaster also has a so-called Programme Complaints Unit to which the public can address their criticisms and complaints. The newspaper and magazine sector created a Press Complaints Commission (PCC): there is a professional code, complaints are heard and conclusions are published. The fact that the media are supposed to serve public interests is being put to the test through forms of public consultation.

Canada offers an interesting public accountability model in which citizens - in all their geographic and ethnic diversity - are actively involved in the evaluation and possible steering of the concrete expression of public responsibility by the media. One example of public consultation is the so-called Public Hearings that the CRTC (Canadian Radio-Television Telecommunications Commission) regularly organizes. These are fora on the 'Public Accountability' of both public and commercial broadcasters throughout the country, including in remote areas. These public consultations take place whenever a broadcasting license is up for renewal or when the CRTC wants to collect information about new policy directions or licensing decisions. These consultations, in the form of semi-structured interviews, are broad; anyone can participate, including industry representatives, organized public interest groups or ordinary members of the public.

The process of such forums has been archived as audiovisual material and can be consulted through the Internet. One of these forums - e. g., Deciding What's News - deals with convergence of media conglomerates and its impact on the news user, and tries to find an answer to the question how the Canadian audience can continue to consider the public broadcasting service as the most credible news source. The Inuit and Indian peoples are not left aside, as is illustrated in the so-called 'First Nations Accountability Coalition.'

Transparency and openness of government policy towards citizens in each and every area are considered paramount in Canada, as is testified in the Access to Information Act, which stipulates that everyone who pays $5 within thirty days should be provided with the necessary clarifications on every government decision (with the exception of national security files, decisions related to the private realm, etc.).

Journalism, Media and Society

The history of journalism is often confused with the history of the newspaper because newspapers were one of the earliest and most common methods of distribution of information about public life, the two are separate and distinct. Newspapers are a delivery system. Today the delivery systems for journalism include radio, television, magazines, books, and sites online. Some people define journalism as an act-a method and art of collecting and presenting information that ultimately is distributed through various channels; others describe it as a ritual-a way of sustaining, enriching, and challenging societal norms; still others see it as the mere dissemination of information. Journalism-reporting on government, politics, policies, economics, and other news and issues-has become a cornerstone of our life. Newspaper editors and printers sought to inform the people about the happenings of the day.

Political journalism has helped guard against secrecy and governmental power. Thus journalisms primary purpose has been to inform. But in different periods, it also has been a powerful persuasive tool. And from the earliest times, it has sought to entertain by providing information about unusual happenings and humorous incidents. In recent years, a move by many media industries toward infotainment, a blur of information and entertainment, has caused many journalists to worry about redefining the essence of journalism.

During the early colonial period, journalists were not a separate occupational group; they were editors, postmasters, and elite businessmen who sought to earn a living by printing information and who wanted to play a role in the founding of a new country. These writers were citizens first and intellectuals or commentators second. Some argue that journalists were quite cautious, rarely challenging the status quo. Others point out that despite the fact that governors in the colonies did not like criticism of themselves or the British government, journalists still spoke out.

For example, in 1733, John Peter Zenger, printing the New York Weekly Journal for a radical attorney named James Alexander, was charged with seditious libel for openly criticizing the royal governor of New York. At that time, the law allowed a jury to determine only whether a printer had actually published specific material, not whether the material was true or was, indeed, seditious.

After a highly publicized trial and an eloquent defense by Andrew Hamilton, the jury acquitted Zenger, thereby establishing a political, although not a legal, precedent for the right to criticize government. Hamilton argued that truth should be a defense in any seditious libel trial and that a jury should be able to judge not only whether an accused printer actually printed the material, but also whether it was libelous. He appealed to the colonists' dislike of arbitrary power, an aversion that would become even stronger as colonists began to consider independence.

Independence and the Marketplace of Ideas Journalists played an important role during the late-eighteenth-century struggle for independence. They not only recounted events but also presented competing ideologies for discussion in the marketplace of ideas. During the mid-eighteenth century-especially after the French and Indian War, which required colonists to contribute to what they considered a British cause-colonists began to entertain the idea of increased independence from Britain.

Many of the imported books, local newspapers, and pamphlets read by the colonists spread the ideas of the Enlightenment, a philosophical movement during the seventeenth and eighteenth centuries that generated new ideas about scientific reasoning, democracy, rule by consent of the governed, and free criticism of government. These ideas challenged authoritarian control and championed individual rights and democratic participation.

Chief among intellectuals and editors who challenged British authority was Benjamin Franklin. He established a prominent newspaper in Philadelphia, ran a bookshop, printed a newspaper and various pamphlets, attempted publication of a magazine, and helped found a public library system. He extended his printing network to the southern colonies by financing printers so they could start bookshops and printing establishments in growing cities. He gained fame for both the lightning rod experiments that later earned him a place in elementary school science books and the "Join or Die" snake, a graphic representation of the need for the colonies to stick together in their fight against England or else undergo separate deaths.

When the British Parliament passed the Stamp Act, which assessed a tax on paper, newspaper publishers rebelled. The tax was designed to help pay for the French and Indian War, which started in 1756. The colonists argued that they had no say in whether or how the war should be fought and therefore should not have to pay the tax. In protest some of the newspaper publishers printed woodcuts with skull-andcrossbones emblems; other ceased publishing and refused to pay the tax. By the time of the Revolution, most printers were notoriously patriotic.

A lack of tolerance for diversity of political opinion characterized most communities, and printers who remained loyal to the British Crown were quickly exiled. Despite protests against British control of the press, colonists readily exercised their own control of public opinion by suppressing unpopular opinions. The resistance to free expression for everyone during times of stress became a characteristic of American media during the next two centuries, and the media often felt free to demonize and stereotype America's enemies in times of social strife or war.

Newspaper editors and pamphleteers such as Thomas Paine cheered the colonists onward. During the struggle for independence, when George Washington's troops were mired in winter snows in Trenton, New Jersey, Paine offered eloquent pleas for steadfastness, such as, "These are the times that try men's souls. " Although the states ratified the Constitution with no provision for a free press, within three years (in 1791) a Bill of Rights was added to ensure civil liberties: among others, the right to assemble, to choose a religion, to speak and write freely, and to be tried fairly.

Chief among the Bill of Rights was the First Amendment: From 1790 to 1830, during the constitutional debates and the establishment of political parties, most editors and commentators argued vociferously on one side. Eighteenthcentury political writers did not value objectivity as an ideal. Journalists, often members of the social elite and appointed by a politician, helped establish the function of the press in a newly created democratic society. They sometimes overstepped the boundaries of good taste, but they established the right of journalists to comment on political competition, a right that has fueled the political process ever since.

These commentators sided with either the Federalists, who wanted a strong central government, or the Anti-Federalists, who argued to preserve the powers of the states. The period of rabid political rhetoric has been labeled the Dark Ages of American journalism by many historians. Anti-Federalist Benjamin Franklin Bache, the grandson of Benjamin Franklin, accused the revered George Washington of having "debauched" the nation and argued that "the masque of patriotism may be worn to conceal the foulest designs against the liberties of a people. " Bache was so outrageous that even his friends at times turned against him. But he stuck to his political principles, "in which he said that government officers were fallible, the Constitution good but not obviously 'stampt with the seal of perfection,' and that a free press was 'one of the first safeguards of Liberty. '" A vituperative editor on the Federalist side, William Cobbett, called Bache black-hearted, seditious, sleepy-eyed, vile, and perverted.

Despite the First Amendment, a Federalist Congress in 1798 passed the restrictive Naturalization, Enemy Alien, and Sedition Acts. These laws, commonly called the Alien and Sedition Acts, made it possible to indict those who "shall write, print, utter, or publish... false, scandalous and malicious writing or writings against the Government of the United States, or the President of the United States, or either house of the Congress... with intent to defame... or to bring them into contempt or disrepute. " Those who were convicted could be punished by a fine of not more than $2,000 and could be imprisoned for two years.

Anti-Federalist editors across the land were indicted and jailed, and only when Thomas Jefferson took office as president of the United States in 1801 were those editors released. The Alien and Sedition Acts indeed marked a low point, with their restrictions against the criticism of government in a time of peace. Because those acts were passed but not renewed, such restrictions generally have been reserved for times of war.

Press Journalism and Social Responsibility

When the First Amendment was written, idealists adhered to the Enlightenment philosophy that all individuals are born equal to learn, improve, and make proper decisions from which to lead productive lives. The government was thought to exist only as an extension of the people. It was the responsibility of the press to provide information to individuals, who were considered rational beings who could discern truth from falsehood. The founders of the United States believed that if a variety of people contributed ideas to the discussion, a free marketplace of ideas would be created and the truth would emerge.

For the marketplace of ideas to succeed, the market needs to provide free access for those who would contribute. By the twentieth century, the Industrial Revolution had changed society and the press. Individuals became more interdependent, and national media developed as radio and television expanded. During the Great Depression, Franklin Delano Roosevelt introduced federal programs based on the concept that government has the responsibility to make sure people live in acceptable conditions. In addition, with the implementation of compulsory education, people gave government the responsibility of educating the children.

To some degree, U. S. society had exchanged individualism for protectionism and collectivism. With that change came renewed calls for offering individuals information that would allow them to put events and issues into context. In 1947 a commission chaired by Robert Hutchins expressed the change in society's expectations of the press system. The Hutchins Commission, funded primarily by Henry Luce, founder of Time and Life, said that the great influence of media and the concentration of ownership required that media be socially responsible. The commission, after reviewing press behavior, decried the state of American journalism. The commission listed five "ideal demands of society for the communication of news and ideas:

1. A truthful, comprehensive, and intelligent account of the day's events in a context that gives them meaning
2. A forum for the exchange of comment and criticism
3. The projection of a representative picture of the constituent groups in society
4. The presentation and clarification of the goals and values of society
5. Full access to the day's intelligence

After evaluating the press in light of its ideal demands, the commission found freedom of the press in the United States to be in danger because of the monopolistic nature of the press. Concentration meant, the commission noted, that fewer people had access to communication channels and that those in charge had not provided a service adequate to society's needs. Concerned with the potential of new technology to be developed for either good or evil, the commission discussed guidelines for regulation of new technology and international communications systems.

The commission chose, however, to assign the press the responsibility of "accountability," rather than recommending increased government regulation. The commission suggested that retraction or restatement might better serve victims of libel rather than suits for damages, and it recommended repeal of state syndicalism acts and the Alien Registration Act of 1940, saying they were of "dubious constitutionality. " The commission also suggested that the government assume responsibility for disseminating its own news, through either private channels or channels of its own.

The commission suggested that the press should accept the responsibility of being a "common carrier" of information and discussion rather than assuming that ownership meant dissemination of a personal viewpoint. It encouraged owners to experiment with new activities, especially in areas in which profits were not necessarily assured. The commission also encouraged vigorous mutual criticism by members of the press and increased competence of news staffs. It also chided the radio industry for giving away control to soap sponsors and recommended the industry take control of its programs by treating advertisers the way the "best" newspapers treated them.

Focusing on freedom as "bound up intrinsically in the collective good of life in society," the commission further suggested that the public had a social responsibility to ensure continued freedom of the press, requesting that nonprofit institutions help supply variety and quality to press service. It requested that educational centers be created for advanced research about communications and emphasized the importance of the liberal arts in journalistic training. Renewing the discussion of the importance of a free and accessible press to a democratic society, the Hutchins Commission finally recommended that an independent agency be established to appraise and report annually on the performance of the press.

The commission worried, however, that too much emphasis was being placed on that recommendation. Nevertheless, it seemed to be the only solution commissioners could agree on, after acknowledging that the concept of laissez-faire, not government control, would eliminate the effects of monopoly. Needless to say, the owners of the agencies of mass communication reacted negatively.

During the twentieth century, social responsibility has become the dominant theoretical model for media. As coauthor of Four Theories of the Press, Theodore Peterson wrote, "freedom carries concomitant obligations; and the press, which enjoys a privileged position under our government, is obliged to be responsible to society for carrying out certain essential functions of mass communications in contemporary society. " In addition, media should continue to be free from government in order to watch over government. Although most journalists and media critics accept social responsibility in some form, not all do. Communication scholars John Merrill and Jack Odell have written about the hazards of the social responsibility approach:

> We simply (1) cannot understand exactly what is meant by a *theory* of social responsibility, and (2) cannot help feeling that a growing emphasis on such a theory will lead a nation's press system away from freedom toward authoritarianism. In the eyes of individual persons in *any* society various media at times will perform what they see as irresponsible actions; for irresponsibility, like beauty, is in the eye of the beholder. Some critics see social responsibility as self-censorship that could deprive the marketplace of ideas of potentially beneficial information. They also fear that standards of responsibility will come from the powerful and not from ordinary citizens.

The shift from editor/printer/intellectual to reporter/editor came with the advent of the penny press in the 1830s. Urban editors wanted to expand circulations, hoping that revenues would follow. In doing so, they recognized that strong political affiliations with parties would jeopardize the expansion of their readership. They began to rely more strongly on advertising and sought to report news that would be of interest to all.

Fictional accounts of reporters in the late nineteenth and early twentieth centuries depict them as semieducated "tough guys" who were out to expose corrupt businessmen and government officials. Women, though they began to enter the ranks, are relatively invisible in the fictional accounts. The intellectual role of the newspaper was relegated to the editorial page, and editors who often were heavily involved in politics made editorial decisions. The editors continued to separate themselves financially from political parties, but most editors strongly supported a particular party.

During the mid-1800s, newspaper journalists began to expose the wrongdoings of city officials and to focus on city services and politics. During the late 1800s, reporters established the form of reporting called muckraking, unearthing corporate greed and exposing it to the masses. The food and drug industry had expanded quickly without regulation, and reporters found that many commercial food-handling situations were dangerous to the consumer.

Broadcast Journalism and Social Responsibilities

Print journalism-and print and wire reporters-dominated journalism through the first third of the twentieth century. At first radio was merely a voice for the newspaper; newspaper copy fashioned by print journalists was read across the air. Later, reporters developed specific styles oriented toward listeners and viewers. In July 1922, the Norfolk [Nebraska] Daily News started the first regularly broadcast noon news program. In 1932 radio reporters covered the Roosevelt-Hoover presidential race and launched radio news. They also started a major industry battle between newspapers and radio, and publishers sought to keep radio from competing with them by limiting radio access to news from the major wire services. Newspapers could not stop radio, however, and by the late 1930s radio news was becoming a standard feature.

Radio journalists became popular sources of news with their dramatic and complete coverage of World War II. Before radio, war news took hours, days, or even weeks to reach the general public. Radio was instantaneous. Furthermore, print could never match the immediacy of Edward R. Murrow broadcasting from London as German bombs ripped through the city. Murrow developed a radio style, an intimate conversation with his listeners.

During the 1938 coverage of Germany's invasion of Austria, Murrow set up the first simultaneous broadcast with reporters in Vienna, London, Paris, Berlin, and Rome. By the time Hitler invaded Poland in 1939, CBS and NBC had placed experienced reporters throughout Europe. By 1943 the amount of radio news in the networks' evening programming had tripled, and a majority of people in the United States rated radio as more accurate than newspapers in war coverage.

Newsreels, shown in movie houses, and television offered the first electronic visual journalism. Although some experimentation with television news occurred as early as 1940, development of news programming was delayed until after World War II; the half-hour television network news shows did not appear until the 1960s. In 1945, NBC set up an organization for production of news film. In 1948 the network presented NBC Newsroom, a program produced by radio journalists and broadcast from the NBC radio newsroom. Critics argued that pictures of a man reading the news did not add much to an understanding of world affairs, but ratings were sufficient to keep the program on the air and attract competitors.

The current evening newscast format dates to NBC's Camel News Caravan, a fifteen-minute nightly program starring John Cameron Swayze. CBS inaugurated a similar program, Douglas Edwards with the News. Camel News Caravan solidified NBC's news operation for the short term. By May 1951, forty stations carried the program, which mixed newsreel footage with visual reading of the news. NBC Television News established bureaus in New York, Chicago, Washington, D. C., Cleveland, Los Angeles, Dallas, and San Francisco. It recruited stringers from abroad, hired camera crews and photographers, and signed exchange agreements with affiliate stations for news film.

Initially, this meant additional jobs for journalists, but in 1952/1953, as production costs increased and NBC's news programs encountered financial difficulty, the network dramatically reduced its news division. Meanwhile, CBS also expanded its news operations. William Paley, along with his second-in-command, Frank Stanton, shaped CBS into a leader in entertainment and news programming. Paley solidified CBS's financing, then demonstrated an uncanny skill for negotiating with affiliates and with celebrities. He was willing to allocate resources to programming, and it didn't take Paley long to ensure that CBS would surpass NBC as a leader in news and information programming.

Veteran news reporters remember the Edward R. Murrow days as the Golden Age of Television News, when money flowed through CBS newsrooms and news shaped the reputation of the individual network. Murrow, famous for his radio news broadcasts during World War II, debuted in television in 1951 with the first network public affairs series, See It Now. In later years, Murrow made CBS famous for its documentaries, such as Harvest of Shame, which depicted the plight of migrant farmworkers.

Just as television restructured U. S. entertainment patterns and the process through which people got their news, so it also reshaped the process of reporting on government officials. Television combined with expanding education, increasing mobility, participatory democratic legislation, and sophisticated research methods during the 1950s and 1960s to weaken political parties in the United States and increase the role of the media in selecting leaders. Network journalists covered the presidential campaign of 1952, a race between the popular General Dwight D. Eisenhower, a hero of World War II, and Illinois Governor Adlai Stevenson, one of the nation's foremost intellectuals.

During this race, politics began to conform to the requirements of television. Stevenson's long commentaries bored too many of his listeners; Eisenhower, although anything but a polished television star, at least learned the value of short spots. Soon after being named Eisenhower's running mate, Richard Nixon was accused of being the beneficiary of a secret trust fund set up by wealthy businessmen. The public was scandalized. Fearing that Eisenhower would drop him from the Republican ticket, Nixon chose television as the medium for his defense. It was through television that Richard Nixon was able to bypass journalists.

Television provided this politician the opportunity to present himself in public without editing by journalists. In what became known as "the Checkers speech," Nixon detailed his financial condition and vowed that, though his children's dog Checkers had been donated by an admirer, the family loved the dog and "regardless of what they say, we're going to keep it. " This personalized use of television built on what Franklin Delano Roosevelt had accomplished with his "Fireside Chats" over radio before and during World War II. Politicians began to go directly to the public, rather than having information first sifted through reporters and editors for newspapers and magazines.

Image has always played a role in politics. Image helps to define candidates for voters. Television, with its strong visual impact, enhanced the ability of media and politicians to manipulate political images. John Kennedy used presidential debates and press conferences to shape his image. His ready wit and handsome smile made him a natural for the cameras. In the first televised presidential debate between Kennedy and Richard Nixon in 1960, Kennedy established himself as a man with a vision for leadership and placed Nixon in the position of defending the status quo.

The Kennedy-Nixon debates set a precedent for future presidential campaigns. Debates are now an expected part of the campaign process, and their effectiveness or lack of it is controversial and thus interesting to voters.

In the 1992 elections, the questioning of candidates in a town hall format, with citizens rather than journalists asking questions, gained more attention than did the formal debates. However, as the 2000 election debates showed, formal encounters continue to be a significant part of presidential campaigning.

In 1968 Richard Nixon hired people who understood the art of television advertising, and paid media became a significant force in political campaigning. Nixon's people knew how to research public taste and to create advertising. Although disarray in the Democratic Party in 1968 aided Nixon's victory, some critics charge that without the mastery of the television image devised by his advisors, Nixon might never have become president.

Today political candidates work hard to control their images through advertising and by making arranged appearances. Many candidates limit their exposure to journalists, preferring to display a crafted image rather than respond to impromptu questions. Whenever candidates do respond to the press, their spin doctors work to get the candidate's interpretation of an event or issue into journalists' stories. The promotion of image rather than issues and substance is also fostered by some of the current production values of television. News values that promote higher ratings through ever shorter sound bites allow candidates to shape a planned, desirable television image, no matter what their actual political history.

In 1963, only a few weeks before the assassination of President John F. Kennedy, whose funeral made television history, NBC expanded its evening news coverage from a mere fifteen minutes to a thirty-minute newscast featuring the anchor team of Chet Huntley and David Brinkley. CBS followed suit with a news program anchored by Walter Cronkite. ABC, whose newscasts were at best a fledgling operation, didn't expand to a half hour until 1967. Since the 1960s, the networks have often explored expanding their evening newscasts to an hour.

However, the affiliated stations continue to run their own profitable local newscasts in the lead-in time slot and retain the time slot following the network news for profit-making syndicated shows such as Wheel of Fortune and Jeopardy. By the end of the 1960s, television had become the country's dominant medium for the visual display of social controversy. The civil rights movement, the war in Vietnam, environmental damage, and women's demands for equality were the big stories of the decade. Television covered them all.

Expansion of network news came not in the prestigious and expensive evening hours but in morning news, in which a softer format appealed to audiences with shows such as Good Morning America. The definition of news also expanded to include newsmagazines such as 60 Minutes, which began in 1968 but did not achieve a permanent slot on the weekly schedule until the late 1970s. The expansion also includes late-night news programs such as Ted Koppel's Nightline, which ABC introduced in 1979 during the height of the crisis arising from Iranian militants' seizure of hostages in the U. S. embassy in Tehran. In the late 1980s, the number of newsmagazines in prime time grew. By 2000, ABC, NBC, and CBS were producing as many as a dozen newsmagazines a week.

American journalism has emerged from two separate traditions, that of objectivity and that of storytelling, or the narrative tradition. Modern journalism exhibits a tension between these traditions, with many editors and station managers arguing that objectivity is the golden norm of journalism, while others struggle to retain and understand the narrative tradition and its importance. We know that impartiality or objectivity was a criterion used as early as the colonial days. Benjamin Franklin speaks of being an "impartial printer. "

During the Civil War, J. Thrasher, head of the Press Association in the Confederate states, tells editors to be "objective. " When Adolph Ochs strives to make the New York Times a newspaper of record in the mid-1800s, he speaks of "objectivity. " Traditionally, objectivity has included five components: detachment from the object of the story, nonpartisanship, a reliance on facts, a sense of balance, and use of the inverted pyramid style of writing. However, many journalists believe it is impossible to be totally objective.

In fact, journalists have dropped the word objectivity from such documents as the Society for Professional Journalists' code. Whereas Walter Cronkite, the renowned anchor of the CBS evening news from 1962 to 1981, ended his newscast saying, "And that's the way it is," Dan Rather ends his with the words, "And that's part of our world. " The strive for objectivity has been replaced by use of the words truthfulness, accuracy, and comprehensiveness. However, journalists often endorse objectivity as a principal tenet. Leonard Downie, managing editor of the Washington Post, reveres the concept to the degree that he claims he does not vote because doing so would force him to take sides and make him less objective.

The tradition of narrative journalism has remained strong. Telling stories was a component of colonial and frontier newspapers. Sometimes they were totally factual; at other times, they were representations of reality. Narrative journalism, or "literary journalism," was controversial as early as the 1880s, when it threatened literature, whose predominant form during the period was realism. The controversies centered on some themes that are still heard today: the conflict between "high" and "low" culture and the blending of fiction and fact.

Many narrative journalists actually aspired to be novelists. During the late 1960s, when a young generation of journalists evaluated the role of journalism in the social change brought about by civil rights and Vietnam activities and debates, they turned to what they labeled "new journalism" as a way of expressing the social context of political arguments. Some of these young reporters abandoned the objective, straightforward approach of "Who? What? When? Where? and Why?" The demands of interpretation and the political and cultural context of the decade demanded new techniques, new language, and incorporation of styles that had distinguished alternative media for many years.

Everette Dennis, in the Magic Writing Machine, divided New Journalism into five types:

(1) the new nonfiction, also called "reportage" and "parajournalism";

(2) alternative journalism, also called "modern muckraking";

(3) advocacy journalism;

(4) underground journalism; and

(5) precision journalism.

David Halberstam wrote a journalistic account of Vietnam (new nonfiction); the Village Voice advocated political positions on issues such as free love (alternative and advocacy, which sometimes blend); underground newspapers were printed and distributed without acknowledgment of authorship; and precision journalists used new statistical methods to prove points. Today, narrative journalism appears in books by journalists such as Mark Bowden, whose account of the disastrous U. S. intervention in Somalia is chronicled in Black Hawk Down. Controversy about the method still abounds, especially in relation to books such as Midnight in the Garden of Good and Evil, a supposedly nonfiction account of a high-profile murder in Savannah, Georgia. Many critics contend that although the basic structure is nonfiction, the narrative is embellished considerably with fictional constructs.

Today's journalists operate in a highly competitive marketplace. Both the objective and the narrative traditions are used in reporting news for newspapers, radio, television, and the Internet. However, the marketplace has become increasingly competitive, and media companies have "gone public," or begun to sell stock on the markets, thereby creating a need to pay dividends to those individuals who buy the stocks. This has increased the attention paid to ratings of television and radio news, as well as to the circulation numbers of newspapers and to the numbers of hits on Internet sites.

Entertainment has assumed more importance. Although journalism has always been a business, during the last thirty-five years it has evolved into big business. Whether television, radio, newspapers, or online, the corporations that increasingly own large news outlets require ever-higher profit margins to please the stock analysts and mutual fund managers. The results have varied. In some cases, publicly owned companies such as the New York Times produce award-winning journalism. In other cases, such as Thomson newspapers, the journalism got so bad that companies lost large numbers of readers.

Thomson eventually sold its newspaper holdings. When newspapers seek profit levels that exceed those of most other industries, the result is often a reduction in the number of journalists and a corresponding decline in local, quality coverage. Despite these problems, journalism today is supported by thousands of devoted journalists in all media who aim to serve the public and society. The quality of journalism often rests on the initiative of the individuals who put in extra time just to get the story right. However, the tension between profit and quality journalism will continue as long as journalism is a commercial enterprise.

An often debated question in newsrooms is whether the journalist should give the people what they "need" or whether the journalist should provide the material that audiences "want. " Such an argument assumes that the journalist and editor know what people need to read. The public certainly does not agree and through its purchasing power does make its own decisions about what kinds of information it needs and wants. The marketplace of ideas assumes that all ideas should be discussed in the open. The more ideas, the better. Only when ideas (even those thought radical) gain access to the public forum can social change occur. Women fought for almost a century before gaining the right to vote through a constitutional amendment adopted in 1920. Their ideas were considered radical by many men-and women. The marketplace of ideas involves social discourse, and social discourse can lead to policy formation. For example, the state of Oregon adopted strict recycling standards for its population by the early 1970s, ten to twenty years before most other states did the same. Oregon's marketplace of ideas considered the recycling issue important, and the discussion in that marketplace led to policy changes that other states eventually adopted. The audience demands information that it can discuss; thus journalism provides the discussion points that help to create the marketplace of ideas. Through the marketplace, the public-individually and in groups-makes political, social, and economic decisions.

Because information available through new technology requires that someone purchase a technological device, the possibility exists for a society divided into information- poor and information-rich segments. In such a society, information is the golden key to success, and the information is available only to those with money. Research has consistently shown that those with already high levels of information gain even more information as they begin to use new technologies, and even if informationpoor consumers become more knowledgeable, they continually fall behind in the socioinformation struggle. Therefore, the knowledge gap, the distance between those who use information technologies at the highest levels and those usually with lower socioeconomic status who do not, increases rather than decreases.

The creation of a knowledge gap is of concern for many reasons. A 1972 study showed that information distribution inequities in a society could be directly related to inequities in the distribution of other elements of social life such as education, affluence, and exposure to communication channels. The United States has long succeeded as a democracy at least in part because of its high literacy rates and its emphasis on maintaining a solid middle class; democracies are known to survive longest in countries with a strong middle class. If class begins to be defined not only by education and social status but also by access to and possession of information, the creation of a knowledge gap may signify the weakening of the middle class.

The supply for the marketplace of ideas comes from all sources of information, including individuals, newspapers, movies, television, recordings, and radio. Consumers, journalists, lobbyists, public-relations personnel, and government officials determine, both as individuals and as groups, what content has use in the marketplace of ideas. Because people are both information sources and information consumers, they make the mass communication system an important part of the political and social process.

Media serve as agenda setters: the content of media helps determine which topics and issues society considers important. Who gets to comment affects the information we all receive, so if only one political party were permitted to comment, content presented by the media would not reflect the social and political world we all must deal with. Likewise, if social issues were presented from only one point of view, such as that of the businessperson, the social context of those on welfare, of working single parents, or of educators would be excluded from the picture. When the agenda setters fairly present all points of view, society is best served.

Consumers want varying kinds of news. The bulk of nonadvertising information is news. News can be soft, hard, or deep. Soft news includes a variety of feature stories, such as the story of the first woman to serve as drum major of a university band or the story of the birth of a Siberian tiger at the local zoo. Soft news also includes advice columns, such as "Dear Abby. " Hard news focuses on current events that have serious effects on people, such as crime, politics, and disasters. If a child dies in a house fire, the story is hard news. In-depth news requires the story to go beyond breaking stories to incorporate background details and trends.

Investigative articles often fall into this category. A series of stories about the impact of changing federal regulations on student loans is an example. News in newspapers comes from three sources: the newspaper staff, wire and news services, and feature syndicates. Staff and news service reporters share similar standards for selecting which events and issues become news. These standards are called news values, and their application to particular stories is called "news judgment. " Over time, several news values have evolved. The following values are usually cited as the reasons behind news selection and are even taught in reporting courses in journalism school:

— Impact applies when a large number of people are affected by an event or issue or when a small number of individuals are intensely affected.

A car accident that kills three people has a greater impact than one that causes a small cut on one person's forehead.

— Proximity deals with the geographic location of an event. The more local the event, the more news value it has. A story that shuts off electricity for eight hours in Lansing, Michigan, will be reported in the Lansing State Journal but not in the Detroit Free Press because the Journal is proximate to Lansing readers.

— Prominence concerns how notable or famous a person is. Politicians, sports figures, and entertainment stars are prominent figures. An illicit affair by a shoe store clerk would not be news, but President Clinton's affair was because of prominence.

— Timeliness deals with recency of an event or issue. A bank robbery that happened yesterday has more news value than one twenty years ago. The focus is on breaking stories.

— Conflict relates to disagreement among people. The conflict can be physical, as in crime and war, but it need not be. Much political news involves conflict in the marketplace of ideas.

— Disaster includes both natural calamities such as earthquakes and human-caused catastrophes such as an oil spill in the ocean.

— Human interest relates to personal details that intrigue readers. The story of an eighty-year-old woman who drives a school bus and is called "Grandma" by elementary students has human interest.

News values may change as society changes. The penny press, for example, emphasized crime news, which contained conflict and impact. A more recent type of news is called "coping information. " Life in the United States has grown more complicated. More readers want information that will help them live more efficiently. Articles about how to stay healthy through better eating and exercise help people cope with daily stress. A story can have more than one news value. The more of these values in a story, the more likely it is that people will read it. In addition, some values are more important than others. Because newspapers tend to emphasize local news, proximity is important for most staff-prepared stories.

Journalists don't sit with a checklist of news values when picking events to be covered. Rather, they internalize these values and judge whether stories will be of interest to their readers. As the audience changes, however, the match between the journalists' and the audience's news values can change. Coping information emerged because readers wanted it. Many readers criticize newspapers for emphasizing too much bad news, another term for conflict and disaster. Journalists counter that some bad news is important and must be understood if people are to be effective citizens.

Many readers grew tired of reading about the Clinton and Lewinsky controversy. The debate centered not only on the amount of coverage but also on the nature of the coverage. Readers and journalists can agree on a story having news value but disagree on how that story should be presented to readers. Information can be supplied in many forms through many different media.

Media organizations are becoming increasingly global. Multinational companies own media outlets in multiple countries. Ownership ultimately has an impact on journalism. In World War II and in Vietnam, for the most part U. S. citizens covered the war and reported on it in U. S. media for U. S. consumers. Other countries relied on various systems for gaining information. Some of that information was U. S. based, such as international news broadcasts by Voice of America, the government-owned information service. Today, however, CNN employs news reporters from around the world. They may or may not be U. S. citizens. This means that the view of reporters in regard to international incidents may vary considerably more than reporter views varied during earlier international conflicts.

CNN executives also are searching for audiences around the world. An example of this was apparent during the spring and summer of June 2002, when many Israeli groups charged CNN with biased coverage of the Palestinian-Israeli conflict. Media watch groups charged that CNN humanized Palestinians and merely noted the number of dead in Israel. Ted Turner's comments to the London Guardian didn't help: "The Israelis, they've got the most powerful military machines in the world.

Throughout history, journalistic trends have come and gone. Sometimes they involve technology and delivery of news, and other times they involve the impact of business and journalistic practices on what people receive as news. Currently, four major trends are shaping journalism: issues of credibility, journalism and political participation, the future of journalism online, and the impact of profits on journalism.

Journalists have come on hard times-their credibility with the public has taken a nosedive. In an attempt to address these issues, several associations and "think groups" have studied the credibility issue. A study conducted by Time magazine in 1998 found that newspaper credibility had sunk to a level at which only 21 percent of Americans believed all or most of the content in the local newspaper, representing a decline from 28 percent in 1985.

The American Society of Newspaper Editors (ASNE) began a $1 million project to improve credibility. They discovered that the public finds too many factual and spelling/grammar errors in newspapers, too little respect for and knowledge about their communities, too much influence of reporters' biases on what is covered and how it is reported, too much sensationalism to increase sales, and too much concern with profit. Following are some principles:

1. Journalism's first obligation is to tell the truth.
2. Journalism's first loyalty is to citizens.
3. The essence of journalism is a discipline of verification.
4. Journalists must maintain an independence from those they cover.
5. Journalists must serve as an independent monitor of power.
6. Journalism must provide a forum for public criticism and comment.
7. Journalists must make the significant interesting and relevant.
8. Journalists should keep the news in proportion and make it comprehensive.
9. Journalists have an obligation to personal conscience.

These principles are not exactly new. They closely parallel codes of ethics by such organizations as The Society for Professional Journalists. However, they point to a significant trend-and to an important issue. The trend is actually twofold: (1) Journalism has declined in credibility and the public doesn't believe journalists; and (2) critics and journalists are striving to address the issue because they believe credibility to be important not only to their profession but also to the society in which they live. The issue is whether journalistic principles can survive in the modern-day cacophony of entertainment noise and profit-seeking values.

Journalism and Political Participation

Being able to participate in the selection of political leaders is one of the characteristics of a democracy. However, in the United States declining percentages of eligible voters participate in the process. In 1964, 69. 3 percent of people of voting age actually cast a ballot. That number has declined until in 2000 it fell just short of 55 percent. In 2000, because of large immigration numbers, the Census Bureau reported the statistics slightly differently. It reported the percentage of voters of eligible age and eligible citizenship who voted. Using that population, the percentage of eligible voters actually casting a ballot rose to 60 percent, up 2 percent from 1996.

Only 64 percent of those eligible to vote registered to do so. You might ask, "Isn't that a political issue? Is that an issue for journalism?" It is an issue for journalism because journalists deliver most political messages to U. S. voters. And when an election is so close that journalists cannot adequately report it-indeed, the vote counters cannot accurately count the votes-the role of journalists in the political process becomes even more apparent. The election of 2000 caused many reporters, editors, and managers to rethink how they cover elections.

In addition, journalists and political critics have become increasingly concerned about the reliance on popular culture media for political news and about the trend toward increased political advertising and decreased political coverage. In 1992, President Clinton appeared on the Arsenio Hall Show and on Donahue, in addition to responding to journalists on traditional political shows such as Meet the Press and the MacNeil-Lehrer NewsHour. He played his saxophone in an effort to establish a link with the American public. He participated in a new style of debate in Richmond, Virginia, responding to questions from the audience rather than to questions from journalists.

By 1996 this type of media behavior did not seem unusual. In the 1998 midterm elections, the major television networks carried 73 percent fewer stories about the elections than they did in the 1994 midterm elections. Political advertising on broadcast television alone amounted to over $400 million dollars in 1996; in 2000 it reached $606 million. However, television stations billed $531 million in political advertising, the highest election billing year ever. Michael Kelly, in a New York Times Magazine article, argued that "the conversation of politics now is carried on in the vernacular of advertising. The big sell, the television sell, appears to be the only way to sell.

Increasingly, and especially in Washington, how well one does on television has come to determine how well one does in life. Kelly describes

Washington, D. C., as a national capital where increasingly the distinction between reality and fantasy has been lost.... Movie stars show up with their press agents and their bodyguards to 'testify' before Congress. Politicians and reporters make cameo appearances as movie stars, playing themselves in fictional scenes about politics and reporting.

The effectiveness of the marketplace of ideas in different societies varies with the type of government and with the extent of commercialism in each country. In authoritarian countries, the government often limits access to the public forum. In a country where ordinary citizens participate in governance, extensive participation in the marketplace of ideas is crucial for effective government. In the United States, media critics recently have become concerned about the quality of political participation because of the commercialization of the political process through TV advertisements and the sensationalism of quasi-entertainment political talk shows. Some argue that television has corrupted the marketplace of ideas into a showplace for images rather than a public forum for issues and that it has destroyed any possibility for rational political discourse. Others argue that popularization of politics through television and other avenues has brought-and will continue to bring-more individuals into the political process.

References

Barnett, C. . Media, democracy and representation: Disembodying the public. In C. Barnett & M. Low (Eds.), *Spaces of Democracy: geographical perspectives on citizenship, participation and representation* (pp. 185–206). London, UK: Sage.

Bogart, L. . Media and Democracy. In E. E. Dennis & R. W. Snyder (Eds.), *Media & Democracy* (pp. 6-8). USA: Transaction.

Flew, T. . Democracy, participation and convergent media: case studies in contemporary online news journalism in Australia. *Communication, Politics & Culture, 42*(2), pp. 87-115

Habermas, J. . Information and democracy. In F. Webster (Ed.), *Theories of the Information Society* (pp. 161-163). New York, NY: Taylor & Francis.

McQuail, D. . *McQuail's Mass Communication Theory.* Vistaar Publications.

Pelinka, A. . *Democracy Indian Style: Subhas Chandra Bose and the creation of India's political culture.* (R. Schell, Trans.). (pp 109-111). USA: Transaction.

5

Responsible Journalism

A journalist writes what for the society that he observes.He presents whatever,is consumed by the society people which may consist of different classes, religions, categories and characteristics.So,while presenting the report on any event,a journalist should be very careful and aware of his responsibilities in disseminating it towards the present sensible society. He must deliver such news as it serves a common purpose and fulfills major people's interests as well.Any presentation or writing of a journalist, should never inflict or hit any part or group of our society regarding its belief, ideals,religion and rituals anyway. The writing of journalist should be inspiring not only in keeping 'social harmony' but also in achieving social development at the sametime.

Basic Responsibilities of Journalism

There are three basic responsibilities that are to be considered by any journalist. They are social, legal and professional.

Social Responsibiliy

Press reflects the social images or pictures of our society.The whole activities of the press imparts many events of our society with a view to present them later on, in decent manner to the society people. The intention behind such approaches and activities, is to make the society people tobe well-informed as well as well-aware of round about happenings.So,every presentation of any journalist should be fair, balnce, truthful,inspiring and meeting the needs of common consumers of the news. Beside the usual events ,a journalist can highlight so many unsolved areas of the society by seeking solution for the same through the activity of journalism and must not overlook or avoid this great part of responsibility towards the society.The presentation of journalist should, initiate an environment of understanding within the society and shoul continue the same in sustained manner, in upholding it satisfactorily.Development of any society mostly, depending upon the imparting of creative and objectful journalistic activities.

Legal Responsibilty

While working as a journalist, one should be well conversant with all legal clutches as to avert the generation of complicacy as well as to keep the organization 'troublefree' any way. For this reason, a journalist must not intervene or inflict to someone's privacy or confidential matter until it is required to be brought to the notice of public. Any libellous or defamatory presentation taking with someone, any organization or group, is not permittable and should strictly be avoided by the journalist. Libellous and defamatory writings or pictures, may earn instantly resounse or reply from the public with larger acceptance, but it is not pertinent as well as not complying with the standard of professionalism.

Professional Responsibility

A journalist should have sincerity and commitment towards its profession. The news ofany event that is going to be published for the audience, should be delineated very clearly and faiely. A very good homework in this regard is essential for each and every event, and should be done by the journalist with a view to present the same to the audience confidently and satisfactorily.. The presentation must be truthful and unbiased above all and shall never bring any embarrassment or complicacy to the organization anyway in future. The objective of any journalist is to disseminate the correct and fair report in undistorted manner to the audience rather than crowding them intentially or allegedly to meet the present challenging situation.of the news world.. A news report should be created with greater care and responsibility as to maintain its degree of standard at higher level by avoiding anytype inclusion of undesireable and provocative part or portion.A journalist definitely,would require a high degree of professionalism in presenting any performances to the audience on behalf of any organization, and could be achieved so. by dint of die-hard efforts and unending searching abilty, and being respectful to the works ,understanding with the surroundings and accountability towards the society as well. A journalist must follow the newspaper editor's deadlines.

Socially Responsible Journalism

Responsible journalism does not strengthen the government in power, nor does it insist merely on the individual right to publish and make a profit. The press must remain free from government and business pressure and serve society instead. Socially responsible (SR) news is defined by its duties to the community. For SR theory, it is the duty of the press to provide "a truthful, comprehensive, and intelligent account of the day's events in a context which gives them meaning". The press should serve as "a forum for the exchange of comment and criticism," give a "representative picture of the constituent groups in society," help in the "presentation and clarification of the goals and values of the society," and "provide full access to the day's intelligence".

The major mission of mass communication, the Commission argued, is to raise social conflict from levels of violence and vulgarity to the plane of discussion. The impact of the Hutchins Commission in the United States has been limited, but SR thinking has resonated well around the world. Essentially, the same theory of the press has won wide global recognition over the last 50 years, with or without direct reference to the Commission. Great ideas are seldom unique; they surface in several places, triggered by similar conditions and needs. Accordingly, the Hutchins Commission is not an American landmark for the world to emulate, but an American variant of a need in democratic societies to develop a workable philosophy of and policies for the press.

The late 1960s saw an exciting experiment in Finnish public broadcasting, known as "informational mass communication" for its emphasis on informing the public against ignorance and prejudice. The main idea was essentially the same as that of the Hutchins Commission: to improve the account of the day and to promote a better informed public and democracy. The Finnish broadcasting policy of the late 1960s was indeed a radical reform program, rejecting a passive establishment-oriented policy and adopting an active role for broadcasting as a participant in the political and cultural life of the society. Therefore, the conventional conservative and entertainment approach was replaced by a philosophy that stressed the importance of conveying socially relevant information not only from the point of view of the prevalent hegemony, but especially from the perspective of those interest groups who were left outside the official channels of information and influence. Accordingly, the new objective was to cover the social reality in all of its aspects, each under equal conditions, regardless of the priorities set up by the traditional hegemony.

On this basis, quite a detailed philosophy was elaborated, including an application of semantic information theory that defined news criteria in terms of the potentially new knowledge that resulted from covering the world. A core concept in this approach was the individual's worldview, which was supposed to be influenced by broadcasting to become more and more realistic-in line with the Hutchins Commission's first objective of an accurate and comprehensive picture. In hindsight, this approach bears a striking resemblance to the ideas of Hutchins, although the architects of the Finnish broadcasting experiment had absolutely no knowledge of Hutchins at the time.

This international case reminds us of a historic commission headed by the Irish lawyer and activist Sean MacBride (former president of the International Peace Bureau and founding member of Amnesty International). The MacBride Commission worked in 1977 through 1980, and its report served as the basis for a resolution unanimously adopted by the General Conference of UNESCO in autumn 1980, with the United States and the United Kingdom still members. Akey paragraph of this landmark resolution lists the "considerations" on which the much debated New World Information and Communication Order (NWICO) was supposed to be based:

1. Elimination of the imbalances and inequalities that characterize the situation.
2. Elimination of the negative effects of certain monopolies, public or private, and excessive concentrations.
3. Removal of the internal and external obstacles to a free flow and wider and better balanced dissemination of information and ideas.
4. Plurality of sources and channels of information.
5. Freedom of the press and information.
6. The freedom of journalists and all professionals in the communication media, a freedom inseparable from responsibility.

These points read as if taken directly from the Hutchins Report. Indeed, the same sociopolitical approach adopted by the Hutchins Commission toward the American media scene of the mid-1940s was applied by the MacBride Commission to the global media scene of the late 1970s. The fact that the approach was shaped in a way so strikingly similar in two very different documents can be taken as a test of reliability for the media philosophy in question-what is at issue is very basic, solid, and transnational.

On the other hand, one could cynically comment that scholarship had made little progress in 30 years. Furthermore, one could note that in both cases the Commission's basically moderate thinking provoked a sharp reaction from the press' proprietors-effectively eliminating chances to win wider political support for the reports and their recommendations. In any case, the MacBride Commission stands as a reminder that the ideas raised by the Hutchins Commission were still alive and, indeed, traveled well in the pre-Reagan world dominated by a balance among the so-called East, West, and South.

In addition, as in the previous case of Finnish broadcasting, there was no copying of ideas from the Hutchins Commission to the later platform. To be sure, there was at least one prominent actor in the MacBride platform who had studied the Hutchins Report, but he used it as an ex post facto argument in a political debate to persuade Americans (who were reluctant to accept any reference to responsibility for the media) rather than to generate the thinking itself. The Hutchins Commission proved significant not only because its message remained alive for decades but also because its message was rewritten by a truly international Commission.

SR Policy in the European Union (EU)

Most of Europe takes SR for granted. It is the dominant, mainstream doctrine in journalism and media policies, including public service broadcasting. A significant reminder of this was given by the Summit of the EU in Amsterdam in June 1997 through the adoption of the following Protocol on Public Service Broadcasting: The High Contracting Parties, considering that the system of public broadcasting in the Member States is directly related to the democratic, social and cultural needs of each society and to the need to preserve media pluralism, have agreed on the following interpretative provisions, which shall be annexed to the Treaty establishing the European Community:

The provisions of this Treaty shall be without prejudice to the competence of Member States to provide for the funding of public service broadcasting in so far as such funding is granted to broadcasting organizations for the fulfillment of the public service remit as conferred, defined and organized by each Member State, and that such funding does not affect trading conditions and competition in the Community to an extent that would be contrary to the common interest, while the realization of the remit of that public service shall be taken into account. The introductory paragraph makes the vital point that public broadcasting (vs. commercial broadcasting) should be understood in the EU as part of the cultural and social sphere based on national priorities, instead of the economic sphere based on free competition within the broader European scale.

Accordingly, public service broadcasting is defined at the constitutional level as an exception to the principle of a free European market. The rest of the aforementioned text specifies that the funding of public service broadcasting, notably license fees paid annually by consumers, is protected at the national level against normal EU-wide competition rules. These rules have already been invoked by commercial broadcasters who claim that the public broadcaster with its subsidies violates the principle of the free European market. The protocol averts such claims and provides legal security for public funding.

In reality, the protocol strengthens the dual broadcasting system in Europe, whereby strong public and private sectors coexist. The protocol clearly reflects the spirit of Hutchins already in its reference to media pluralism. This means to oppose media concentration (i.e., commercial media concentration in the free market). It is ironic that what is supported instead is public service broadcasting, which typically becomes institutionalized in really big monopolies like the British Broadcasting Corporation (BBC). At a closer look, however, public service monopolies are in perfect accordance with the idea of media pluralism-after all, their whole philosophy is to provide equal access to and fair coverage of all sectors of society regardless of socioeconomic status, place of living, home language, and so forth.

Although the Amsterdam protocol offers legally hard evidence in support of Hutchins thinking in the particular area of public service broadcasting, a number of other documents both by the EU and the Council of Europe define the broader area of European Audiovisual Policy and what is known in Europe as the Information Society (more or less the same as the American Information Super highway or National Information Infrastructure). In these emerging policy areas one can also trace Hutchins thinking as exemplified in resolutions by the European Parliament.

For example, in June 1995 a resolution was adopted relating to the EU Green Paper on pluralism and media concentration in the internal market, whereby the European Parliament inter alia

> Having regard to the negative consequences of having an information society which is subject solely to market forces, and the need to take account of the cultural, ethical, social and political implications, ...a balanced apportionment of resources of all kinds is essential in order to safeguard the pluralism and diversity of the information media.

In October 1997 the European Communities returned to the theme in its resolution on the impact of new technologies on the press in Europe based on the Daskalaki Report, including the following provisions:

> Having regard to the European Parliament's repeatedly-stated position that information is not a product comparable to other products; having regard to the undisputed role that the press has played-and continues to play-in promoting democracy, freedom and human rights; having regard to the positive impact of the new technologies on public information, notably more rapid and extensive access to a greater number of sources of information, interaction between the recipient and source of information, the globalization of information, the more immediate and more democratic access of citizens to proposals and decisions taken by European, national and regional authorities and the easier participation of citizens in the decision-taking process; having regard, however, to the concerns expressed by the European Parliament in the past regarding the new communications environment, and notably the deluge of information and news that is not always sufficiently evaluated or processed and whose source is not always established; the danger of the marginalization-even temporarily-of certain social groups that are not yet sufficiently familiar with the new technologies or do not have equal access opportunities to them; the dominance of the networks by products that are predominantly commercial in character at the expense of products that express Europe's multilingual and multidimensional cultural identity and heritage; and finally, a tendency toward human isolation.

In short, the contemporary European policy approach to journalism and mass communication has a distinct social and cultural orientation that separates it from the predominantly market-oriented philosophy of the EU. There is a clear corollary between the Hutchins Commission's defense of the press against what it saw as an excessively commercial market and the European defense of the media against the purely commercial market. However, this is not the whole story. Contemporary European media policy, particularly in the audio-visual field including cinema, also has an industrial dimension that to a certain degree contradicts the sociocultural perspective of Hutchins. There is a strong political will to preserve European production in this field, and therefore, even commercial media monopolies are tolerated as long as they remain in European hands.

The overall objective is to create a strong European media market against competition from the United States, Japan, and elsewhere. Policy reasoning is not the classic free market but a common market of "Fortress Europe" where, for example, the Television Directive legislates that no less than one half of the air time must be filled by programs of European origin. Consequently, most European media policies today are schizophrenic. On the one hand, media concentration is seen as evil, but on the other hand, strong media companies are welcome to stand against non-European competition.

However, the main point to be noted here is that public service broadcasting remains strong in Europe, and that there is no reason to deplore — or celebrate, depending on your media politics line-the decline of national broadcasting institutions like the BBC. The United States and its Public Broadcasting Service is a different story. In Europe, the SR theory prevails in the deep structures of political economy and media policy. Therefore, one is entitled to say that the spirit of Hutchins is very much alive in Europe today. The spirit of Hutchins is very much alive in Europe today.

Professional Journalists

The aforementioned cases represent more or less official media policies or models of thinking related to media policies in a country (Finland) or international organizations (UNESCO and the EU). The following picks up the thinking from among media professionals, rank-and-file journalists -often referred to as working journalists to distinguish them from editors and publishers. It is taken from a document prepared in 1988 by the Consultative Club of international and regional organizations of professional journalists-altogether 400,000 working journalists, the majority of the organized profession in the world-after a thorough review of the Mass Media Declaration of UNESCO.

The principal view that the operation of the mass media should be determined primarily by the practice of professional journalism in the public interest without undue government or commercial influence. The role played by information and communication in national as well as international spheres has become more and more prominent during the past decade with a growing responsibility being placed upon the mass media and journalists. This calls, increasingly, for the professional autonomy of journalists as well as a measure of public accountability.

More systematic research is needed to discover and understand all the nuances and subtleties of professional thinking among journalists around the world. However, two generalizations are obvious: First, a common core of professional doctrine is surprisingly similar in various parts of the world; and second, this universal common core is practically identical with the Hutchins Commission's approach.

Civic Journalism

American journalists in the 1990s confronted disturbing trends: weakening demand for serious news, cynicism about the news media, and flagging interest in civic affairs. "Constitutionally guaranteed media libertarianism no longer seemed adequate to propel people into democratic participation;" the press had evolved into "a multifaceted mass media -print, broadcast, and electronic (cyberspace)" -reflecting people's "predilection for entertainment rather than for knowledge of public affairs and political involvement". Faced with a crisis in their craft, reporters, academics, and media professionals began searching for a new kind of journalism, "one tuned more to the needs of an ailing democracy than the rules of a hidebound profession".

> Democracy and its discontents was thus a major theme in the inquiry and many who joined in it were discontented themselves with their work, their sinking standing among citizens, the places they had carved out for themselves as professionals. Amid a mood of anxiety and alarm, they set out to understand democracy in a new way, so they could see journalism from another angle: as democracy's cultivator, as well as its chronicler.

Public journalism-also called civic or community journalism-was born, seeking to restyle the press toward greater citizen involvement and a healthier public climate. One of its architects, public journalism involves a variety of shifts away from conventional journalism: moving "beyond the limited mission of telling the news to a broader mission of helping public life to go well"; instead of detachment, becoming "a fair-minded participant in public life"; shifting from worries "about proper separations to concerns with proper connections"; and moving "from people as consumers …to seeing them as a public, as potential actors in arriving at democratic solutions to public problems".

The term public journalism and the movement it spawned have their roots in America, Sam Chege Mwangi identified similar "experiments carried out by media houses around the world" (p. 24) to engage citizens for a healthy democracy. A version of development journalism in Kerala, India, is a well-known example of this, where a community of scholars, in service to their people, have perfected the art of using indigenous knowledge and forms of communication to improve the lives of communities around them. Using traditional group meetings, oral narratives, and media in local languages, they share innovative practices in agriculture, health, and architecture with local peasants to help them improve their lives.

New Zealand was one of the earliest countries to adopt the American public journalism model. During the 1993 general election campaign, two New Zealand newspapers, The Evening Standard and Waika to Times, abandoned the conventional strategies: adversarial reporting, sound bites, reliance on bad news, and their own news staffs as professional experts. Instead, readers identified the campaign issues through discussions together as citizens, journalists lived among and became a voice for the public, and members of the community had access to newspaper space usually reserved for outside pundits writing in generic terms about their own agendas.

Similarly, in 1997 the Australian Broadcasting Corporation developed public forums on government and politics in Brisbane and other municipalities, but broadened the issues to include race and crime. In Latin America, according to Mwangi, more public journalism projects have been carried out than in any other continent. El Neuvo Dia and La Razon have identified corruption as the main threat to democracy in Bolivia and are highlighting citizens' responsibility to come to grips with it. In Costa Rica, Radio Reloj, the leading news media radio station, and San Jose's Channel 6 television station are engaged in community forums.

Journalists in Kingston, Jamaica, involve citizens in serious efforts to engage health problems such as HIV and prostate cancer. The Swazil and Broadcasting Corporation has a weekly feature on rural communities that arises out of the people's issues and involves them in resolving them. Siyaya and The Cape Times, through public forums, have covered democracy in the new Republic of South Africa from the citizens' perspective. They demonstrate that the strategies of public journalism can work in young democracies as they do here and likewise in Bolivia and Jamaic). Peter Parisi concluded correctly that public journalism enters similar territory to the Hutchins Commission. Hutchins anticipated public journalism in its call for news reporting that projects "the opinions and attitudes of the groups in society to one another".

The Commission's second and third recommendations (the media are to serve "as a forum for the exchange of comment and criticism" and "present and clarify the goals and values of society") are central to the philosophy that drives public journalism. Hutchins and public journalism both turn from dependence on business and government, situating news media within society instead. Lambeth saw parallels in their key ideas, but concluded that public journalism makes the social role of the press more explicit.

Ethical Principles of Journalism

As these cases indicate, SR has become a worldwide phenomenon, and its ethical basis needs to be articulated in global terms. The neoliberal perspective of the Hutchins Commission was satisfactory for the United States in the wake of World War II, but is an inadequate foundation for SR today. The principal philosopher of the Hutchins Commission, William Earnest Hocking, contended that freedom of expression was not an inalienable natural right but an earned moral right. Hocking's Framework of Principle is a carefully reasoned argument that liberty is not unconditional. Given our human status as social beings, liberty involves the necessity of obligations beyond self-interest. Although particular errors are inevitable, wrong-doing motivated by selfish interests cancels the rationale for freedom.

SR is therefore founded on accountable freedom, human freedom with responsibility as its integrating center. Without accountable freedom, the press as a social institution can be coopted by professional privilege and self-interested power. However, therein lies SR's challenge. If the press's freedom is a moral right, who will guarantee its moral rectitude? Business pressures are to be resisted and government authority is unacceptable to serve society. Where then does one turn to ensure that society will be served responsibly? Who guards the guardian? If external restraints are seen to violate the press's very being, why should journalists be uncontrolled? Democracies, by definition, prohibit elite autonomous pockets of power.Loose cannons on the deck of the ship of state are intolerable. Self-regulation has offered to SR theory the pathway out of this conundrum. The conventional wisdom is that a free press can abide no governance except that self-imposed. Therefore, the focus has been on what the press can do internally to regulate itself convincingly. Codes of ethics developed as intra media mechanisms among news professionals are typically understood as the most effective agent of self-regulation. In the SR model, professional ethics has become a central visible institutional indicator that the press takes internal constraints seriously.

Obviously, a host of other internal mechanisms have emerged by which reporters, editors, and news directors police their own ranks: office memoranda, ombudsmen, staff conferences and training, visits by ethics specialists to the newsroom, journalism reviews, professionals who make media criticism their specialty, and so forth. However, in setting guidelines for these internal mechanisms to operate and in positioning itself vis-à-vis the public it seeks to serve, professional codes of ethics have pride of place. Regardless of their role and possible effectiveness when SR theory took root, codes of ethics are not an adequate foundation for the worldwide SR paradigm of today.

Professional codes are limited by professional concerns and by the local, regional, or national contexts in which they are formulated. Global SR needs an ethical basis commensurate in scope, that is, universal ethical principles rather than the parochial moral guidelines represented by codes.

Significance of Professionalism

The evolution of professions in society has inspired a number of scholarly excursions on the nature and significance of professionalism. These contributions boil down to two main approaches that can be labeled functionalist and critical. The functionalist approach, in the spirit of Durkheim, took the view that professions gradually occupied the place of religion and the pre-industrial moral order to uphold social harmony and balance under the new conditions of capitalist economy. According to this view, professions with their rational and ethical standards, collegiality, and status, helped to solve the problems of the Hobbesian pursuit of crude self-interest on the one hand, and those created by bureaucratization on the other.

Professions brought much-needed social cohesion and new morality into the process of modernization, with scientific specialization and social service as prominent characteristics of professionalism. Professionalism was seen as a positive element in a fundamentally optimistic prospect of socioeconomic development, that is, modernization. Diametrically opposed to such a functionalist view of professionalism was the approach following Max Weber, which perceived professions as bastions of narrow and elitist interests rather than of overall societal and democratic interests. This critical view of professionalism emerged in the 1960s, along with a number of other similar intellectual tendencies, casting doubt on the conventional wisdom that professions as such were functionally positive and suggesting that far from being altruistic, they served in modern society as repressive mechanisms that undermine democracy and turn active citizens into passive consumers-targets instead of sources of power.

Accordingly, Illich called professions a form of imperialism and wrote with others a book on "disabling professions." Others exposed how professions turn into ideologies and how their analysis should be based on the concepts of power, control, and autonomy. This antifunctionalist view was elaborated into a true neo-Weberian approach by Giddens and others who analyze the professions not only in terms of social power but above all in terms of market. Accordingly, the big question was how the professions had succeeded in gaining a monopoly position in the market of services, and how they had succeeded in closing off competitive groups that also sought the privileged position in society.

Furthermore, developments in postmodern societies suggested that what is crucial to professions for a market monopoly position are narrow intellectual techniques and a narrow specialization. Journalism as a profession fits perfectly into this overall picture. On the one hand, its evolution over the last 100 years provides a textbook example of a functionalist approach, with a surrounding ideology supporting the profession. On the other hand, reflections around media professions over the past two decades include more and more critical voices alongside those legitimizing the conventional wisdoms of the functionalist approach.

Therefore, one can indeed speak of a democratic shift. In fact, the current debate on professionalism in journalism-with the prospects of an information society and its new interactive technologies-not only leads us to ask for more specialization but also invites us to question the rationale of traditional professionalism. When a media-centered paradigm is replaced by a citizen-centered paradigm, one is moving away from a functionalist approach to a critical (neo-Weberian) approach. The more one is acquainted with international norms and values, the less that person is committed to conventional professionalism. One begins to doubt the value basis of professionalism, and sees it more and more as an ideological smokescreen to protect the proprietors' interests instead of the workers' rights.

This is a paradigm shift away from an approach that understands media and journalists as the owners of communication rights and freedoms toward a paradigm whereby the citizens and their civil society are seen as the ultimate owners of freedom of information. This paradigm shift is highlighted by White, who criticized an individualistic ethics of media professionals and advocated that media ethics be seen as "an integral part of the responsibility of all members of a given society for the quality of information available for collective decision-making in the society". Ahard line is documented by the empirical results of case studies, notably those carried out in Sweden and Finland.

A Swedish study exposed great contradictions between the ideals and the reality of journalistic ethics. The study found that critical examination of power holders proved to be only theory, which did not carry on to journalistic practice; a free and independent profession proved to be so highly routinized that practically no room was left for individual initiative; broad ethical norms proved to be neither broad nor stable but something that could be characterized as technocratic and opportunistic.

The Finnish case study that exposed the problems of journalistic professionalism was a large project on the role of media in Finland's entry into the EU before the referendum on this question in October 1994. The study demonstrated that people were quite prepared for an open and many-sided debate, but the media largely missed this historic opportunity to provide a platform for a true exercise of freedom of expression. Instead of serving the civil society, journalists served the power elite-not in a vulgar and partisan way but professionally by letting the elites (then mostly in favour of joining the EU) set the agenda and letting the routines shape the discourse.

In other words, the media and journalists were more or less extensions of the political and corporate powers without performing as a true fourth branch of government. Consequently, professionalism, instead of stopping such intellectual corruption, legitimized it by providing journalists with a host of routines and cognitive conventions. Professionals were seen to be guided by self-censorship rather than self-criticism. Understanding professionalism as a form of self-censorship may sound surprising coming from the authors who are dedicated to the professional education of journalists. It should not be understood as a principled position against professional competence as such but as a warning of the risks that professionalism brings for democracy-particularly in the media. True, these risks are obviously more real and present in industrialized countries than in developing ones. In many developing countries there may indeed be good grounds to promote professionalism without casting doubt about its potentially undemocratic consequences.

Journalistic Codes of Ethics

In the context of professionalism, journalistic codes of ethics may be assessed from three angles. First, one may look at them positively as vehicles of professionalization, as a means of professional education, or as instruments of consciousness raising. Such a constructive-or naïve-approach has been typically taken since World War II, and it continues to be widespread in so-called developing and post-Communist countries. Second, one may look negatively at codes as mere rhetorical devices, as deliberate window dressing and camouflage, or at best as manifestations of hypocrisy.

Such a cynical approach is held today by many in so-called Western developed countries, with a marked discrepancy between high ethical principles and the low practice of commercial media. Third, one may take an analytical look by seeing codes as a mechanism of self-regulation. In this approach, the codes are understood as part and parcel of a broader system of media regulation, extending from legal imperatives to cultural conventions. They are seen not just as an excuse to refrain from legislating the media but also as a true means of regulating the media. In light of the earlier mentioned reflections on professionalism, there are good grounds for each of these three ways of approaching the codes, but the most important angle is opened up by the last approach.

Taking the broader perspective of political science, at issue is not just journalism and the media but ultimately democracy as a system of governing society. Medias in the contemporary world have become so vital that there are indeed good grounds to take them as a fourth branch of government -

not just rhetorically but even in political theory and legal and ethical practice. Following up earlier studies from the 1970s, in 1989 an inventory of the journalistic codes of ethics adopted in the countries of the Conference on Security and Cooperation in Europe (CSCE) was initiated.

Based on 24 codes, the conclusion was that there is developing among the CSCE countries some sort of basic, universal model of journalistic codes where the accent is on truth, freedom of information, and protection of the individual. Since 1989 to 1990, Europe had fundamentally changed, and therefore, a new inventory was made in 1994 to 1995 of the codes that were then valid in Europe. Thirty-one contemporary codes adopted by journalists' associations or other bodies, notably media councils, were located.

This inventory shows that most of the codes are quite fresh; over two thirds of them were adopted in the 1990s. Between 1995 and 2000, 10 new codes were completed (including Armenia, Belarus, and Estonia), and others are underway. By and large we can say that there are current codes of professional ethics, adopted by journalists' own associations, in about 40 European countries-Europe understood from the Atlantic to the Urals. As shown by Laitila, the most widely covered aspects in these codes are journalists' accountability toward the public, their accountability toward the sources and referents, and the protection of the journalist's integrity.

Least salient of various functions of the codes is the journalist's accountability toward the state and employers. It is significant how much emphasis is placed by the codes on the public, as well as to the sources and referents (some 60% of 61 provisions mentioned in the 31 codes), seen against the natural functions of protecting the integrity and status of the journalist (some 30%). This means that the codes are designed not just for the selfish purpose of safeguarding the journalists' fortress but also for an idealistic purpose of serving the public interest.

Accordingly, the contemporary ethics of European journalists, as reflected in the codes of ethics, is dedicated not only to journalists' but also to peoples' rights and is committed not only to professional but also to political values. This suggests quite a balanced approach to professionalism, far from the doubtful perspectives opened up by the earlier discussed reflections on professionalism as such. Obviously, codes are invaluable as an instrument of self-reflection by helping practitioners understand the nature of their work and relating their practice to broader moral and ethical values. In other words, the codes serve as vehicles of sensitization or, in Paulo

Freire's words, conscientization. On the other hand, one could choose to cast doubt on the codes of ethics and the way they are taught in schools of communication, which typically prepare professionals "more for conformity with media organizations than for creative questioning".

However, one could also point out how conventional professionalism, with its routines and even protective walls, is functional and indeed much needed in countries that have moved from one sociopolitical system to another, with the media remaining not only free from earlier controls but also turning into a chaotic playground void of any rules. Therefore, the main point is not to discover who is the hero and who is the villain but to see that the concept of professional ethics contains a contradiction between media-centered professionalism and citizen-centered ethics. Indeed, it is a genuine contradiction-in the sense of a true dialectic, where both sides are vital.

The profession of journalism is not, after all, a closed fortress but a relatively open institution along the lines of the SR theory of the press. There are indeed good grounds to speak about a paradigm shift, whereby the citizen moves from the audience to the arena. Still, we should not forget that journalists have a built-in tendency to resist such a democratic shift by placing their professional associations-national and international alike-at the service of self-centered professionalism.

Therefore, it is particularly important that codes of ethics are used to stimulate debates on media philosophies and to sensitize media professionals about their own dependencies. Also, journalism education should pay more attention not just to affirmatively strengthening narrow-minded professionalism, but to emancipating professionalism from its antidemocratic tendencies. The best way to accomplish this is by revising our concept of ethics, from a profession-based to a citizen-based paradigm. In addition, if the framework grounded in the public is universal, based on our universal humanness rather than specific obligations as news professionals, then worldwide SR theory has an adequate foundation that truly brings its emphasis on society to the forefront.

Instead of appealing to rational abstractions to ground worldwide SR thinking, we argue for a morality rooted in animate nature. The rationale for human action is reverence for life on earth, respect for the organic realm in which human civilization is situated. The Age of Science in the West defined nature as spiritless material. This reduction to matter and motion enabled the technological revolution-leitmotif of modernity-to prosper. The history of how humans have valued their natural world is long and torturous, but the scientific view cannot account for the purposiveness of life itself. Living nature reproduces itself in terms of its very character. Therefore, within the natural order is a moral claim on us for its own sake and in its own right.

Our duty to preserve life is similar in kind to parental obligation to their offspring. When new life appears, the progenitors do not debate their relation to it as though their responsibility is a matter of calculating the options with neutral protoplasm. The forbears' duty to their children is an imperative that is timeless and non-negotiable. Nurturing life has a taken-for-granted character outside subjective preference. Reverence for life on earth is a pretheoretical given that makes the moral order possible. From the sacredness-of-life perspective, the biological world provides a rich arena for seeing the permanent and universal value of human life in its brilliant diversity.

In a study of ethical foundations in 13 countries on five continents, the veneration of human life is consistently affirmed as bonding humans universally into an organic whole. The primal sacredness of life is a protonorm-similar in kind to the proto-Germanic language, a lingual predecessor underlying Germanic languages as we actually know them in history. Reverence for life on earth establishes a level playing field for cross-cultural collaboration on the ethical foundations of SR. It represents a universalism from the ground up.

Various societies articulate this protonorm in different terms and illustrate it locally, but every culture can bring to the table this fundamental norm for ordering political relations and such social institutions as the press. Human responsibility regarding natural existence contributes the possibility of intrinsic imperatives to moral philosophy. It demonstrates the legitimacy of concluding that collective duty can be cosmic, presuppositional, and irrespective of our roles or contracts. This is a protonorm that precedes its reification into ethical principles. There is at least one primordial generality underlying systematic ethics. In addition, its universal scope enables us to avoid the divisiveness of appeals to individual interests, cultural practices, and national prerogatives. The primal sacredness of life is a protonorm that binds humans into a common oneness.

Respect for another person's dignity is one ethical principle on which various cultures rest. Different cultural traditions affirm human dignity in a variety of ways, but together they insist that all human beings have sacred status without exception. Native American discourse is steeped in reverence for life, an interconnectedness among all living forms so that we live in solidarity with others as equal constituents in the web of life. In communalistic African societies, likute is loyalty to the community's reputation, to tribal honour.

In Latin American societies, insistence on cultural identity is an affirmation of the unique worth of human beings. In Islam, every person has the right to honour and a good reputation. In Confucius, respect for authority is necessary because our authorities are human beings of dignity. Humans are a unique species, requiring within itself respect for its members as a whole. From this perspective, one understands the ongoing vitality of the Universal Declaration of Human Rights issued by the United Nations General Assembly in 1948.

As the preamble states it, "Recognition of the inherent dignity and of the equal and inalienable rights of all members of the human family is the foundation of freedom, justice and peace in the world" (Universal Declaration, 1997). Every child, woman, and man has sacred status, with no exceptions for religion, class, gender, age, or ethnicity. This common sacredness of all human beings regardless of merit or achievement is the shared commitment out of which we begin to generate notions of a just society.

Truth is another underlying principle about which there is cross-cultural agreement as well. The most fundamental norm of Arab-Islamic communication is truthfulness. Truth is one of the three highest values in the context of the Latin American experience of communication. In Hinduism, truth is the highest dharma and the source of all other virtues. Among the Sushwap of Canada, truth as genuineness and authenticity is central to its indigenous culture. Living with others is inconceivable if we cannot tacitly assume that people are speaking truthfully. Lying, in fact, is so unnatural that machines can measure bodily reactions against it.

Language is the primary means of social formation, and therefore, human existence is impossible without an overriding commitment to truth. Imagine a society, no matter how ideal in other respects, where word and gesture could never be counted on. Questions asked, answers given, information exchanged-all would be worthless. Were all statements randomly truthful or deceptive, action and choice would be undermined from the outset. There must be a minimal degree of trust in communication for language and action to be more than stabs in the dark. This is why some level of truthfulness has always been seen as essential to human society....

Even the devils themselves, as Samuel Johnson said, donot lie to one another, since the society of Hell could not subsist without truth any more than others. In Sissela Bok's terms, deception is as blatant, destructive, and morally outrageous as physical assault. In an intellectual trajectory connecting to Aristotle, the positive worth of truth telling has been generally accepted at face value, with deception an enemy of the human order: Falsehood is in itself mean and culpable, and truth noble and full of praise. Although often only a rhetorical flourish and reduced in meaning, media codes of ethics typically appeal to truth as the cornerstone of social communication; therefore, they reflect in their own way its intrinsic value.

As a primary agent of the symbolic theater in which we live, the public media have no choice but to honour this norm as obligatory to their mission and rationale. The result is a richer epistemology than minimalist notions of accurate representation and objectivist ways of knowing. Truth telling is axiological rather than a problem of cognition per se; it is integral to human consciousness and social formation.

Nonviolence is a third ethical principle entailed by the sacredness of life-or in negative terms, no harm to the innocent. Ghandi and Martin Luther King developed this principle beyond a political strategy into a philosophy of life. In communalistic and indigenous cultures, care for the weak and vulnerable (children, sick, and elderly) and sharing material resources are a matter of course. Along with dharma, ahimsa (nonviolence) forms the basis of the Hindu worldview. The death and violence at Columbine High School (United States), and in other secondary schools around the world, cut to our deepest being.

The public's general revulsion against physical abuse at home and our consternation over brutal crimes and savage wars are glimmers of hope reflecting the validity of this principle. Darrell Fasching's comparative study of religions identifies hospitality to strangers as their common commitment. Out of this invitational regard for others, a cross-cultural ethics of nonviolence is established. Under this principle, civil disobedience through movements of liberation always protect the dignity of the stranger.

To postmodernists, universalist positions have discredited themselves because over history they have seemed to breed totalitarianism. "Once any group or individual lays claim to knowledge of universal, transcendental truth, then dissenters must be either converted or controlled. This is the genesis of the Inquisition, of the Gulag, and of any ideological oppression". Universalism is said to threaten diversity, whereas relativism liberates us to reject all oppressive claims to truth.

In light of this objection, it must be reiterated that the protonorm of human sacredness is not a foundational a priori. This universal, in fact, belongs to a different category, philosophically speaking, than that of objectivist absolutes. Adherence to presuppositions is A matter of commitment, not epistemic certainty. Cartesian rationalism and Kant's formalism presumed non contingent starting points; universal human solidarity does not. Nor does it flow from Platonism, that is, the finite participating in the infinite and receiving its essence from it. Without a protonorm of universal scope, ethical theory and politics are trapped in the distributive fallacy-one ideological bloc presuming to speak for the whole. A commitment to universals does not eliminate all differences in what we think and believe.

Normative ethics grounded on to logically is pluralistic. The only question is whether our values affirm the human good or not. As our philosophies of life and beliefs are lobbied within the public sphere, we have a responsibility to make public the course we favour and to demonstrate in what manner it advances our common citizenship. The issue is whether our values help to build a civic philosophy and thereby demonstrate a transformative intent. This is worldview pluralism, which allows us to hold our beliefs in good faith and debate them openly rather than be constrained by a superficial consensus. The standard of judgment is not economic or political success but whether our worldviews and community formations contribute in the long run to truth-telling, human dignity, and nonmaleficence. Ethical principles grounded in being do not obstruct cultures and inhibit their development. On the contrary, they liberate us for strategic action and provide a direction for social change.

Power of Journalism

Journalism is a problem at two levels. There is something essentially pathological about the whole activity that daily satisfies our often pointless curiosity about what is going on in the world. But there is a less extreme position that accords more with common sense: namely, that in our educated and democratic world, a great deal of information is indispensable, and journalism is the only way we can have it. Even here, however, large events such as the Iraq war of 2004 have caused many critics to judge that journalism has lost such integrity as it ever had and is being used to nudge us towards some version of right thinking.

Journalism had slid, it has been suggested, into propaganda. Event-making is an art that turns familiar routines and facts into patterns having a certain uniqueness. Some people are better at it than others, but once the art has been learned, most people can do it to some extent. It is all a matter of scale: the Bible tells some stories in a few sentences, while writers of fiction can spin someone's day into a long novel. Responding to stories is one way of conducting life, distinguishable from the times when we are responding to routines, sensations, classifications, or reflections. No life can avoid gossip, ritual, and response to overriding events such as war or famine, but most people, especially if they are illiterate, have hitherto been interested in little beyond what affects them directly.

Journalism is the cultivation of concern for things that are for the most part remote from us. The basic contrast is with religion, which is concerned with rituals and sermons revolving around beliefs about our eternal situation. Kierkegaard mistrusted journalism because he thought it would feed our love of the ephemeral, and he was no doubt right about this. Hegel remarked that in his time, newspapers were replacing morning prayer. Perhaps the earliest writer to regard our involvement with daily events as a pathology distracting us from the realities of the human condition was Pascal.

As journalism in the contemporary world has extended its range, it has certainly taken in churchly events and concerned itself with the beliefs of different religions, but the very context of such news robs it of the superior status it has for believers, and diminishes religion to the same level as the vast miscellany of other human activities that are also being reported. Religions are composed of archetypes that have a status above the constant flow of ideas and news stories. We respond (or do not respond) to such archetypes in a reflective manner that determines how we view the world, but where journalism dominates our thoughts, reflectiveness is diluted by the passion for novelty. We move from an article on religion to one on fashion, sport, or public affairs. Like democracy, journalism is a manic equalizer.

Historically, journalism emerged from the specific interests of princes, merchants, and administrators. A prince needed to know something of foreign powers, and his ambassador sent him back reports, just as a merchant needed to know of profitable opportunities and conditions of trade. A universal institution such as the Papacy needed a constant flow of information. The Greeks, Romans, Chinese, etc. were great annalists, and Herodotus is credited, as the father of History, with creating prose literature out of an assemblage of contingencies, but the drive of most of these writers was precisely to get beyond contingency and find a broader explanatory structure.

Printing, of course, transformed everything, leading to the movement of power away from grand patrons towards educated city-dwellers. Large political issues were argued out in books, pamphlets, and broadsheets. The writings of diplomats and merchants were soon being supplemented by correspondents writing for a wider audience. It was the beginning of the end for arcana imperii. By the eighteenth century, the flow of material was so reliable that publishers could be sure of filling an annual, a monthly, and ultimately a weekly or daily issue. This was the first and basic mechanical principle by which we became accustomed to a regular flow of news.

Other mechanisms soon emerged to help the editor fill his space-the anniversary, for example, in which nothing related the writer and his subject but an interval of time. Deeper currents were at work. The modern Western world was based upon a close interest in and observation of the things going on around us. The marvels of science in important respects result from a simple propensity to measure things and discover laws relating these measurements. In the early modern period, the value of history, and also of reports of events, consisted in their being able to point a lesson or generate a moral or practical bit of wisdom.

The meaning of an event was to be found in its outcome. The Boston Museum of Fine Arts has a painting by Tiepolo, dated 1745-1750, called (in a rather Heideggerian idiom) Time unveiling truth. The allegory is complex and the painting not without grossness, but the broad idea captures something of how practical men came to understand wisdom. The contrast must be with the religious assumption that the essential truths of life have been revealed, but that the human world is dark and devious, and the connection between events is obscure. Here we have the view that time will tell whether we have been right or wrong to rely on someone.

The interest of a contingency is precisely that it cannot be assimilated to a law. To follow the course of events over time is therefore to discover truth. And one possible implication of this view is that to come later is to know more truth. Journalism thus emerges from deep currents in our civilization. It has roots in Greek and Roman experience, and, from the Middle Ages onwards, a passion to follow the actual events of the world seems to have continually grown. Prose literature and the novel were part of that development, and whole new areas of event-making came to be opened up. The narratives relating to kings, aristocrats, and saints were broadened to include a more general concern with individual life.

In a religious idiom of life, such diurnal events were mere froth on the surface of the infinite. But as Kierkegaard saw, the ephemeral was coming to dominate our interests. The steady diffusion of a journalistic interest in what is going on affects our consciousness of the world we live in. A nun has a different mind-set from a housewife, a philosopher from a man of affairs, but journalism equips them all with a generalized interest in the world. One dimension of how journalism affects the way we think is our propensity to become bored.

Someone who is focussed on the novelty of events as they unfold in the newspapers is to that extent less reflective about the events to which he responds. The details of change crowd out the time and energy that would otherwise go into reflection. Religious people, philosophers, or scientists-people who are genuinely educated, we might say-will think about God, or Nature, or literature, and will find new things in quite exiguous materials, whereas the less educated become increasingly miserable without a continual flow of novelty, and since most of reality is repetition, the novelty is a function of triviality.

People become, in a word, shallow. Here then is a new form of consciousness evolving under the spur of improving technology to the point where twenty-four-hour news and comment is available to us. Journalistic consciousness is imperialistic. It invades every sphere of life and takes it over. Consider the world of scholarship, in which men and women dedicate themselves to exploring some area of reality in terms of a particular mode of inquiry-as historians, scientists, or literary scholars, for example. Scholarship is hard, focussed work, continually retracing its steps to check on its validity as scholarly discussion proceeds. It knows nothing of the urgency of the deadline.

The scholars who practice this art are often pedantic and stuffy, and certainly impatient with those who think they can master the subject in question without a lengthy apprenticeship. And for centuries scholars used to defend themselves against the contempt of practical men for what is "academic" with an entrenched disdain for journalism and popularization. Good journalism gains some of its impact from responding to the mind of the moment, and that is precisely what cannot fully be captured at a later moment. And indeed, it is hard to read journalism critically without realizing the element of padding that goes into it.

The self-protective disdain of the scholar for the popularizer has now gone, or largely gone, and with its disappearance, journalism has been sloshing about in the world of scholarship. Scholars can now become popularizing celebrities without losing face, a further spread of the journalistic imperium. Worse, journalism has begun, by a curious conjunction of cultural tendencies, to invade the world of education. It has long been felt by teachers of subjects in the social sciences that a pupil's reading of the newspaper is an important part of his or her education.

And with the decline of discipline in schools, the teacher can no longer command that his charges must learn what he thinks is the next part of their education. He is forced to seduce them, by the guile of a popularizing involvement with their own interests. Journalism's empire thus lies behind the rise of the impulse to make relevance the test of what is worth teaching in schools. A similar development is happening in universities as they expand to take in students with less native wits than before.

Instead of the focus on method and discipline basic to education, many university courses have become interdisciplinary, which consists in focusing on some subject of broad popular interest, such as the environment, and investigating its problems in terms of a bit of science, a bit of history, a bit of practical wisdom, etc. Journalistic consciousness, then, has spread into the wide field of the humanities and the social sciences. A journalist is the master of the gist of things, and gist is king of the world. The way it dominates contemporary politics might perhaps help to explain why in our time so much legislation has so frequently to be amended, corrected, and replaced.

Journalism may thus be taken as a systematic defiance of the Socratic maxim that wisdom consists in understanding one's own ignorance. We who belong to the world of journalism know a great deal, and are proud of it, and sanctify such knowledgeability in quiz programs and a disdain for those who cannot tell in what century the Civil War happened, or how many states make up the U.S. Stanley Baldwin thought that journalists were prostitutes-but how can knowing a lot be thought to be the satisfaction of a kind of lust? The answer is that journalism satisfies curiosity, a distant relative of the "wonder" thought to be the source of philosophy and science.

How then, one must repeat, can curiosity be a vice? The answer is that we are often curious about things that are none of our business. The malicious village gossip is the most curious creature on earth, and finds her successor in the "door-stopping" journalist and the paparazzo infesting the lives of famous people. Further, curiosity is one of those learned human responses that is dependent on what other people are interested in. In a shallow way, we can easily be influenced to take an interest in something merely because others are curious about it. The most evidently vicious kind of curiosity is morbid. Plato recognized this in arguing that the mind was an arena of conflict rather than a Pythagorean harmony.

In the Republic, Socrates tells the story of Leontius, son of Aglaion: "On his way up from the Piraeus outside the north wall, he noticed the bodies of some criminals lying on the ground with the executioner standing by them. He wanted to go and look at them, but at the same time he was disgusted and tried to turn away. He struggled for some time and covered his eyes, but at last the desire was too much for him. Opening his eyes wide, he ran up to the bodies and cried, 'There you are, curse you; feast yourselves on this lovely sight!'"

Some modern press photography is remarkable, almost an art (that of sport for example), but much that we see in tabloid journalism would disgust us had our sensibilities not been corrupted by learning to enjoy the satisfaction of this particular version of lust-the lust to see and know things of no concern to us. As Pascal remarks: "More often than not, curiosity is merely vanity. We only want to know something in order to talk about it."

Here then is another arena in which journalism has "colonized" our minds. The very availability of a rather illicit satisfaction has developed in us the very appetite itself. All of this is given some kind of ethical coloring in terms of the public's right to know, and indeed, it would be impossible in the modern world to draw a consistent line between genuinely appropriate objects of our curiosity and the bits of knowledge generously thrown our way. Indiscriminate absorption of information is the way we live. But there is another side to this richness of information available to us about the world we live in.

It is that an endless preoccupation with ourselves as subsumed under social categories-as pensioners or teenagers, married or single, heterosexual or homosexual, and so on-dilutes our consciousness, and our identity spills out in all directions. We lose the focus that belongs to real individuality. We meld into others, becoming part of a strange kind of informational collectivity. Until the twentieth century, people did not much consider the category of journalism. Some of what we would now recognize as such was the writing of educated men in books and quarterlies, and some was popular report for the masses.

Reporters and newspapermen had relatively little professional standing. One thinks of twentieth-century newspaperman, according to the image in The Front Page and other fictions, as hard-headed drunks working with green eyeshades as they subbed copy in large offices. These were men who thought that journalism reported and therefore reflected the world, and that (as C. P. Scott put it) “facts are sacred and comment is free.” They were empiricists who took the description of “reporter” seriously; they purported to “tell it as it was.” To use the old logical formulation, “twenty killed in earthquake” was true if, and only if, twenty people had been killed in the earthquake. But at some point in the twentieth century, a familiar type of social evolution occurred.

Journalism became a “profession” (rather than just a trade), and succumbed to the culture of universities. The new sophisticated journalist had picked up a little learning and knew that a news story cannot be a mere “reflection” of events, because every event is infinitely complex, susceptible of many descriptions, and therefore that its meaning depends on the prior selection of the reporter. Journalism was something constructed. This view thus reflected the then popular vogue for mechanical images of “construction” and “invention” in the humanities and social sciences. Here was a theory that transformed the life of your humble journalist. He, or she, was no longer a mere agent of transmission, transferring facts to print.

The journalist became an actual creator of news. Journalists were not, indeed, quite the same as novelists, but some element of creativity was thought necessary to report even the least significant bit of news. It was in part this cast of mind that led to the explosion of signed reports and photographs of the contributors to newspapers, and of the proliferation of columns. The result was an immense vogue among young people for becoming journalists. It was for the most part clean regular work, allowing plenty of self-expression without accountability, and it required no vast input of learning, or indeed remarkable talent of any kind.

Up to a point, both the reflection and the construction views of journalism capture some of its real features. A little light epistemology might have been a pretty harmless addition to journalistic self-understanding had it not soon mutated into a kind of Salvationism. Quite how this mutation occurred is a very large question indeed, but it can best be understood in terms of a similar process happening in most of the professions in the second half of the twentieth century. Teachers came to think that, because they were custodians of the minds of the rising generation, they held the key to social progress. Spreading the right ideas in the classroom would diminish violence and prejudice in the next generation, so molding the attitudes of the young became at least as important as education itself.

Similarly, lawyers sought to expand beyond the dry technicalities of the law in order to make society more just, and many a doctor embracing epidemiology was less concerned with curing his patients than with instructing them about a better lifestyle. The idea of social responsibility-that we are all the molders of our society-spread far and wide, even into the temples of profit. We may summarize this by saying that all of these professionals began to acquire the affectations of an elite possessed of saving knowledge. In the case of journalists, this encounter with epistemology turned into a form of political partisanship.

The issue was often expounded in terms of the concept of "bias." In the game of bowls, a certain distortion (known as "bias") tests the skill of the player, and metaphorically, the subjective element in the interpretation of an event might be described as "bias." No one doubted that such subjectivity was a distortion, but it was generally held that truth could emerge from discussion and criticism. The new doctrine insisted-at its least sophisticated-that since no judgement was unbiased, any utterance was as good as any other. Any claim to neutrality was treated with particular scorn. Whereas a generation before, facts had been distinguished as the hard stuff of truth by contrast with values, which were merely the porous vehicles of feeling and preference, now facts themselves lost their claim to superiority.

Cultural analysts dissolved truth into power, following the lead of Michel Foucault. It is a familiar feature of the history of philosophy that skepticism's partner is dogmatism. The dogmatism emerging from this particular bout of skepticism held that all cultures were equally valid, and that all utterances, as expressing opinion, were equal, at least in this fundamental respect. They could only be discriminated in terms of some sort of notional "correctness." The Salvationism in this doctrine consisted in the belief that in being skeptical of all universal claims, the journalist as critical thinker was revealing a sophistication superior to that of the average voter. The test of such critical sophistication was that the journalist held opinions liberated from the influence of his or her milieu, and the milieu was taken to include not merely class or nation, but European civilization itself.

Journalists saw themselves as "free floating intellectuals" in a world of prejudice and superstition. This pleasing self-image was often complemented by the further opinion that the critical thinker had unmasked the hidden partisanship in our common belief that Western civilization was superior to other forms of life. This civilizational self-criticism commonly took a moral form, applying the higher moral abstractions (such as human rights, anti-imperialism, and racial equality) to European societies themselves, and projecting this criterion back down the ages in a massive indictment of our ancestors. Collective guilt was discovered to be the appropriate response to a great deal of Western conduct, ranging from the Crusades to Slavery and Apartheid.

Some enthusiasts demanded official apologies, and some politicians (Tony Blair among them) gave them. Skeptical non-judgmentalism had strangely morphed into dogmatic condemnation, generating a strange kind of collective guilt, from which the critic could absolve himself by his very recognition of it. The history of this process, in the universities (especially the universities) and journalism schools of the Western world, is of course immensely complicated, but without referring to it, one cannot begin to understand why our addiction to journalism is virtually inseparable from our dislike of it.

The crudest way of formulating our dislike would be to say that the picture of the world presented in newspapers and television programs jars with our political opinions. The discontent is greater among those on "the right" than those on "the left" but both share it. And here the discontent must seem odd, because journalists pride themselves on covering, or trying to cover, all points of view. "Points of view" is, of course, a vulgarizing simplicity that can recognize only those for, and those against, some all-too-familiar opinion. We have all, no doubt, been amused by the absurdities of the television interviewer swinging back and forth between two opposing personages, putting in a mechanically extreme way the opposed opinion (suitably made extreme) to its opponent.

No one seriously believes that the academic sophistication that journalists have acquired helps them give a better account of the world. We are no better informed today than we were when reporters told us how it was. Indeed, all shades of opinion regard "the media" with deep suspicion as giving a biased account of reality. Some bold journalists embrace this universal unpopularity as proof of a perverse kind of integrity, but early in the twenty-first century, it is hard to resist the view that, indispensable as it is in modern democracies, journalism is an increasingly pathological influence on the way we live. For all their affectations of the critical spirit, journalists are putty in the hands of the latest intellectual fashion.

What they have to say is dangerously linked to the posture they intend to reveal in saying it. Their basic moral stance must be an unrelenting concern with truth, and it is in this sense that journalism reveals itself as an essentially Western practice. For it has often been observed that ours is a "truth-obsessed" civilization. By "truth" here, we mean something rather beyond mere correspondence with facts; we must incorporate in the word an element, harder to define, of integrity. A really good journalist needs a sturdy ballast of good sense and an almost scholarly revulsion from the quick and the glib in order to transcend the corruptions that have surfaced over the last century.

It would no doubt be perilous to think that all Victorian journalists were more serious than our contemporaries, but in writers like Bagehot and Leslie Stephen we have figures who worked on the frontiers of journalism and scholarship without losing their integrity. It may be merely that the temptations of cheap sensationalism were less at that period than they are now, or it may just be that they had more space. It was, however, in the nineteenth century that literary realism took the form in which it became the guiding star of modern journalism.

Novelists such as Dickens and Zola were certainly not the first to explore "low life," but they extended the boundaries of social understanding in order to incorporate the experiences of socially insignificant people into the materials of drama, and also to reveal some of the realities-usually poverty, vice, and oppression-"behind" the facades of the time. The crucial ideas of this literary movement were those of journalists themselves-indeed both Dickens and Zola had been journalists in their time. The basic idea of literary realism is that life is a theater put on for show, and that reality is what you find when you go behind the scenes.

Reality, in other words, is something concealed by those whose interest lies in concealment. The posture of the journalist is thus that of the investigator debunking institutions by exposing secrets. This general theory clearly domesticates scandal and conspiracy as instruments of revelation. The custodians of ritual and authority are, of course, particularly vulnerable to criticism of this form. Their outward aspect is their essential point, and what lies behind them may well be banal, or worse. We have here a view of reality that cannot distinguish between those things whose inwardness has no bearing on their force, and those things where hypocrisy or dissimulation may be usefully revealed.

Journalism begins, then, in genuinely "sensational" events such as wars, earthquakes, and the rise and fall of governments, but it can multiply sensation by getting "behind" the events. Some social personages-royalty, politicians, actors, etc. -are worthy of note in themselves, but even better is to discover how they behave "behind the scenes." Spontaneous irritation is thought to be more revealing than measured dignity, a little light lust than a policy of self-control. Recent philosophy has been strongly influenced by the so-called "philosophers of suspicion"-Marx, Nietzsche, and Freud-but in journalism we find suspicion as the constitutive passion of an entire practice.

The rational basis of modern journalism, its claim to our attention as bringing us knowledge of the world, thus turns out to be the practice of revealing what other people want to hide from us. This is, of course, particularly true of what authority wants to hide. The First World War was a watershed in the growth of cynicism about authority. People came to think that the official account of almost anything was generally wrong. Here then we find the beginnings of the journalistic posture of indignation as the reporter demands "full disclosure" of whatever the public might be thought to have a right to know. Such is the rational basis of journalism, but it is important never to ignore the passions it may be supposed to feed?

What journalism most obviously supplies is "sensations" or small shocks of pleasurable surprise because something unexpected has happened, and the journalistic "story" itself may incorporate the contexts within which it was unexpected. But what if the small shock is the discovery of some change in the private life of someone celebrated? Here we would have a case of Pascal's idle and pointless curiosity, the malice of the village gossip in earlier times writ large. Perhaps the best comment on this is Goethe's "No man is a hero to his valet de chambre," to which Hegel added: "not because the hero is not a hero, but because the valet is a valet."

It is in expressing this impulse towards psychological valetism, a lowering and demeaning passion, that journalism clearly loses any real contact with its immemorial mission to understand political realities, the mission of the ambassador writing to his prince. As it has evolved, journalism has bent to conform to that universal passion of our civilization: entertainment. So far as most people up until quite recent times were concerned, amusements and entertainments were rare treats. This seriousness of workaday practicality may well have made church services more tolerable, and it certainly conduced to a more reflective cast of mind, for, as Pope remarked, "amusement is the happiness of those that cannot think."

In our time, however, radio, television, books, magazines, and a ubiquity of music have had the result that a quiet mind is a rare luxury for many people. Given that most of the information in our ever-expanding journalistic world is of no direct concern to us, it follows that the basic point of most journalism is to entertain. Just as freaks and bearded ladies amazed us in the past, so too do the remarkable private contortions of people we do not know arouse our wonder and astonishment today. This merger between journalism and entertainment is unmistakably evident in the way newspapers treat the news, and at a higher level it is replicated in the corporate expansion by which, for example, the same company may control film, television, and newspapers.

We are all familiar with many of the corrupting devices of modern journalism-the hopeless addiction to pointless puns in headlines, the treating of politics as if it were a sports contest, the turning of rivalries into "rows" by talking up competition into conflict and hatred. In its pursuit of revelations, journalism has corrupted the servants and employees of famous people and made the vilest of crimes a paying proposition. But evident corruption is the least danger we face from journalism.

To act and to philosophize action are two separate and incompatible activities. One cannot do both at once. But the journalist takes up a posture notionally above the battle, and therefore thinks he has little difficulty avoiding the obvious peaks of partisanship with which he is familiar, so long as he can recognize them. Is he then, a kind of philosopher? If he is a passably honest journalist, he will give "left" and "right" more or less equal time, at least so long as he gets the difference right. He understands that there are two sides to a war, and may well parade his neutrality by giving extra mileage to our opponents. Accused of distortion, he takes satisfaction in his own consistency: he is not reporting conflict as a partisan, but as a neutral observer, though he would today be edgy about the term "neutral." Here is indeed a kind of integrity, but it is integrity whose orientation depends on fluid and moving points.

In religious activities, the point is ritual and feeling, not truth, and an insistence upon truth (as empirically understood) is a category error, and often a destructive one. With too much truth, the glory in war gets lost in the details of blood and body bags. Universities depend on finding themselves in a dark and obscure corner of social life largely free from social pressures. Were they to be forced to explain themselves partially or prematurely, they would sound foolish and pretentious, and scholarship would be diverted into righteousness. The ceaseless glare of light from journalism illuminates the dark places in our civilization-and sterilizes many of them. No doubt a significant part of this illumination may prevent evils and expose things that ought to be exposed, but it also takes some immemorial human activities to the brink of extinction.

Indeed, journalism exposes things that perhaps ought to be exposed, and prevents evils, but by that very token, it becomes a practical player in the world, and thus finds itself in contradiction with its own posture as a critic above the battles of partisans. In adopting a posture of oppositionality to everything powerful, established, pretentious, and superior, it embraces a kind of universal skepticism, perhaps indeed of nihilism. Some journalists can indeed sustain an opportunistic negativism about everything, but most cannot, and in fact a meta-moralistic addiction to tolerance, secularism, ecumenism, and anti-discrimination becomes evident as what one might initially call "the journalistic ideology."

To hold an opinion is to mortgage a certain amount of pleasure and pain to the turn of events. What confirms one's opinion gives pleasure, what seems to refute it, pain. The journalist, living amidst opinions, knows by instinct the pains of being caught out holding a vulnerable opinion. The first move in his professionalization, as it were, must therefore be to evacuate any position that might be explained by others as arising from his own interest: anything having to do with class, nationality, or civilization: all such inherited baggage must be abandoned by the journalist.

The problem is that whoever abandons interests-which have about them a certain discussable reality, where compromise is possible-finds that his stock of opinions consists of abstract ideas. These will usually take an ethical form, and that impels them towards righteousness. Any such package of opinions is likely to irritate patriots and partisans of all kinds. The holder of such a position is usually enormously self-satisfied, because, having arrived there by the process of identifying extremes as things to be challenged and questioned, he fancies himself as having all the rationality of an Aristotelian mean.

It seems a vile thing to take so serious a view of the newspapers we read with pleasure every day, and the radio and television that entertain us endlessly, but it is no business of philosophers, any more than of journalists, to reinforce our lazy habits. All civilizations are built upon specific distortions of reality, and ours is particularly concerned with observing, measuring and responding to the discrete objects in terms of which we construe reality. Journalism is a development of this cast of mind, and may be contrasted with other possible worlds, in one version of which we might focus our attention upon what we conceive to be eternal things.

Christian writers have been prominent in stigmatizing an interest in ephemera as a dissipation of spiritual energies. The very fact that the journalistic world can focus its attention on nothing for more than a few days at a time, forever seeking a new sensation, makes it clear that this judgment on journalism as one of the pathologies of our civilization should be taken seriously. Change the focus, and we may take journalism as an inescapable development of our Western adventures into literacy and education for all, so that it becomes the mode by which we take our bearings in a rich and exciting world.

Journalism now becomes a category of its own, alongside science and history, as something to be valued in its own terms. But what are its own terms? We cannot avoid discovering that these terms constantly change, partly in response to ideas about truth, such as reflection and construction, and partly in response to the demands that the customers of journalism make upon it. We have suggested that the terms of journalism conceal self-contradiction. A pseudo-philosophical commitment to evade partisanship turns at this level into a partisanship of its own. And not the least of the paradoxes we find in examining journalism is that this most Western of all practices should embrace so anti-Western a stance. The logical problem journalists face parallels that of liberals who embrace all lawful forms of freedom, only to be told that this apparent openness is itself a form of concealed partisanship.

References

David Grayson. (2007). *Business-Led Corporate Responsibility Coalitions: Learning from the example of Business in the Community*. CSR Initiative of the Kennedy School of Government, Harvard.

Grayson and Hodges. (2004). *Corporate Social Opportunity: Making Corporate Social Responsibility work for your business*, Greenleaf.

EU Commission Green Paper. (2001). *Promoting a European Framework for Corporate Social Responsibility*, COM.

John Battelle. (2005). *The Search: How Google and its rivals rewrote the rules of business and transformed our culture.* Portfolio Hardcover.

Jonathan Sachs. (2002). *The dignity of difference – how to avoid the clash of civilisations.* Continuum.

Paul Hawken. (2007). *Blessed Unrest: How the Largest Movement in the World Came into Being and Why No One Saw It Coming.* Viking Penguin.

Michael Robert Evans. (2004). *The Layer of Magazine Publishing.* Columbia University.

6

Media and Its Influence on Society

In the last five decades or so, the media and its influence on the societies, has grown exponentially with the advance of technology. First there was the telegraph and the post offices, then the radio, the newspaper, magazines, television and now the internet and the new media including palmtops, cell phones etc. There are positive and negative influences of mass media, which we must understand as a responsible person of a society.

Before discussing the influence of mass media on society it is imperative to explain the three basic functions of mass media; they are providing news/information, entertainment and education. The first and foremost function of the media in a society is to provide news and information to the masses, that is why the present era is some time termed as the *information age* as well. People need news/information for various reasons, on one hand it can be used to socialize and on the other to make decisions and formulate opinions. Entertainment would be the other function of the mass media where it is mostly used by the masses to amuse them in present day hectic environment. Educating the masses about their rights, moral, social and religious obligations is another important function of mass media, which needs no emphasis.

In present era of globalization, majority of people in the society depends on information and communication to remain connected with the world and do our daily activities like work, entertainment, health care, education, socialization, travelling and anything else that we have to do. A common urban person usually wakes up in the morning checks the tv news or newspaper, goes to work, makes a few phone calls, eats with their family or peers when possible and makes his decisions based on the information that he has either from their co workers, tv news, friends, family, financial reports, etc. we need to be conscious of the reality that most of our decisions, beliefs and values are based on what we know for a fact, our assumptions and our own experience. In our work we usually know what we have to do, based on our experience and studies, however on our routine life and house hold chores we mostly rely on the mass media to get the current news and facts about what is important and what we should be aware of.

We have put our trust on the media as an authority to give us news, entertainment and education. However, the influence of mass media on our kids, teenagers and society is so big that we should know how it really works. The media makes billions of dollars with the advertising they sell and that we are exposed to, every single moment. We buy what we are told to buy by the media. After seeing thousands of advertisings we make our buying decisions based on what we saw on TV, newspapers or magazines. These are the effects of mass media especially in teenagers, they buy what they see on Tv, what their favourite celebrity advertise and what is acceptable by society based on the fashion that the media has imposed on them.

There are some positive and negative influences in young people of our society due to these ad campaigns in the media. Here is a positive influence example, if there is a quiz show on education that is getting a lot of attention by the media and gains popularity among your friends and society, you will more likely want to actively participate and watch these quiz shows. These activities are good for the society and will promote literary activities in the youth. However a negative influence in teenagers is the use of guns and ammunition by celebrity movie stars, the constant exposure of which would seduce the teen to replicate the same behaviour in the real life. When we watch tv or a action movie we usually see many images of violence and people hurting others. The problem with this is that it can become traumatic especially in our children as they see it more and more. Our kids that are starting to grow and are shaping their personality values and beliefs can become aggressive or they can lose a sense of distinction between reality and fiction. Another problem is that real war is used as a form of entertainment by the media, we should make our kids and teen aware that war is not a form of entertainment and that there is no win or lose like in video games, in real war everyone lose.

Teens, youngsters are in a stage of life where they want to be accepted by their peers, they want to be loved and be successful. The media creates the ideal image of beautiful men and women with all the ingredients of a successful person, you can see it in movies and tv. It's a subliminal way to persuade the masses that if you want to be successful and look like them then you have to buy that particular brand or product. Another negative influence in teenagers, especially in the USA, that has grown over the last years is obesity. There are millions of adolescents fighting obesity, but at the same time they are exposed to thousands of advertisements of junk food, while the ideal image of a successful person is told to be thin and wealthy.

The media has a huge impact on society in shaping the public opinion of the masses. They can form or modify the public opinion in different ways depending of what is the objective. For example, Pakistani media influenced the public opinion against the Taliban in Swat by repeated telecast of a video clip showing whipping of a woman by a Taliban. Before that the public opinion over the military action against the Taliban in Swat was divided, but repeated telecast of this short video clip changed the public opinion over night in the favour of the government to take action. Other ways to influence are with polls and trends, especially in political campaigns. The candidates that can pay for more TV and media exposure have more influence on public opinion and thus can receive more votes.

Role of Mass Media in Creating Public Opinion

Mass media plays a crucial role in forming and reflecting public imagination, opinion, connecting the world to individuals and reproducing the self-image of society. In the last 50 years the media influence has grown exponentially with the advance of technology, first there was the telegraph, then the radio, the newspaper, magazines, television and now the internet.

Our society is centered on media, it is the most influential factor in constructing our culture, but is it a positive culture? If we examine the effect that media has on children, we can say that it breeds a harmful culture, one that throws values and morals out the window. This is because the media is profit driven and has developed its own code of ethics of "anything-goes". As a result, children are exposed to things that they should not necessarily be exposed to yet and as a result it rushes their mental development and in fact moulds their mentality. This is a scary fact because these children's minds are susceptible to the trickery of those who run the media. With the media luring in the children, they are able to sell their own value system to the kids through actors, cartoon characters, and even musicians who are puppets in the media's propaganda. They in turn tend to become role models to the kids and can influence the children and manipulate their behavior

The media have a strong social and cultural impact upon society. This is predicated upon their ability to reach a wide audience with a strong and influential message. Marshall McLuhan uses the phrase "the medium is the message" as a means of explaining how the distribution of a message can often be more important than content of the message itself. It is through the persuasiveness of media such as television, radio and print media that messages reach their target audiences. These have been influential media as they have been largely responsible for structuring people's daily lives and routines. Television broadcasting has a large amount of control over the content society watches and the times in which it is viewed. This is a distinguishing feature of traditional media which New media have challenged by altering the participation habits of the public.

Media strongly affects youth culture. The media executives are quick to defend their role in youth violence and bullying while selling millions of dollars in ads focused on youth. TV producers, network executives, motion picture companies and others in the media deny any impact of their programs on the attitudes and actions of youth. Meanwhile they continue to spend millions on special effects and marketing geared to increase appeal to youth markets. While corporations spend millions on market research and advertising to create products and campaigns targeted at a youth demographic, they still deny their ability to influence youth. If this were true to fact, would NIKE continue spending millions every year on product development, marketing and advertising? Would McDonalds still be using cartoon like characters to sell hamburgers? Would music labels be increasing the level of violence and sexual content in the music geared towards the youth audience? Would liquor companies be using youth oriented activities in their advertising? Of course it works on influencing youth and its ideals advertising would not be a multi-billion dollar a year business. If it had no influence, M-TV would not have consultant on staff spending huge amounts of money to ensure them keeping up with youth culture.

The internet creates a space for more diverse political opinions, social and cultural viewpoints and a heightened level of consumer participation.

They include licensing in advance;censorship of offending material before publication;seizure of offending material;injunctions against publication of a newspaper or book or of specified content;requirement of surety bonds against libel or other offense;compulsory disclosure of ownership and authority;post publication criminal penalties for objectionable matter;post publication collection of damages in a civil action;post publication correction of libel and other misstatements;discrimination in granting access to news source and facilities;discrimination and denial in the use of communications facilities for distribution;taxes;discriminatory subsidies;and interference with buying, reading and listening.

Media should encourage art, science and literature but it is focusing on astrology, rebirths, religious myths, beliefs and aliens. Now days almost every news channel telecast astrological programmes where an astrologer or some baba is sitting and predicting about deaths, marriages and relationships. The funny part is that sometimes statements made by each astrologer are contradictory which confuses the audience. Superstition and myths are also encouraged as recently in one of the news channel there was programme based on a tantrik who claimed that he can kill a person within three minutes. It was telecast but the action failed and to escape from humiliation the tantrik said that it can only be performed at night.

In the 2000s, Bollywood began influencing musical films in the Western world, and played a particularly instrumental role in the revival of the American musical film genre.Bollywood films are mostly musicals, and are expected to contain catchy music in the form of song-and-dance numbers woven into the script. A film's success often depends on the quality of such musical numbers. Indeed, a film's music is often released before the movie itself and helps increase the audience

The release of "Aja Nachle" enthused a dance craze. The teenage crowd completely overshadowed us with their enviable knowledge of Indian songs and dance moves. One such enthusiast, 14 year-old-Faiza confessed "I enjoy Indian dramas and films especially the remixed songs.

Television is very influential when it comes to new trends and fashion. Peoples get in touch with all the new trends related to dresses and same kind of things because of this.

Programs like Kaun Banay Ga Crorepati, Tariq Aziz Show and many others are doing a good job by providing information in an entertaining way. The Public Service Messages on Television are really influential.

Most importantly, by reading columns, peoples learn a lot about writing. They admit that their creative writing is good because of reading books and news papers' columns.

As Television is the most common and powerful media form that is why it has a number of negative influences. Some peoples really get impressed by new trends of fashion and they waste their money on those foolish things after watching them in any program or advertisements.

Wasting time on surfing different channels of Television is the biggest negative point of peoples. Some times, young girls get impressed by different beauty products just because of their eye capturing advertisement campaigns and then they often get allergy. Cross-promotions between food products and popular TV and movie characters encourage peoples to eat more high calorie food.

Some times young boys keep long hair and say, "it is fashion", a very negative influence of media. Furthermore, the constant ambush of messages from the media especially Television to lose weight and to appear waif-like in order to meet society's expectations of the ideal woman are possibly behind youngsters little eating.

The time youngsters spend using internet displaces time they could be doing physical activities. Whenever peoples get some time spare, they listen to Radio. Again, that time could have been used for any other useful activity.

These were just few examples of media influence but I think, they were enough to show that how convincing and influential media is. The growth of media as an industry has accelerated over the past few years with new forms such as DVD and the internet changing the way we, the audience, consume and receive media.So concluding this topic, I would say that it is up to us that how we consume media. It has both pros and cons but let us try to focus on positive points, not the negative ones.

What remains to be seen is how tomorrow's young adults will show the effects of growing up in a time of computers, Britney Spears and supremacy of Indian media. We may just end up paying a higher price than we bargained for. In the race to "Indianise" our media, are we evolving with the times or burying our own heritage? Will we be successful in statue our own position eventually, or will the technologically know-how Indian industry usurp our culture and society?

Influence on Education

Communication includes all methods of disseminating information, knowledge, thought, attitudes, and beliefs. Modern mass media like newspapers, cinema, and television, and traditional media of social communication like the bazaar, puppet show, drama, dance, local meetings, as well as inter-personal communication media like posts and telegraphs, teleprinters, and telephones all impact language use. The underlying and basic factor of these categories of mass media is language. Hence for the effectual and proper utilisation of these mass media, language education is very essential and material.

Inter-personal communication media helps meet the demand for mutual communication and exchange of information among people and institutions. In recent years, the use of computer has far reaching effect on language education and communication. In this field also language education is of paramount importance. The special feature of radio, television, and cinema is that they serve the needs of both literates and illiterates. They will also entertain people in remote areas not within the reach of newspapers. On the other hand, newspapers present the 'written word' and serve as 'record,' while at the same time give local coverage. Language education to the audience, readers and spectators is very essential.

Language and Communication

In India, various forms of language are in competition with each other to draw the attention of the public. These forms range from the extremely informal style of speech found in the radio and the cinema to the formal styles found in newspapers and news broadcasts. Different language styles perform different functions in society. The styles of standard languages constantly undergo changes and development through the impact of various mass communication media.

Formal public education is one of the most powerful tools that influences linguistic norms and linguistic attitudes. Another important aspect of language education in India is culture learning. One learns a language through being culturally aware. Thus there is inter-relationship and reinforcement between language and culture. They are inter-dependent. News texts are part of what a particular culture thinks of as significant, and show a hierarchy of values.

The newspaper is 'talk' about world affairs and current events, having multifarious functions in society such as disseminating information, socialisation, motivation, education, cultural learning, entertainment, integration, etc. Most newspapers in Indian languages appear to focus on the readability of the material or news they present. They recognize that the way language is used is an important factor in enabling their readers to come back to them.

But language alone does not help a newspaper to increase its sale in the market place. In a country where everything is looked at from a political angle, the support base for a newspaper in Indian languages often comes from the shades of political opinion that a newspaper supports and highlights. The manner a news item is presented and highlighted depends on the "ideology" of the newspapers. This "ideology" controls and regulates language use.

Of the different mass media, newspapers assume great importance as they deal every day with dissemination of current information pertaining to different aspects of human life, such as social, economic, political and cultural, both at national and international levels. In a newspaper, headlines occupy a prominent position by summarising the most important news of the day in a nutshell, which facilitates the reader with quick reading and comprehension.

The choice of expression plays a vital role in making the headlines more effective. Thus language plays a prominent part and it aims at educating the reader. At present Indian language newspapers show a tendency to use simpler and colloquial forms of expression more frequently. Newspapers in Indian languages at present have also begun to use loaded expressions with sarcasm and cynicism, because the growing middle class around the nation that buys and reads the newspapers is basically cynical about politics and politicians. The newspapers are educators of the literate and not so literate public. Now-a-days newspaper reading habit is growing rapidly and widely. Thus there is the steady and expanding process of language education through newspapers. The educated families in south India a generation ago made it a point to read THE HINDU daily newspaper as part of their daily English education.

History reveals that the Press Acts against vernacular press in British India actually helped the people to seek greater freedom and ultimately independence from Britain. Political, social, and economic revolutions in

India are closely related to the active involvement and development of newspapers in Indian languages. The prose of every Indian language is critically developed and guided by the language style used in the newspapers published in these languages.

In order to establish their own identity, newspapers deliberately coin and choose their own language expressions. For example, there is a great tendency these days to combine various native words with English words to create special expressions. Translation is no more a fashion with most Indian languages newspapers. Some thirty years ago, most Indian languages newspapers made special effort to translate words and phrases in to Indian languages. Now they tend to simply transcribe foreign words in the native script. This tendency is supported by the spread of cable TV as well as by the globalization process.

Further in a democratic country like India, the newspaper acts as a powerful weapon in exposing the irregularities, shortcomings, and failures of government policy and also function as an eye-opener of the public. But newspapers should not abuse their status and functions. They should be above bias and should be fair and impartial. The language used should be of high standard aiming at educating the public not only in terms of news content but also in terms of language use. This twin function is not wholly appreciated or even discerned in some newspapers that seek only sensationalism in content and expression.

Radio has greater potential in mass communication than the newspaper for two reasons. Firstly, it reaches even the remote corners of the country and has no physical impediments. Secondly, it imparts language education and provides entertainment and disseminates information to both literate and illiterate listeners. Radio is under government control for fear of its misuse and powerful influence. There are indications that soon we will have privately owned radio stations with their own programs of broadcasts all over the country. The range of programmes includes a wide variety of educational, cultural and entertainment items, aimed at a broad spectrum of classes of people.

The type of language used in government-controlled radio stations, unfortunately, seems to be artificial in its idiom in the broadcasts done in all Indian languages. The broadcasts for farmers and workers try to use a style that is supposedly understood by less literate groups. We are yet to find a balance in the broadcasts that suit the audience for which these are intended. But the broadcasts are not as appropriate as these should be for the simple reason that these broadcasts are still largely government-controlled. Radio has a major role to play in language.

The language used in radio impacted the previous generation very much. News broadcasts introduced chaste language, closely modelled after the written variety. The newsreaders introduced standard pronunciation values to the phonemes, words, phrases, and sentences. The impact of radio language was heavy upon the written style, rather than on the spoken idiom. This is somewhat strange, considering the fact that radio is mainly an audio form. It appears that Indian radio is more closely associated with news and music than with dialogue.

Television is the audio-visual non-literary media having the additional advantage of being able to use visual cues to reinforce the information being presented in spoken form. Thus even in this field language education plays a vital role, because additional cues compensate for dialectal differences between speakers and hearers.

The potential of television as an educative device is very great. But exploiting this potential depends upon the choice of appropriate language. TV programs are telecast through satellites. The satellite TV offers a dazzling array of channels and programme choices in many different languages. The divide between the literate and less literate or non-literate classes is covered up in the television media.

Media discourse provides a fertile ground for traditional cultural learning, even as it provides opportunities to entertain and educate the viewers in novel and wholly modern ways that work against traditional values. Unfortunately, TV is more cinema-centered than radio. Entertainment takes precedence in TV. The impact of TV on Indian languages, in terms of their lexicon and structure, so far seems to be negligible. Privately owned TV channels often follow the models set by the leading newspapers in their coverage.

The language of cinema, on the whole, is more accessible to the average person than that of other media. The movies, in general, make use of colloquial style of speech. The language of the cinema, like that of other media, also shows considerable variation. The cinema, being closer to informal popular speech, has two advantages:

1. It appeals to mass audience, and

2. it portrays everyday situations wherein popular language is more appropriate than the more formal variety.

In the village context the cinema competes with other forms of entertainment because it assesses a more popular language. There is, however, a serious problem. Until early seventies, most movies in Indian languages often followed a style that was closer to the written style. These days, movies are produced mostly in the colloquial idiom, except those movies that try to depict the heritage through mythology, etc.

A movie viewer does not get introduced to the written variety now a day. Since in many Indian languages the distinction between the formal and informal styles of language or the distinction between the colloquial/spoken and written styles are still maintained, the usefulness of watching a movie in order to improve the competence in mother tongue is practically less significant.

The computer Revolution in teaching Indian languages is still not yet widespread, despite the fact that computer software engineering is the most preferred profession for the educated young men and women in India. Driven by economic pursuits and greed, Indians seem to be competing with one another in offering their services to enrich the already rich nations. And yet, it is a fact that the presence of Indian languages in the world-wide-web is more significant than any other group of languages in the developing world.

Certain Indian linguistic groups such as Kannadigas, Telugus, and Tamils seem to be more advanced in taking advantage of the computer revolution to improve their language education. There is a significant impact in language use brought out by the use of e-mail. Abbreviations even in Indian languages seem to be used more commonly these days. Once upon a time, inscriptions in copper plates and stones used abbreviations as a means to communicate information in short sentences, etc. Time was not the main consideration when a few generations ago Indians used lots of abbreviations in spelling and combination of letters in their written documents. But, for this generation, time is an important consideration and they use abbreviations of different sorts in their e-mails, and chats.

People want to be different from one another, especially from one generation to another. Wireless, cell phone abbreviations become the dominant feature of urban young men and women these days. Languages are mangled or deconstructed in an idiosyncratic manner. Indian languages find a significant place in the Unicode. This is a great contribution from the energetic Indian software engineers. However, just like the technical terms created by committees constituted by various governments and their agencies, the use of Unicode characters allotted to Indian languages are not yet popular with the Indian public.

Computers store material and keep them in memory. They express the correct use of language. They furnish valuable information concerning various subjects. They operate at high speed and provide opportunity for rectifying and correcting mistakes and errors. Thus the computer, mainly having literary merits, plays a very significant role in language education. It provides knowledge and information in almost all the major languages, both national and international.

Educational Radio Projects

The main projects that describe the growth of educational radio are:

School Broadcast Project: This project was commissioned in 1937 and the target group was School students. This programme started from Delhi, Calcutta, Madras and Bombay. In the beginning the school programme were not strictly governed by the curriculum. With the passages of time and acquisitions of more experience, the AIR tried to make its radio broadcasts more curriculum oriented, but in absence of common syllabi and time tables in schools, even within the same state, it could not succeed in it's aim.

Adult education and community development project (Radio Forum): Commenced in 1956, the Villagers of 144 villages in the vicinity of Poona (in Maharastra state), were the main beneficiaries of this project. This was agriculture-based project, which was originally designed and tried out in Canada. With the help of UNESCO, it was tried in 144 villages of Poona and was named as ' Radio forums Project' (defined as a listening cum-discussion-cum-action group). The members of the forum could listen thirty-minute radio programme on some agricultural or community—development programme, then discuss and decide regarding it's adoption in their own village. This project was a great success. Many action programmes were planned and put into practice.

Farm and Home Broadcast Project: This project was commenced in 1966 and again targeted at Farmers and villagers. These broadcasts were designed to provide information and advice on agricultural and allied topics. The aim was to educate the farmers and provide them assistance in adopting innovative practices in their fields as per the local relevance. The experts also conducted occasional farm radio schools, which proved to be very effective.

University broadcast project: This project for University students was initiated in 1965, with an aim to expand higher education as widely as possible among the different strata of society. The Programme consisted of two types- 'General' & enrichment'. The general programmes included topics of public interest and enrichment programmes supported correspondence education offered by universities in their respective jurisdictions. School of Correspondence studies, University of Delhi and the Central Institute of English and Foreign Languages, Hyderabad is well known for preparation and broadcast of their programmes through AIR.

Language Learning Programme: The project, popularly known as 'Radio Pilot project' was started in 1979-80 jointly by AIR and Department of Education Government of Rajasthan, with an aim to teach Hindi to School going children as first language in 500 primary schools of Jaipur & Ajmer districts on experimental basis. The project was found useful in improving the vocabulary of children. With its success, similar project was repeated in Hoshangabad district of Madhya Pradesh with some modifications but had limited success.

IGNOU-AIR Broadcast: In collaboration with IGNOU, AIR stations of Mumbai, Hyderabad and Shillong started radio broadcasts of IGNOU Programmes from January 1992. Main target group of this project were students of Open / Conventional Universities. Although Shillong started this but discontinued later on. Therefore presently it is being broadcast from AIR Mumbai and AIR Hyderabad only. This programme is still popular in the respective region.

IGNOU-AIR Interactive Radio Counselling (IRC): Started in 1998 for students of Open / Conventional Universities, this project is also very successful. In order to bridge the gap between Institutions and learners by instantly responding to their queries and also to provide Academic Counselling in subject area, IGNOU in collaboration with AIR Bhopal started this project in May 1998 as an experimental programme for one year. With the success of the experiment, it was extended to 8 other AIR stations (Lucknow, Patna, Jaipur, Shimla, Rohtak, Jalandhra, Delhi and Jammu). Presently Interactive Radio counseling is being provided on every Sunday for one hour from 186 radio stations of All India Radio. This includes two Sundays on the National hook-up.

Toll-free telephone facility is available from 80 cities enabling the learners to interact with experts and seek clarification, without paying for their telephone calls. The first and third Sundays of the month, AIR stations of Delhi (Hindi) and Kolkata (in English) broadcast from national hook-up, which 186 radio stations relay either of them. The 2nd and 4th Sunday are slotted for programmes of various regional centers of IGNOU and State Open universities respectively. The slot of 5th Sunday (if any) has also been given to region-based programmes of IGNOU. This programme is gaining popularity day by day.

Gyan-Vani (Educational FM Radio Channel of India): This project is recently launched (in year 2001) and again the target group is students of Open / Conventional Universities. Gyan Vani (Gyan = Knowledge, Vani = aerial broadcasting) is Educational FM Radio Channel of India, a unique decentralised concept of extending mass media for education and empowerment, suited to the educational needs of the local community. It is operating presently through Allahabad, Banglore and, Coimbatore FM stations of India on test transmission mode. The network is slotted to expand to a total of 40 stations by June-2002.

Gyan Vani stations will operate as media cooperatives, with day-to-day programmes contributed by different Educational Institutions, NGO's and national level institutions like IGNOU, NCERT, UGC, IIT, DEC etc. Each stations will have range of about 60-KM radius, covering the entire city /town plus the surrounding environs with extensive access. It serves as ideal medium addressing the local educational developmental and socio cultural needs (IGNOU, 2001). Gyan Vani is not only for the conventional educational system but also a main tool in making available the dream of education for all come true. Gyan Vani's main intention is to take education to the doorsteps of the people.

Gyan Vani, in addition to giving the hardcore education will also deal with awareness programmes including the ones for Panchayati Raj Functionaries, Women Empowerment, Consumer Rights, Human Rights, the Rights of the Child, Health Education, Science Education, Continuing Education, Extension Education, Vocational Education, Teacher Education, Non-formal Education, Adult Education, Education for the handicapped,

Education for the down trodden, education for the tribals and so on. Gyan Vani is available through commercial FM radio set.

Radio-Vision (Multimedia through Digital Radio): Pioneered by the BBC, the technique of radio-vision allows the subject matter to be presented through two channels, the audio and the visual. The visuals are presented in the form of still filmstrips, charts, slides, models, etc, while the explanation is given through recorded narration. Educational institutions use this as a substitute for educational television. Radio-vision has its own advantages:

— It is economical

— It can cater to different categories of learners

— It is easy to produce such programmes at the institutional level or at the learning centers

— It provides visual support to the concept that is taught.

A small experiment in the use of radio-vision technique was carried out by The National Council of Education Training and Research, India in 1975-76 using it as one of the components of the multi-media package for in service teacher training designed and operated during SITE. A series of charts and picture cards were presented to about 24,000 participating teachers 2400 centres alongwith verbal explanation provided through specially prepared radio broadcasts. The results were found to be encouraging.

A pilot project was carried out in IGNOU in 2001 under UNESCO support for testing the feasibility of using the new digital technology for cost effective transmission of audio-visual courseware. The project proved that FM Radio transmitters and Satellite Radio transponders can be used successfully to transmit, downlink and download multimedia courseware, in this case using the Asia Star of WorldSpace.

Radio-text: Radio has been used along with textual data transfer via computer networks simultaneously to create a 'radio-text' environment. The teaching end is normally a FM radio station having data broadcast facility through a computer network. The main points of the radio broadcast are sent through textual mode to the receiving end via a computer network. The learning end has radio listening facility as well as a computer screen to receive the textual data. Since both audio and text are broadcast simultaneously, the learner at the receiving end gets high quality and low cost teaching. An experiment on the use of radio-text at Yashwant Rao

Chavan Maharashtra Open University, Nasik, India resulted in the satisfaction of more than 80 percent the learners. It also used for peer group discussion at the receiving end after the broadcast, which indicates radio-text could be used for varieties of objectives.

Role of Women in Media

Stereotyped portrayal of women in media messages is a universal axiom, though definitions of what constitutes a stereotype way vary across cultures. Likewise one can find similarities in feminist reactions towards advertisements across cultures and geographical boundaries. So much so that portrayal of women in media has become a global sensitivity. Furthermore, in the past decade media analysis has become an important agenda of action for many women activists groups and other organisations.

Among young women (college going) there is a strong perception that obscene film songs lead to eve teasing and harassment. The positive sign in this situation is some increase in women's programmes of greater variety. But these kind of positive efforts have always remained limited. Hence we are one step forward but two steps backward. There is manifold increase in vulgarity in the programmes and using women as commodity that cannot shape the attitude of gender equality.

It is generally perceived that the main reason for exploitation of woman is her lack of control over these media. There is a constant demand to increase the representation by hiring and promoting more and more women at least in the government owned media organisations. However studies have indicated marginal or no improvement in this sector.

It had been estimated that women formed 25 per cent in broadcasting in India in 1979. A need to increase women's participation was felt by all the concerned hence greater participation in the future was expected. Especially when new developments had taken place like the development of the television.

Instead the percentage of women in television centres was found lower than in `broadcasting ` in 1979. Among full time permanent employees 84-88 per cent are men and only 12-15 per cent are women in Doordarshan in 1994. However it seems that there is no substantial difference over the period of five years as the sample study states the range of 7% to 13% of women in administrative and 11% to 15% in production jobs in Doordarshan during 1989.

There is no simple explanation for the frequency of violent crimes against women, but it has been suggested that one contributing factor may be the way women are portrayed in the media. Women are often depicted as victims of violence or as sexual objects, and researchers have found that these media portrayals may influence how women are viewed and treated in society. Film, television, music, music videos and computer games have all been criticized for content considered demeaning to women, such as sexual objectification, depictions of violence against women, and the frequent association of violence with sexuality. Over 40 years of scientific investigation has led researchers to conclude that media violence significantly contributes to aggressive attitudes and behavior in society.

Mounting evidence suggests that negative perceptions of women in entertainment can affect women in real life. Research examining onscreen violence toward women finds that emotional desensitization can occur after viewing as few as two films with sexually degrading and violent themes. Studies also show that men who view a number of films in which women are portrayed in sexually degrading or violent situations become increasingly less disturbed by violence against women and less sympathetic toward female victims of violence. In addition, films initially found demeaning to women are judged to be less so after prolonged exposure. Some people target pornography as the medium most likely to depict women in an offensive manner.

Mainstream films and magazines are often more violent than pornography. In fact, the American public considers many movies demeaning to women; a survey found that 68% of the public believes sexual portrayals of women in American movies "often" amount to exploitation. Recent studies have found that college men exposed to just a few of these films tend to lack empathy towards female victims of rape, believing she "deserved what she got." In addition, these men often do not believe the rapist should be punished.

On television, a disproportionate amount of violence is directed toward female victims. For every 10 male characters on primetime network TV who commit violence, 11 other male characters fall to violence, but for every 10 women who inflict violence, 16 women become victims. Studies have shown that viewers who strongly associate with the victims (i.e., women) feel more susceptible to violence in the real world. More often than not, these viewers become the "real life" victims.

Movies and television alone do not foster changes in attitude. Other media, including music and music videos, may also contribute to negative perceptions of women. Researchers have found an average of 18 instances of aggression each hour on Music Television (MTV), 35% of which depict sexual violence against women. One study of 144 undergraduate males determined that after watching a significant amount of violent or demeaning music videos, desensitization occurs which may foster an antagonistic attitude toward women. Forty percent (40%) of the men in this study indicated some likelihood of committing rape if they could be assured of avoiding punishment.

Studies show that the dominating theme of "love relationship" in songs has increasingly shifted to include explicit sexual references that are often demeaning to women. In particular, gangsta rap, a popular West Coast music style distinguished by lyrics that graphically describe scenes of gunplay, sex, drug use and violence, often depicts women negatively; their roles rarely extend beyond being kidnapped, held hostage, brutally gang raped at gunpoint, or murdered.

Studies have found that exposure to rap music does, in fact, "tend to lead to a higher degree of acceptance of the use of violence (including violence against women)." These types music videos communicate a dangerous message to both men and women—that the invasion of the female body is welcomed and desired, which may translate to rape in the real world.

Video games can also portray violence against or degradation of women. In many, "women are usually cast as persons who are acted upon rather than as initiators of action; in extreme cases, they are depicted as victims." A study of 47 popular Nintendo games revealed that among 115 male and 9 female characters, 20 male and zero female characters had dominant roles. Twenty-eight percent (28%) of the games in the study contained scenes depicting women as inferior and powerless.

Some video games also perpetuate negative stereotypes about women and encourage players to participate in violence against them. In Duke Nukem, 3D players earn points by killing prostitutes. In addition to presenting women as sex objects, the game awards players for harassing women by throwing cash at them.

One icon in computer games is the animated fantasy girl Lara Croft, who stars in Playstation's Tomb Raider. She is a female referred to as a "sex symbol with attitude." According to sociologists, games such as Tomb Raider encourage sexism and condition adolescents to view the world as they do the computer screen: with female sex symbols, female kidnapping, and female rescue and submission. In one study, up to one-third of parents were concerned about possible anti-social behavior (i.e., violence) influenced by these games.

As computers and Internet access become widespread, real-world crimes of harassment and stalking have moved on-line. It is estimated that one in twenty women will become targets of stalking behavior at least once during their lifetimes, and evidence suggests that the majority of cyberstalkers are men victimizing women. The Internet makes stalking, or "cyberstalking," much easier for the perpetrator than off-line stalking. The anonymity of e-mail and chat rooms cloak stalkers well, and stalkers can easily access private information about their victims via the Internet. Many on-line services and directories also enable individuals to obtain e-mail addresses, home addresses, and phone numbers without their intended victims knowing, since few people realize that their personal information is publicly listed online.

Cyberstalking is a relatively new phenomenon, but occurrences are becoming more frequent. In a national survey of college women during the 1996-97 academic year, 13% were stalked and 25% of those incidences reportedly involved cyberstalking. The Web Police, an international crime fighting agency, also estimated that about 30% of the 47,000 complaints it received in 1998 involved harassing or threatening e-mail, and seventeen states now have laws against on-line stalking and harassment. The Clinton administration has called for tougher laws against on-line stalking and encourages Internet companies to launch a web site to educate people about cyberstalking and how to protect themselves.

Influence of Television on Society

Children and Television

Children internalize gender role stereotypes from books, songs, television, and the movies. Television, however, is perhaps the form of media most influential in shaping ideas of appropriate sex roles. Research on television viewing and the socialization of children indicates television has a great impact on the lives of children. Studies have shown preschoolers spend an average of nearly 30 hours a week watching television; it is suggested children spend more time watching television than they spend on anything else except sleeping.

By the time children are sixteen years old, they have spent more time watching television than going to school. Children are exposed to about 20,000 advertisements a year. By the time children graduate from high school, they have witnessed 13,000 violent deaths on television. Prosocial and antisocial behaviors are influenced by television. Also, television influences attitudes about race and gender.

As children grow and develop, they are taking in information and acquiring knowledge at a rapid pace. As children develop their cognitive abilities, they assimilate new information into their existing knowledge base and adjust to the new information by accommodating it to what they already know. Children's ideas about how the world works come from the experiences they have and the attitudes and behaviors they see around them. The young child who comes to understand women are nurses and men are doctors may have come to the realization because the first doctor he or she saw was a man, and he was assisted by a female nurse. This man as doctor, woman as nurse idea may have reinforced by parents reading books; conversations with friends and television may reinforce also.

If the child frequently is faced with gender biases and gender stereotypes, this knowledge will be incorporated and influence perceptions regarding men and women. Keeping in mind young children with developing minds watch many hours of television, and recalling television reinforces gender stereotypes, it is not surprising children come away from this television experience with firmly held beliefs. Frequently these beliefs are stereotyped with regard to gender. Of the various factors which help shape gender-typed behaviors, role models and imitation are extremely influential.

Children are exposed to models throughout their environment, including those on television. Research suggests children who view violent programming on television will behave more aggressively with peers. It is also true children who view prosocial behaviors on television are likely to exhibit those types of behaviors themselves. Young children will imitate and repeat behaviors they see on television. Because children are influenced by gender stereotyped role models they see on television, they will also exhibit gender biased behaviors and develop gender biased attitudes that they see modeled on television.

Positive developmental outcomes for young children during their growing-up years include developing autonomy, initiative, and a sense of industriousness. Children who witness female characters on television programs who are passive, indecisive, and subordinate to men come to understand this is the appropriate way for females to behave. It is less likely for female children to develop autonomy, initiative and industriousness when they rarely see it modeled in those around them. Similarly, because male characters on television programs are more likely to be shown in leadership roles and exhibit assertive, decisive behavior, children learn this is the appropriate way for males to behave.

Regarding gender role development on television, the National Institute of Mental Health has determined:

1) In male-female interaction, men are usually more dominant.
2) Men on television are rational, ambitious, smart, competitive, powerful, stable, violent, and tolerant, while women are sensitive, romantic, attractive, happy, warm, sociable, peaceful, fair, submissive, and timid.
3) For men, the emphasis is on strength, performance, and skill; for women, it is on attractiveness and desirability.
4) Marriage and family are not important to television's men. One study found that for nearly half the men, it wasn't possible to tell if they were married, a fact that was true for only 11% of the women.

While some children's programming has come under attack for being violent, irrelevant, or sexist, other programs for children, such as Sesame Street, are regularly lauded for attempting to meet the developmental needsof children. Sexism, however, can be found even among the Muppets, who all have male names or male voices.

Television and Gender Stereotypes

Gender stereotypes occur with frequency on daytime soap operas; women are often shown as hopeless individuals, unable to solve problems without assistance. Both males and females are shown in gender stereotypic roles on many music television programs. Children frequently watch these programs after school, and receive reinforcement for the notion women are subordinate, passive, and indecisive. About two-thirds of characters in television programs are male. From the 1950s through the 1990s, this figure has remained stable. There is more interaction shown with men (with both men and women) than there is with women. Further, interactions between men and women frequently indicate women are defined by their relationships with men.

Television often does not reflect reality when it deals with the occupations of men and women. For example, programs depict 75% of women as being in the labor force, compared with the truer figure of about 56%. The primary job setting for most women on television is as a professional. Most women in real life, however, are in low paying, low status jobs. Lessthan 10% of women in the United States make more than $50,000 a year. Most females on nighttime television are young, attractive, thin, and ornamental. Most female characters are either under 35 or over 50. Middle-aged women are rare.

Females are consistently placed in situations where looks count more than brains, and helpless and incompetent behaviors are expected. Men are twice as likely as women to be shown as competent and able to solve problems. Gender stereotypes abound on television, with women being depicted as sex objects more frequently than men, and men portrayed as inept when handling children's needs.

On music television, a popular program choice among young viewers, females are often shown in degrading positions. Music videos frequently show women as sex objects. Females are also shown as trying to gain the attention of a male who ignores them. Rap music videos are also popular with young television viewers. Frequently women are portrayed as objects of lust. Women are four times more likely than men to be provocatively dressed; while men are almost always fully clothed.

While early television commercials were criticized for being overwhelmingly biased in favor of males, a study of commercials broadcast between 1971 and 1985 indicated improvement regarding numbers of male and female main characters. However, even though there is currently more equity in the number of men and women appearing in commercials, women are most often shown in the role of wife and mother, or in demonstrating products for the home. Another aspect of television advertising which is overwhelmingly a masculine province is voiceovers and narration, in which 83-90% of the voices are male.

In commercials for children's programs, boys are shown more frequently and in active roles; girls' behavior is much more likely to be passive. Advertisers indicate male models generate more product sales to children of both sexes than female models. It has also been suggested girls watch male-dominated programs and commercials because there are few other options. Girls will become loyal to programming that is more gender fair. Interestingly, children without television have been shown to be less stereotyped in their gender role attitudes. Children who view programs with non-traditional gender roles tend to have non-traditional gender role perceptions. Because children model behavior they see on television, they are likely to perpetuate gender stereotypes they view.

Influence of TV on Youth

The media executives are quick to defend their role in youth violence and bullying while selling millions of dollars in add space focused on youth. Lets take a closer look at the reality of this issue. TV producers, network executives, motion picture companies and others in the media world downplay and deny any impact of their programs on the attitudes and actions of youth. Meanwhile they continue to spend millions on special effects and marketing geared to increase appeal to youth markets. While corporations spend millions on market research and advertising to create products and campaigns targeted at a youth demographic, they still deny their ability to influence youth attitudes and culture.

If this were true to fact, would Nike continue spending millions every year on product development, marketing and advertising? Would McDonalds still be using cartoon like characters to sell hamburgers? Would music labels be increasing the level of violence and sexual content in the music geared towards the youth audience? Would liquor companies be using youth oriented activities in their advertising? Of course it works on influencing youth attitudes and ideals advertising would not be a multi-billion dollar a year business. If it had no influence, M-TV would not have consultant on staff spending huge amounts of money to ensure they keeping up with youth culture.

Clothing companies are spending millions to get young good-looking individuals to make plain and boring clothes look appealing to youth. Youth respond to visual advertising more than other forms. This is due to the fact that youth want to visualize them selves using the product or service. An example of this would be simply as follows. Even adults are manipulated by these practices. For example, Roots comes out with a new hat. You hear an ad for this hat on the radio. You may be curious but you cannot visualize the actual style or yourself wearing this item. Next you see the ad in a newspaper. Now you can visualize the product but it is only a photo. Now you see a television commercial.

The persons in the commercial are snowboarding and having fun. A song is playing in the ad that catches your ear. Now you subconsciously associate the product with fun, excitement and style. Now you want to go and purchase that hat. This is a plain and straight example of how the media in it's simplest for influences youth culture. Now if you consider how often youth are subjected to the idea that you need to look perfect, be thin, use violence and smoke cannabis etc. it is a powerful and effective influence or it would not be such big business. If they took more responsibility in the attitudes they are creating they are scared that they would not make the revenues that they currently enjoy.

This has an effect on society on a whole because of the younger kids looking up to the older youth for guidance. They want to mimic the older youth as they see as "cool". Adults have a desire to look and feel younger and therefore they tend to follow youth trends in order to facilitate this behaviour. Thus the media has a large influence on society as a whole. They effectively manipulate and create false perception to further their own financial objectives.

TV and Adolescents

The mass media is a big part of our culture in terms of entertainment, yet it can also be a helper, adviser and teacher to our young generation. The mass media affects the lives of our young by acting as a substitute for a number of institutions and social contacts, by providing information and entertainment, by creating and mediating art, etc. In this way, it fulfills a variety of functions in human life.

The time spent in front of the television screen is usually at the expense of leisure: there is less time for games, amusement and rest. Most often children look upon television as a certain kind of socially beneficial instrument, an open door into the world of the imagination. Attracted by what is happening on the screen, children not only imitate what they see but directly identify themselves with different characters.

The Surgeon General also states that Americans have been concerned about the prevalence of violence in the media and its potential harm to children and adolescents for at least forty years. During this period, new media emerged, such as video games, cable television, music videos, and the Internet. Current psychological theory suggests that the interactive nature of many of these new media may affect children's behavior more powerfully than they have thought in the past. As they continue to gain popularity, these media, along with television, prompt public concern and research attention.

Another large societal concern on our young generation inflicted by the media, is body image. External forces can influence body image positively or negatively. For one, societal and cultural norms and mass media marketing impact our concepts of beauty. In the mass media, the images of standardized beauty fill magazines and newspapers, beam from our televisions and entertain us at the movies. Even in advertising, the mass media plays upon accepted cultural values of thinness and fitness for commercial gain. Young adults are presented with a narrowly defined standard of attractiveness, an ideal that carries unrealistic physical expectations.

According to The Dairy Council of CA-Educators, both boys and girls are told that they should look like a model, but only one in forty-thousand people, naturally have a model's body shape. This is a problem because adolescence is a time when young adults begin to separate from their parents and identify their own identities. Acceptance by their peers is of utmost importance. This can make teens vulnerable to ideals embraced by our culture and reflected in the media. To obtain the fashionable, ultra thin look, many young men and women restrict their food intake. Sometimes, men or women will result to drastic measures to fit the image they want to be, or the image that they feel society will accept them.

In doing so, disorders can develop, such as Anorexia nervosa and Bulimia nervosa. Anorexia nervosa generally starts between 12-18 years of age, and is characterized by restrictive food intake, weight loss and excessive exercise. One half to one percent of adolescent girls develops anorexia. Another eating disorder that is common is Bulimia nervosa, which is the binge/purge syndrome. It typically develops between sixteen to twenty years of age. Approximately three percent of teenage girls develop bulimia. These percentages do not include all those who have these disorders, only those that have reported their' eating disorders. Many people can hide their disorder very well, and can result in death.

The mass media can affect children's thinking and behaviors. For many young people, the world on the television screen is a more frequent topic of conversation than events and unpleasant moments in school or at work, than the opposite sex, and what friends are doing, etc. Compared with television, the other mass communication media form a substantially smaller part of the daily topics of conversation.

Also, television watchers can be influenced positively or negatively by what they see on the screen and can go out into the world, imitating these acts. Also, the media portrays an unrealistic body image for adolescents and all of society. This struggle to be accepted by society can lead to feelings of depression, anger, and anxiety and even direct to eating disorders.

Two common known eating disorders prevalent in society are Anorexia nervosa and Bulimia nervosa. Both disorders are common in society and can result in death if not treated. In closing, the media should be of great concern to our society. What our youth see and view, is what they feel society wants from them. Delivering wrong messages and unrealistic images by the media can only cause problems and trouble for our youth. Although the sole purpose of the media is enjoyment for society, the public should be aware that it could sometimes cause negative effects on its viewers.

Media Violence and the Audience

The effect of media violence on the human mind has been a subject of debate over decades. Newspaper headlines have linked bizarre crimes to specific examples of media coverage, and the protection of children from media violence crops up periodically as a media issue. Yet although the debate seems no closer to being resolved than it was back in the 1950s, there is a substantial body of research on the patterns of media violence and the possible effects of media violence on the consumer.

The findings of content analysis studies carried out e.g. in the USA, the UK, Israel and Germany all point almost identically in the same direction. The major criteria can be summarised as follows:

Structural violence (social injustice) is of only subordinate importance in entertainment broadcasts. Violence is presented almost exclusively in connection with individual fates, with no insight into possible socio-structural determinants of the violence. The most violent protagonists by far are unmarried men of middle age. Violence is shown as typically linked with the masculine role. As a rule, aggressive dynamic men aged 30 to 40 are surrounded by beautiful soft women aged 20 o 30. In TV entertainment an image of women is drawn that has predominated in European art since the Middle Ages; the woman is passive and seductive.

Typically violent acts occur in the TV broadcasts between protagonists who are strangers to each other, in speaking distance of one another. This depiction is most unrealistic as in most cases violence is the result of an interaction sequence between individuals who know each other, e.g. members of a family. The most frequently shown form of violence is that of a clearly dominant attacker who damages and/or overpowers another. Depiction of the violence itself is extremely unrealistic. Although an act of violence can cause death of the recipient, the suffering of the victim, blood and wounds are shown only rarely.

In the world of TV entertainment hardly a protagonist dies a natural death. The focus is on the performing of violence, i.e. on "action". As a rule the victim is presented only briefly. Violence is shown as an efficient instrument for attaining goals or solving conflicts, When a negative main protagonist who uses violence is punished, this mostly happens at the end of a film plot, after violent behaviour was previously successful in many individual sequences. Violence is not only used by "negative" protagonists but also just as often by representatives of law and order (police or private detectives) to help uphold the law. Whoever becomes violent because of loyalty to the law as a rule has nothing to fear.

Witnesses to violent events as a rule do not try to mediate or help but usually remain passive. In summary, TV violence is linked to the masculine role and is (carried out) between strangers. Although violence can be fatal for the recipient, it is very rarely painful. Television offers behaviour models demonstrating how with illegitimate means (violence) aims recognised as legitimate (prosperity, power, prestige, justice) are achieved. There are, of course, detractors from the notion that media violence causes harm to viewers and readers. A major criticism of the "media effects" theory is that it assumes that readers and audiences are passive sponges, unable to sift what is within a media genre from what is real life.

Active audiences, this theory maintains, are trained through a lifetime of viewing to tell screen violence from real violence, to enjoy the first as a form of entertainment but to naturally eschew the second. Traditional definitions of "violence" have also been criticised. According to Martin Barker the expression "media violence" has to be one of the most ill-informed of all time. "It is supposed to encompass everything from cartoons (ten-ton blocks dropped on Tom's head by Jerry, children's action adventure films (the dinosaurs of Jurassic Park...) news footage from Rwanda and Bosnia; documentary footage showing the police attacking Rodney King in Los Angeles; horror films from Hammer; the range from Clint Eastwood as the voiceless hard man of Dirty Harry to Arnie as the violent humorist of almost any of his films, etc, etc. No single ground has ever been given for us to suppose that such a list has any single property in common...it is a useless conflation of wholly different things."

Yet another exception generally taken is that research methods are crude and you cannot measure human reaction the way you observe Pavlovian dogs. But crude or not, a substantial body of research does exist to show that media violence has definite effects on consumers. Edward Donnerstein found that the level of aggression of male subjects toward females increased after they had been exposed to violent pornography in which a female rape victim was portrayed as becoming aroused by the end of the movie. (Aggression was measured by the intensity of electric shock that subjects were willing to administer.) Violent films that were non-pornographic (depicting, for example, a man hitting a woman) also increased subjects' levels of aggression toward hitting women, but not to the same extent as violent pornographic films.

Other studies have found that prolonged exposure to filmed violence desensitizes subjects. In one particular study, subjects were exposed to five consecutive days of viewing violent films. Subjects' perceptions of the violence portrayed in the films also changed over the five days. The films were perceived to be significantly less violent by the last day of viewing.

Ratings of how degrading the film was to women and of its offensiveness were also significantly lower by the last day. There is a tendency for such desensitisation to "spill over" into subjects' judgements of a female victim in another context. Men who were exposed to the large doses of filmed violence against women judged the victim of a violent assault and rape to be significantly less injured and evaluated her as generally less worthy tan the control group of subjects who saw no films.

Subjects who rated the material as less offensive or violent and more enjoyable by the last day of viewing were much more likely to judge the victim as more responsible. These findings add strength to the mounting evidence that sustained exposure to filmed violence may lower sensitivity to victims of violence in other contexts." If such findings are applied to the news coverage of violence against women, it becomes clear that it is the media's responsibility not to identify, blame or judge female rape victims and not to make judgements of domestic abuse survivors. It also becomes important not to eroticise violence. Some guidelines like those put out by the Philippine Journalism Review go as far as to recommend that reports of violence are not placed next to pin-ups and other items which heighten their titillating value.

Influence of Online Media on Society

After 50 years of controversy over the impact of television on children, a new world of online media is emerging that may have even greater impact on them. Almost one million children in the United States are now using the World Wide Web, according to a research and consulting firm specializing in interactive technology, and 3.8 million have Web access-a figure that will grow rapidly in coming years. Like adults, children will increasingly be connected to a vast digital universe that transcends the family, the local community, and even the nation. Education will expand beyond the classroom and other traditional settings, as more interactive "edutainment" becomes available. New personal and portable technologies will enable children to inhabit their own separate electronic worlds.

The dazzling graphics and engaging interactivity of the new multimedia technologies will make them potent forces in the lives of children. If harnessed properly, the new media could enhance their drive to learn, provide them with access to a rich diversity of information and ideas, and enable them to reach across community and national borders. But there is also peril: Video game channels, virtual shopping malls, and manipulative forms of advertising targeted at children could further compound the problems in the existing media that have troubled parents, educators, and child advocates for decades.

We are in the midst of the formative stage of this new digital age. Government policies are being debated and enacted, marketing and programming strategies are being developed, and services for children are being designed. If we are to believe some hyperbolic visions of cyberspace, the information superhighway will be a great equalizing force that will bring unprecedented opportunity for all. Improvements in education and other benefits for children are often at the center of these visions.

But history offers us cautionary lessons. In this century enthusiasts have hailed every new medium-from radio to FM to television to cable to satellites-with claims that it would reinvigorate our culture, expand educational opportunities, and enhance the democratic process. None has lived up to these claims. In each case, powerful commercial forces have used civic values to gain support for the new medium-and then squelched the very policies necessary to serve the public good.

While traditional media are sometimes viewed as unnecessary diversions, digital media will soon become an integral part of daily life. Those without access to the communications system are likely to fall behind in education and be unable to compete in a highly selective job market. Yet just as access is becoming imperative, the number of children living in poverty, with little or no access to technology, is growing at an alarming rate.

Access isn't the only challenge; the quality of the new media culture for children also raises concern. Unlike TV, online media are dynamic and two-way. This participatory quality makes them particularly compelling to children. Such technological breakthroughs as real-time audio, real-time video, and virtual reality modeling language are transforming online media. Eventually, this interactive online world could supplant traditional television as the most powerful and influential medium in children's lives.

Many online services are now available that seek to challenge children by exposing them to places, people, and ideas far outside their everyday experiences. For example, Plugged In, a Web site created by a community computing center in Palo Alto, California, allows poor children to explore the Internet, produce their own art, and display it to other children around the world. Another Web site, CyberKids, enables children to write and share their own stories in an online magazine. Special networks have been established to foster online communities for children.

These educational and civic services, however, are in danger of being overshadowed by a powerful interactive commercial culture with an unprecedented ability to capture children's attention. Marketing to children has become a multibillion-dollar business. The direct spending power of children, almost all of it discretionary, has risen rapidly in recent years. In 1995, according to Interactive Marketing News and Youth Markets Alert, children under 12 spent $14 billion, teenagers another $67 billion, and together they influenced $160 billion of their parents' annual spending.

In the last decade, these trends triggered a proliferation of new TV networks aimed at capturing a segment of the hot children's market, including the controversial classroom news service Channel One, the highly profitable Nickelodeon cable channel, CNN's Cartoon Channel, and the Fox Children's Network. Character licensing has become the driving force not only in children's television, but also in much of the rest of children's culture. Cross-promotion of licensed products through TV, movies, magazines, discount stores, and fast food restaurants has produced a proliferation of licensed characters that permeate every facet of a child's life.

The new online services for children are being developed in the context of this highly commercialized children's media culture. Children are a disproportionately important market for the new interactive media because they are early adopters of high-tech products. Marketers who view children as the "lucrative cyber-tot category" see the emerging media as a fertile new frontier for targeting children. As an executive from Saatchi and Saatchi, a leader in the online kids' marketing field, recently proclaimed, "There is nothing else that exists like it for advertisers to build relationships with kids."

Advertisers are already aggressively moving into cyberspace.In US a Coalition for Advertising Supported Information and Entertainment (CASIE), led jointly by the American Association of Advertising Agencies and the Association of National Advertisers, is spearheading lobbying efforts to ensure that advertising becomes the dominant mode for funding online content and to ward off government restrictions. The coalition claims that advertiser support for online services is the only way to make information services affordable to all. But the consequences of making advertising the key to universal access for children are troubling.

Advertisers are not just supporting online content; they are shaping much of the virtual landscape for children. At Saatchi and Saatchi, psychologists and cultural anthropologists have perfected a variety of techniques-including play groups, art, and games-to probe children's feelings and behavior when they go online. They are also studying the nature of "kids' culture" as a separate set of experiences and values from that of adults.

Knowing that children often use computers alone, marketers are carefully cultivating this separateness in the design of online services that circumvent parental authority. One online children's service recently published results from a survey that asked children whom they trusted more-their parents or their computers. The majority of respondents said they put more trust in their computers.

According to advertising researchers, going online quickly puts children into a "flow state," that "highly pleasurable experience of total absorption in a challenging activity." This is an optimal condition for advertisers to reach children. Traditional commercials will not work online. "Anything that is perceived as an interruption of the flow state," explained a Saatchi and Saatchi executive, "whether it's artwork being downloaded or an ad that is obtrusively splattered on a screen, is going to get a negative reaction." So the solution is the seamless integration of content and advertising in "branded environments." The goal of these environments is to "get kids involved with brands"-including "brand characters, brand logos, brand jingles, and brand video."

Major children's advertisers have Web sites where children are encouraged to come and play for extended periods of time with such product "spokescharacters" as Ronald McDonald, Kellogg's Snap, Crackle, and Pop, and Chester Cheetah. The aim is to encourage children to develop ongoing relationships with the characters-and the products. Within days of visiting the Kellogg's Web site recently, for example, one child received unsolicited e-mail from Snap, Crackle, and Pop, urging her to return for more fun.

The new interactive media are being designed to compile personal profiles on each child to help in developing individually tailored advertising known as "microtargeting" or "one-to-one marketing." The sites get children to volunteer such personal data as e-mail address, street address, the identity of other family members, and purchasing behavior and preferences. Sophisticated computer software can track every move a child makes online and give marketers "clickstream data" or, in the vernacular of the business, "mouse droppings."

American Federal regulations limit TV advertising to children, but no such rules exist in cyberspace. Marketers can pursue children with few restraints. Nothing prevents them from collecting personal information from children and selling it to third parties. The lines among advertising, entertainment, and information-already dangerously blurred in television and other media-are likely to disappear entirely in the new online environment. "What is really happening," explains one industry expert, "is what will ultimately happen on interactive television: the infomercialization of all programming." Adds another: "The blending of entertainment with advertising will work if packaged correctly: just look at how the toy industry has taken over production of Saturday morning cartoons."

Even traditionally noncommercial services are likely to be shaped by the norms of this new unregulated media environment. While laws prohibited from most forms of advertising on television, there are no restrictions on its use of advertising online.

Online Hate

The Internet has been rightly hailed as a groundbreaking interactive marketplace of ideas, in which anyone with the necessary hardware and software can set up a cyber-stall. But the downside of this unparalleled information exchange is that, alongside its many valuable online resources, the Net also offers a host of offensive materials—including hate materials—that attempt to inflame public opinion against certain groups of people.

This section explores the ways in which hate-mongers use the Internet to promote their agenda, examines the line between hate speech and free speech, provides an overview of relevant legislation and voluntary industry codes, and suggests ways in which to safeguard children and teens. It is also the place to find seminal articles and the latest reports and surveys on the above issues.

Most definitions of hate focus on the ways in which hate-mongers see entire groups of people as the "Other." For example, U.S.-based Tolerance.org argues that "All hate groups have beliefs or practices that attack or malign an entire class of people, typically for their immutable characteristics." Raymond A. Franklin, author of The Hate Directory, focuses on groups that "advocate violence against, separation from, defamation of, deception about, or hostility towards others based on race, religion, ethnicity, gender, or sexual orientation."

Canadian communications scholar Karim Karim points out that the "Other" is one of a number of human archetypes common to all cultures. When people transfer their fears and hatred to the "Other," the targeted group becomes less than human. Hate-mongers can then "justify" acts of violence and degradation because they have denied the humanity of their victims.

Online Privacy

Privacy is a fundamental human right. It underpins human dignity and other values such as freedom of association and freedom of speech. It has become one of the most important human rights of the modern age. Privacy is recognized around the world in diverse regions and cultures. It is protected in the Universal Declaration of Human Rights, the International Covenant on Civil and Political Rights, and in many other international and regional human rights treaties. Nearly every country in the world includes a right of privacy in its constitution. At a minimum, these provisions include rights of inviolability of the home and secrecy of communications.

Most recently written constitutions include specific rights to access and control one's personal information. In many of the countries where privacy is not explicitly recognized in the constitution, the courts have found that right in other provisions. In many countries, international agreements that recognize privacy rights such as the International Covenant on Civil and Political Rights or the European Convention on Human Rights have been adopted into law.

Definitions of privacy vary widely according to context and environment. In many countries, the concept has been fused with data protection, which interprets privacy in terms of management of personal information. Outside this rather strict context, privacy protection is frequently seen as a way of drawing the line at how far society can intrude into a person's affairs. The lack of a single definition should not imply that the issue lacks importance. As one writer observed, "in one sense, all human rights are aspects of the right to privacy."

Privacy can be divided into the following separate but related concepts:

Information privacy, which involves the establishment of rules governing the collection and handling of personal data such as credit information, and medical and government records. It is also known as "data protection";

Bodily privacy, which concerns the protection of people's physical selves against invasive procedures such as genetic tests, drug testing and cavity searches;

Privacy of communications, which covers the security and privacy of mail, telephones, e-mail and other forms of communication; and

Territorial privacy, which concerns the setting of limits on intrusion into the domestic and other environments such as the workplace or public space. This includes searches, video surveillance and ID checks.

The World Wide Web is an exciting new marketplace for consumers. It offers easy access not only to a vast array of goods and services, but also to rich sources of information that enable consumers to make better-informed purchasing decisions. It also offers the convenience of shopping from the office or home. This information-rich medium also serves as a source of vast amounts of personal information about consumers. Commercial Web sites collect personal information explicitly through a variety of means, including registration pages, user surveys, and online contests, application forms, and order forms. Web sites also collect personal information through means that are not obvious to consumers, such as "cookies."

Emergence of Online Communities

Information technology can link geographically separated people and help them locate interesting or compatible resources. Although these attributes have the potential to bridge gaps and unite communities, they also have the potential to fragment interaction and divide groups by leading people to spend more time on special interests and by screening out less preferred contact.

With the explosive growth in Internet connections worldwide, networked communication has the potential to shrink geographic distances and facilitate information exchange among people of various backgrounds. Telecommunications policy in the US-and other countries-resolves to extend access to all levels of society, assuming that this will foster greater information exchange while boosting economic growth (NTIA).

Empowered by information technology such as search engines and automatic filters, IT users are spending more of their waking hours plugged into the Internet, choosing to interact with information sources customized to their individual interests. No longer limited to sources or companions in their geographic neighbourhoods, these users presage an interactive world without borders.

An emerging global village represents only one outcome from a range of possibilities. It is also possible that improving communications access through emerging technology will fragment society and balkanize interactions. If IT provides a lubricant that allows for the satisfaction of preferences against the friction of geography, then more IT can imply that people increasingly fulfill their preferences. A preference for contact that is more focused than contacts available locally leads to narrower interactions.

Thus local heterogeneity can give way to virtual homogeneity as communities coalesce across geographic boundaries.

The Internet has enormous potential to elevate the nature of human interaction. Indeed, we find that if preferences favour diversity, the same mechanisms might reduce balkanization. Bounded rationality, a limit on the human capacity for calculation, also promotes balkanization. As IT eliminates geographical constraints on interaction, bounded rationality imposes a new constraint.

Improved technologies have increased information transmission speeds and bandwidth across all distances except the last 12 inches-between the computer monitor and the brain. The amount of data one can absorb is bounded, regardless of how fast it scrolls across the screen.

The Internet can provide access to millions of other users and a wide range of knowledge sources, but no one can interact with all of them. As of May 1996, the AltaVista search engine had indexed more that 33 million articles and web pages. It would take over five years to read just the new listings added each month. Even if people wished to do so, creating a global community which depends on individuals consuming vast amounts of disparate and topically unrelated information would simply be infeasible.

As long as human information processing capabilities are bounded, electronic media are unlikely to dramatically change this total. When geography no longer narrows interaction, people are able to select their acquaintances by other criteria such as common interests, status, economic class, academic discipline, or ethnic group. The result can easily be a greater balkanization along dimensions which matter far more than geography.

In this world-without-walls, historical biases stand in for geographic barriers and limit integration just as effectively. Because the Internet makes it easier to find like-minded individuals, it can facilitate and strengthen fringe communities that have a common ideology but are dispersed geographically. In many cases, their heated dialogues might never have reached critical mass as long as geographic separation diluted them to a few parts per million.

Once like-minded individuals locate each other, their subsequent interactions can further polarize their views or even ignite calls-to-action. The Internet can also facilitate the de facto secession of individuals or groups from their geographic neighbourhoods. Because time is limited, spending more time interacting with online communities necessarily means spending less time interacting with geographic communities or even family members.

The Internet has apparently led him to spend less time interacting with his geographic neighbours, isolating him on some dimensions even as it integrates him on others. Existing literature provides useful indices of "centrality" and "vulnerability" in network structures which help measure how well-connected or pivotal individuals are within their networks.

Social network literature also identifies blocks of related ties within interconnected communities and describes the effects of weak ties or the absence of ties i.e. "structural holes" on information flows. A formal model of dyadic or pairwise communication also shows integration occurring as a result of face-to-face interaction and print communication.

As communication costs fall generally, the cost of connecting individual agents also falls. If the costs are too high, no two agents communicate; if the costs are negligible, all agents can communicate. With IT costs falling dramatically, inter-connectivity is likely to increase. When communication costs are prohibitive, these twelve agents operate in isolation with incomplete knowledge of global information.

As communication costs fall, clusters of communication emerge allowing agents to share information and gain a less fragmented understanding. This is shown in intermediate frames. Once costs become negligible, a fully connected community emerges permitting everyone access to full knowledge of events. From left to right, knowledge profiles grow from their greatest fragmentation to their least fragmentation while community "balkanization" decreases.

Different agents, represented by different shapes may have different information requirements or communication interests. These potential preferences will motivate subsequent observations on how much communication actually occurs. The decline in balkanization associated with the improved access of this simple model is consistent with the common view that telecommunications, and the Internet in particular, can help foster the emergence of a global village.

The trouble with simply eliminating geographic constraints lies in assuming the absence of any other constraints such as bounded rationality or vetoed interaction. Physical connectivity does not imply logical connectivity when either party at one end of a connection is either too preoccupied or otherwise unwilling to interact.

In practice, limitations on interaction exist due to (1) cognitive capacity constraints (2) missing or unshared vocabulary, e.g. medical terminology (3) insufficient bandwidth, e.g. even video-conferencing may provide insufficient context for first meetings and (4) lack of trust, e.g. Japanese business relationships may require bonding time to establish reputations.

Unconstrained communication can actually be burdensome. During one police investigation, an Internet posting of a request for information resulted in too many false leads during a time-sensitive abduction. Netiquette also addresses wasteful communication. Newsgroup readers actively discourage posting irrelevant material-off-topic news, solicitations, personal attacks-partly because of the time and nuisance costs it imposes on the community.

Since time and rationality are finite, agents prioritize their connections based on a combination of access to and preferences for certain types. The figure below depicts expanding geographic access. Nearer agents are more likely contacts as are agents of a preferred type. Geography imposes an unavoidable heterogeneity.

Adam Smith's butcher, brewer, and baker rubbed shoulders in a local town of physical neighbours. A virtual community of like-minded citizens, however, might be entirely homogeneous. The baker might learn from and contribute to the collected information on baking, indulging his passion for learning more and more about breads even as he learns less and less about meat and drink.

As virtual citizens leave their physical neighbourhoods behind, they inadvertently withdraw their contributions to their physical locales. Increasingly unaware of each other's communities, specialized vocabularies, and nouveau contributions, the butcher, the brewer, and the baker might each provide better meat, drink, or bread individually but lose the ability to provide a balanced meal. This is not without the caveat that incentives can coax groups into working together.

If there are benefits to cooperation, then IT is likely to facilitate interaction among them. A caterer, for example, might contract with providers from each community. Without geographic constraints, incentives can push interaction towards fragmentation or integration, which raises the issues of how incentives operate and of which pathways emerge.

Evidence suggests that better communications can strengthen interactions within special interest groups. In describing what might characterize the emerging "Global Village," McLuhan and Powers nevertheless recognize the power of satellite technology to aid "super-regionalisms" and "separatisms" like the Parti Quebeçois in Canada. As an historical example, the telephone strengthened affiliation among teenage peer groups.

In the field of economics, the number of out-of-state and out-of-country coauthorships in four top journals grew from 4.6% in the 1960s to 27.6% in the 1990s. Similar evidence appears to hold for academia in general: "Historically, the strength of an academic department rested with its resident faculty. Now it depends on the extent to which each faculty member is interconnected with other professionals-worldwide-pursuing similar interests.

The Internet has the attractive property that a person might communicate with a very large group of associates, and this might integrate the population. For example newsgroups and chat rooms have few, if any, physical limitations on participation. Broader participation will unbalkanize resources and groups insofar as more people choose to access the same information and insofar as information flows across the boundaries of distinct groups.

These represent important gains from increased connectivity. There are, however, two important qualifications. The first qualification is that if broader participation is restricted to members of the same community then information resources are less fragmented (i.e. falls) but intergroup fragmentation remains unchanged (i.e. stays constant). People might also find that the sizes of their groups increase but that the number of group memberships they hold remains relatively constant.

By analogy to journal publication, the variety of choices and the number of subscribers might increase but the number of simultaneous subscriptions held by individuals might not increase much. Due to bounded rationality, the median subscriber base might even fall as mass publication gives way to niche publication. This appears to be a strategy of many increasingly focused, or even personalized, net "e-zines" and news feeds.

Second, participating in a group is not the same as interacting with all of a group's members. The number of subscribers to most newsgroups substantially exceeds the number of people who actually post messages. Joining a new community shortens communications distance (i.e. falls) only if this establishes new and shorter paths and it homogenizes information profiles (i.e. falls) only if members actually communicate.

Universal participation is unlikely to imply universal broadcast. Noise and confusion would likely result. Expressed differently, as a group gets larger, the fraction of members who post communications probably declines after some critical point.

In network organizations, for example, sociologists have recognized that as the number of in-group ties increase, the number of out-group ties tends to decrease due to affinity relations and economizing on time and effort—an empirical finding which supports the possibility of fragmentation.

New channels might reduce balkanization if agents use their added capabilities to reach outside their original communities. In the example above, however, channels have increased by 50% but all agents use their additional resources to communicate with previously unreached members of their existing communities. Resource fragmentation falls but groups are no more integrated than before. Each agent effectively deepens his or her knowledge of a given topic area.

The Internet can, in fact, lend itself to experimentation as when people enter into multi user-domains (MUDs) and alter their virtual personalities, genders, and behaviours. The model and metrics are robust and they can illustrate movement both towards and away from balkanization. Which effect dominates depends on the aggregate distribution of preferences. Narrower preferences balkanize while broader preferences unbalkanize interactions.

Communications research suggests that "what you know depends on whom you know and who you know depends on whom you meet". This can make knowledge profiles path dependent and it also opens the door to information feedback. Historically, positive feedback is damped by geography and unfiltered interaction. Communication technology, search engines, and message filters, however, encourage positive feedback.

In illustrating a theory of communication ecology as mutually defining agents, context, and transmissions, Kaufer and Carley cite several studies in which contact and shared information exhibited a reciprocal relationship. A study of writing students, for example, found a positive correlation between their patterns of interaction and emerging pockets of consensus. Another study found that employees' similarity, shared information, and proximity predicted their social interactions.

Feedback between interaction and shared information also appears to explain differences in observed cohesiveness of certain religious groups.

Recent technology provides a far higher level of control over interaction and contact filtering. Control exists at the message level where previously it extended only to the interpersonal level.

Moreover, filtering and screening may take place on behalf of individuals with or without their foreknowledge and consent. The New York Times will shortly deliver customized news via Netscape's web browser and a patent has recently been issued for software which customizes personalized advertisements over cable channels. Advertising and news stories can be targeted to the level of word choice both to spark interest and to penetrate filters designed to screen unwanted contact.

IT might therefore lead to more focused interaction through the action of choices people make for themselves and the action of choices others make for them. Moreover, if preferences for new information are a function of past information or contacts, then an agent's preferences and connections can become highly path dependent. Small changes early in the evolution of a community can radically affect their character.

Many communities offer examples of increasingly narrow focus and specialization. Numerous academic disciplines, in fact, have progressed to the point where the specialized vocabulary that facilitates interactions within the community hinders interaction across communities. Indeed, Kuhn has observed that a widening gulf "separates the professional scientist from his colleagues in other fields".

As IT improves filtering, tailoring, segmenting, and searching, the more global network becomes the less local village. The principles which govern balkanization across types also hold within types if sufficient differentiation exists to distinguish one classification from another of the same type. Quality can represent one such axis of differentiation.

Given quality differences-analogous to different types the same balkanization phenomena can occur. Associations can form among high, middle, and low quality tiers inducing stratification. There is an implicit competition between choices for interaction only because a limitation on choices means that a decision to include one option results in the exclusion of another.

Under certain conditions, balkanization can be economically efficient and stable in the sense that no individual can be made better off by changing their personal affiliations from those under focused interaction. It might even be possible for this to be welfare maximizing in the sense that balkanized organization produces the greatest output.

Perhaps the greatest production is possible when the most efficient and like-minded producers collaborate. For instance, interconnected "collaboraties" can allow scientists to share data and access remote instruments. Even in those cases where the connections are obvious, the necessary interactions may fail to occur. If the returns to individuals from balkanized interaction do not align with the returns to societies, then persons acting out of pure self-interest will not internalize the spill over effects-the externalities-that would otherwise benefit society.

Voluntary balkanization might then produce direct economic costs. For example, the benefits of knowledge produced by the "intellectual cross-pollination" of having academic researchers interact with business practitioners might spill over into government policy - a positive externality. These two groups will interact too infrequently, however, if they do not internalize the benefits they provide to other groups.

In such situations, reduced balkanization would be optimal from a purely economic perspective. Independent of the potential economic costs or benefits of balkanization, members of a society may wish to reduce balkanization simply to maintain a degree of integration and societal cohesiveness.

With the customized access and search capabilities of IT, individuals can focus their attention on career interests, music and entertainment that already match their defined profiles, or they can read only news and analysis that align with their preferences.

Individuals empowered to screen out material that does not conform to their existing preferences may form virtual cliques, insulate themselves from opposing points of view, and reinforce their biases. Internet users can seek out interactions with like-minded individuals who have similar values, and thus become less likely to trust important decisions to people whose values differ from their own.

This voluntary balkanization and the loss of shared experiences and values may be harmful to the structure of democratic societies as well as decentralized organizations. In addition, the stratification that results from balkanization along a quality dimension raises a concern for equality.

The gap between the information rich and the information poor can widen with virtual communities. Balkanization in one or more dimensions of our interactions may or may not be desirable, but once achieved, it can be difficult to reverse. In any event, at this early stage of developing information infrastructure, no single scenario is inevitable.

Challenges of Online Technologies

The Internet has evolved into a major communications platform that enables new forms of human and organizational interaction. While it should be no surprise that many believe it can indeed become the network of planet earth, a series of difficult technical, industry, and market challenges stand in the way.

There are three different types of networks that most knowledge workers and consumers use on a daily basis. Your home phone has a wired analog electrical connection to a phone company facility called a central office (CO) where your phone wire goes into an automated switching device.

When you place a call, this switch either reroutes the electrical signal to another local phone line or initiates a digital transmission across the interconnected digital networks owned by whatever mix of local and long distance carriers are involved in the completion of the call.

When the digitally transmitted signal reaches the CO local to the party you're calling, it is converted back into an analog electrical signal and sent out across the phone line of the party you are calling. The digital portion of today's telephone networks allocate a fixed amount of transmission capacity (i.e., bandwidth) for each and every call, from end-to-end across the network-ensuring high quality connections and clear, reliable phone calls.

The end-to-end reservation for each phone call is called a circuit, and the network is a called a circuit switched network. The reliability ensured by the bandwidth reservation mechanism of this type of digital network is referred to as Quality of Service (QoS). While we've all come to know and love the conventional phone network, it does have its drawbacks.

Circuit switched networks are inefficient, since considerable bandwidth is dedicated to each call, for the duration of each call, even when no one is talking. Also, the conventional service does not provide for end-to-end integration of multiple media types owing to the local analog connection which is designed for straightforward conversion between electrical signals and sound waves at the phone handset.

The telephone network is also designed to support a limited number of end-points in a single transmission (and most of use the network only for individual, point-to-point conversation). Local radio and television networks and cable and satellite television networks utilize all available bandwidth to transmit high quality media in one direction to large numbers of recipients.

Most of these broadcast networks have historically used analog transmission, although an increasing number now use digital transmission (e.g., satellite television and radio, digital cable, and HDTV broadcasts by local channels). Like the circuit switched telephone network, the conventional broadcast network has significant limitations. It has little or no capacity for interaction (thus, talk-radio is based on a radio broadcast with interactivity provided by the phone network).

Media integration is also not an option: only audio and/or video are supported. And while broadcast networks are very effective, there is inefficient bandwidth utilization in some instances. For example, cable television networks concurrently broadcast all channels into your home even though most of us usually watch only one program at any one time.

The broadcast network is a also a tightly controlled scheduled content delivery mechanism. Listeners and viewers have no direct control over content transmission-the "what" and "when" of content delivery are decided by broadcast programmers. To receive desired content, you must be available at the time that content is broadcast, or you are out of luck, unless you use a recording device.

As you continue to learn more about the capabilities and flexibility of convergence technologies these limitations become more obvious and more frustrating. Packet switched networks decompose all source media-whether audio, video, animation, text, software, or any of a number of other media types-into a series of digital packages, called packets.

Each packet is routed through an open and shared network medium in a burst transmission that utilizes all available bandwidth to get each packet to its destination as soon as possible. When packets reach the destination computer, they are reassembled into the original source media. This burst transmission mechanism is referred to as "best effort" delivery, and it effectively speeds packets along when there is little contention for network resources.

However, all network connected devices are free to send out as many packets as they need at any given time. Congestion can and does occur when too many packets concurrently pass through a particular part of the 'net. When this happens, packets are delayed and sometimes dropped. Packet switched network transmission has been a good fit for the most popular Internet applications:

— email messages,

— Web pages, and

— instant messages were effectively delivered across the 'net in burst transmissions.

However, the best effort delivery of packet switching offers no speed or delivery guarantees. In other words, packet switched networks lack the Quality of Service (QoS) of circuit switched networks. When congestion occurs, the lack of QoS can become annoying for those engaged in Web surfing and other online activities; when it comes to rich media like audio and video, congestion can totally disrupt the flow of media, resulting in an unacceptable end-user experience.

Scaling packet networks for one-to-many media distribution-the core competency of the broadcast network-can also be problematic. This is especially prevalent with synchronous rich media transmissions, such as live streaming media Webcasts. These challenges in the first book, and indicated then that significant funds were being invested within the telecommunications industry to deal with the shortcomings of packet switched networks.

The Internet computing phase of digital convergence, the growth in the use of the Internet as a platform for human and organizational communication and interaction was phenomenal. As a result, the Internet has become a centerpiece of digital convergence, and it is now generally recognized as an innovative global communications platform that offers the following advantages when compared to existing circuit switched phone networks and broadcast television and radio networks:

— *media integration*: Internet technologies enable an ability to combine and transmit text, numbers, animations, audio, video and other media types in any combination.

— *enhanced interactivity*: The Internet can support one-to-one, group, community-based, and one-to-many modes of interaction. Interactions can be either synchronous (videoconference, chat, or live Webcast) or asynchronous (video on demand, email). Interactions to support searching, transaction processing and navigation can be creatively integrated into an Internet interface.

— *network efficiency and reach*: The shared approach of packet switching ensures more efficient network utilization for many applications. Information can be transmitted across any type of physical network infrastructure. Many believe the Internet has the potential to become the basis for all of our communications needs-with broadband Internet eventually becoming so pervasive that the future will see almost any device you can think of, knitted together via a global, ubiquitous Internet network:
  — Internet connected computers and PDAs
  — Internet phones
  — Internet television
  — Internet connected automobiles
  — Internet kiosks
  — Internet vending machines
  — Internet appliances
  — Imagine a world where people just accept that "the network" (i.e., the next generation Internet) is everywhere, interconnecting almost everything and everyone in the developed world.

In the 1980s and early 1990s when people used to talk about the Information Superhighway, which was then a dream-a dream of a high-speed network that offered ubiquitous, high speed digital connectivity. No one knew who would build it. While politicians, business executives, journalists and others were debating the Information Superhighway, a community of geeks and hackers created the Internet which has now assumed the position as centerpiece of our telecommunications consciousness.

The Internet evolved over the past few decades through a grass roots collaboration. It continues to evolve with many new efforts focused on overcoming technical shortcomings that prevent it from enabling innovative new services and eventually replacing legacy broadcast and telephone networks. Let's quickly review the past evolution of the Internet, and further explore some of the technological challenges that are driving its continued evolution.

The original technologies developed by department of defence and academic researchers were designed to create a fault-tolerant communications platform based on a seamless network of interconnected networks: an internet. The Transmission Control Protocol and Internet Protocol (TCP/IP) that came out of these early efforts are intermediate layer standard formats and procedures for transmitting data in packets of information across a heterogeneous mix of interconnected physical networks.

The global public internet that eventually emerged with the broad deployment of these protocols is the Internet with a capital "I." The first versions of TCP and IP were created through a collaborative design process with no purpose other than to create a great network. The designers probably never fully envisioned the potential for this type of network and never anticipated the breadth of applications that would ride on top of today's public Internet.

Initially, development, standardization, and deployment of Internet protocols were voluntary and informal. While this worked remarkably well, there were some coordination issues, and the Internet Engineering Task Force (IETF) was eventually established to provide a structure for the Internet standards process. The IETF enabled a focal point and a set of formalized organizing principles for the collaborative, community based work that has continued to churn out Internet innovations (the World Wide Web Consortium, or W3C, plays a similar role in coordinating Web standards).

The Internet was first widely adopted within the academic and research communities. Email was popular with a larger number of users, but there were still many who eschewed this communications platform, owing to its crude interfaces and user-unfriendliness. When the Mosaic Web browser was introduced in the early 1990s-enabling a graphical interface to hyperlinked pages of text and images-its instant popularity launched the first phase of the digital convergence era.

Through the late 1990s, tens of millions of consumers gained access to the Internet and Web via modem connections from: local Internet Service Providers; regional and national Internet Service Providers such as Mindspring and Earthlink; and proprietary online service providers such as America Online, which, with its easy to use interface, became America's choice for those new to the Internet.

During this period the corporate sector also saw widespread deployment of Internet technology. In the early days, most mainstream computer networking and telecommunications providers didn't take the Internet very seriously. Corporate computer networks were running packet switched networks using proprietary technologies and protocols such as Novell's IPX/SPX and Microsoft's Windows networking.

Cable providers, telecommunications carriers, and local phone companies all used non-Internet communications technologies as well, although organizations such as the International Telecommunications Union (ITU) and the National Television Systems Committee (NTSC) had established standards for these industries. As more and more companies began to understand the flexibility and value of the Internet, and as more and more users jumped on to surf the Web and email their colleagues, business partners, friends, and families, many began to think and dream of ways this infrastructure could be fitted for a wider variety of applications.

This thinking drove extensions to the Web that increased interactivity, supported transaction processing, and stimulated introduction of new rich media capabilities such as Internet telephony, videoconferencing, and streaming media. The open and shared Internet was beginning to grow up, and it wasn't long before many of us began to believe that it was to become the Information Superhighway that had been talked about for so long.

Broadband Internet everywhere became a reasonable expectation for this evolving, expanding-and increasingly general purpose-communications infrastructure. It was easy to imagine a future Internet with incredible potential, and the game was on to extend and enhance the Internet to support all manner of human and organizational interaction, collaboration, communication, and information sharing.

Unfortunately, the Internet infrastructure was not able to adequately support some of these innovative new services and interactions. While there were high hopes, it was also clear that some crucial technical challenges had to be addressed for the promise to become a reality.

Substantial bandwidth is necessary in the last mile Internet connection to ensure speedy transmission of high-resolution digital images, quick downloads of audio files in the compressed MP3 format, or smooth-playing streaming media feeds. Unfortunately, many consumers and small businesses continue to access the 'net through narrowband dialup connections at well under fifty thousand bits per second.

The bandwidth solution for the local loop is in the form of a broadband connection, most often via cable modem provided by a cable provider such as Comcast or Time Warner, or a Digital Subscriber Line (DSL) connection from a phone company. Bandwidth is not only an issue in the last mile. With the open and shared architecture of the 'net there are other network components that also become bandwidth constrained.

For example, a local Internet Service Provider may have a link to a backbone provider that works fine. Then a unique and compelling resource is deployed by a local ISP customer, and the resulting "word-of-mouth" generates traffic that swamps the ISP's connection. Or a crucial backbone link or inter-network router may become overtaxed when a sudden and unexpected surge in traffic hits. Increasing bandwidth at these bottlenecks provides a quick fix.

Unfortunately, it is impossible to anticipate where bandwidth shortfalls will occur, and it seems there are a never-ending set of scenarios that cause bandwidth bottlenecks across the public Internet. Let's focus in on two specific bandwidth-related Internet performance issues that keep the Internet from mounting a real challenge to legacy broadcast and circuit switched networks.

Real-time transmission of rich media or time-oriented text or numeric information (e.g., stock prices) requires a reliable transmission rate-i.e., Quality of Service (QoS)—between source and destination. QoS is a defining feature of the phone network, and it is something that Internet researchers and computer and network engineers have been pursuing for several years.

Unfortunatey, QoS is still not a reliable feature of the public Internet, a fact which has limited the quality, reliability, and acceptance of applications that incorporate real-time feeds. Among alternative Internet QoS mechanisms for the Internet are the following:

— *Over-provisioning*: This is the application of aggregate and ever-cheaper bandwidth to effectively raise the upper limit on transmission capacity to a point that contention and congestion never occurs, even in the presence of extreme traffic conditions. Over-provisioning is not a total network-wide solution, but it is an effective strategy for some network segments, such as the Local Area Network (LAN), where it is possible to deploy enough bandwidth to prevent bottlenecks.

— *Resource Reservation Setup Protocol (RSVP)*: This Internet protocol allows for an end-to-end reservation of bandwidth across the Internet for a particular transmission (e.g., a real-time audio or video stream). Unfortunately, it hasn't been feasible to implement RSVP across the public Internet, given the lack of control over all the routers and other devices that must support the protocol, and the complexities of billing and pricing for this type of fine-grained QoS approach on a totally decentralized network.

— *Multi-Protocol Label Switching (MPLS)*: The MPLS standards effort has resulted in technology that can effectively tag different types of network traffic so that network administrators can program network devices to handle different types based on network "policies." For example, mission critical corporate transactions or Internet video streams may be given priority over basic Web and email traffic. This is a preferred solution for many enterprise and service provider networks.

— *Caching*: Propagating content to the edges of the network in local storage devices enables end-users to retrieve content from a local copy without the need for transmission across the public network. This reduces the potential for network congestion and delay, significantly improving the prospects for a quality experience for the end user. Caching has given rise to the Content Delivery Network which uses caching technologies to deliver quality Web and streaming media experiences.

In the foreseeable future it appears that Internet QoS will be limited to specific enterprise or ISP Internet networks where financial models support prioritization of specific type of traffic or caching of high-end content. Unfortunately, these scenarios do not include the sort of creator-collaborator-centric, free-wheeling media access that many of us had dreamed of when the Internet emerged several years ago.

The Internet excels at supporting millions of concurrent users. Part of this success is due to the fact that the typical aggregate demand is characterized by asynchronous access to an incredibly wide set of Internet accessible resources. However, when many users all decide to access the same resource at the same time, problems arise. Scaling up to synchronously serve content and interactions in real-time to large numbers of users in a reliable, cost effective manner is a huge challenge.

As the horrible events of September 11, 2001 unfolded, news oriented Web sites and ISP networks were swamped. Millions of 'net connected individuals sought the latest in news and video, and access to mainstream Internet news sources degraded terribly. Television and radio, proven technologies for scaling to serve many viewers and listeners, provided the best window into the events of that fateful day.

When many Internet users try to concurrently access a single resource a separate transmission is required for each and every user. This is the root cause of the scalability challenge. There are a variety of solutions designed to enable scalable access to popular Web resources and rich media events:

— *Multicasting*: This is a technical solution for efficiently propagating real-time transmissions across the Internet infrastructure for many users, conserving bandwidth and ensuring a quality experience for end-users. This is particularly promising for some broadcast-style events. Unfortunately, an inability to consistently implement multicasting capability across all Internet routers renders this solution ineffective for public Internet transmissions. Multicasting is only viable in a managed environment such as an ISP or enterprise network.

— *Load balancing*: Responding to sudden spikes in Web traffic will increasingly be handled by load balancing technology that can dynamically allocate bandwidth across service provider networks. This solution is appropriate for large corporate applications, but the small-scale provider with limited resources is still prone to sudden spikes in traffic that degrade the end-user experience.

— *Caching*: Introduced above as a technology that can enable QoS, caching can also be used to scale Webcasts or popular Web content to serve many concurrent users.

Various Internet Service Providers will seek to implement scaling mechanisms to gain competitive advantage, primarily when aiming offerings at well-funded enterprises; and high-end content providers will continue to seek solutions so long as a profitable bottom line is assured. Unfortunately, at this juncture there is no completely reliable, efficient, and cost-effective solution for one-to-many scaling across the public Internet for all scenarios.

While the openness of the Internet is one of the powerful characteristics of this new communications platform, it has also created an ominous dark side as unscrupulous creator-collaborators wreak havoc on the information and processing capabilities of others. But as the growth and use of the Internet has continued to empower those who work in the dark side of the 'net, we've seen a marked increase in the number and severity of security events, with the costs of these events increasing in terms of time and resources.

Peer-to-peer file sharing programs have provided a new platform for transmission of worm and Trojan horse programs. Denial of service attacks, where many broadband-connected PCs are commandeered to launch a packet attack on an unsuspecting network, have become commonplace. Internet connected devices which feature embedded Web servers, such as printers, are being targeted for disruptive intrusions.

The increase of Internet security intrusions has cast doubt on the suitability of this infrastructure for some of our most important services and interactions. If the Internet is to eventually provide us with broadband Internet everywhere, there must be some assurance that our information and our technologies can remain secure.

During a time of increased terrorism in our society, and of decreasing trust among its global citizenry, the suitability of the Internet for doing business and developing reliable, high quality services is increasingly called into question. When the U.S. government became serious about implementing a separate Internet network, called Govnet, it became clear to me that the mounting security problems of the 'net had reached a new low.

A variety of technologies and mechanisms are being put into place to combat new threats to our use of the Internet. Security monitoring tools, undercover efforts to infiltrate hacker rings, and advanced antivirus programs are among the significant Internet security efforts underway. Secure corporate connections across the public Internet are being proactively implemented using Virtual Private Network (VPN) technology.

The design of the Internet is totally decentralized. It features a collaborative set of network interconnections and is based on voluntary support for standard protocols and services. Any organizational network or ISP anywhere can interconnect and provide new communities with Internet connectivity. Any individual is free to connect to the 'net using any of a number of ISP edge networks. This is clearly one of the most powerful advantages of the Internet.

References

Beniger, James, (1986). *The Control Revolution: Technological and Economic Origins of the Information Society*, Harvard University Press, Cambridge, Mass. 1986.

Bourgault, L. M., (1995). *Mass Media in Sub-Saharan Africa*, Bloomington, Ind. p. 127.

Carrolll, R, L., et al., (1997). "Consonance in Local Television News Program Content: An Examination of Intermarket Diversity", *Journal of Broadcasting and Electronic Media,* Vol. 41, No. 1, Winter, pp. 132–44.

Centerwall, B.S., (1989). "Exposure to television as a cause of violence," in Comstock G., (ed) *Public Communications as Behavior,* Orlando, FL: Academic Press, Inc.

Mander, Jerry, (1977). *Four Arguments for the Elimination of Television,* New York: Morrow.

McLuhan, Marshall, (1964). *Understanding Media: The Extensions of Man,* New York: McGraw-Hill.

7

Role of the Media in Peacebuilding

Information is power and insight can impact on public discourse. This way, perceptions can be changed by access to media. Different types of media are utilised globally to distribute knowledge and idealistically, free mass media is a tool of and signpost for democracy. Freedom of expression is not only the core of a healthy media but also a fundamental human right and vital for a democratic structure. It stands for freedom of speech, the right to information and the representation of different opinions in a heterogeneous society. In any culture of prevention, effective and democratic media are an essential part and indispensable for societies trying to make a transition towards peace and democracy. Harry S. Truman once said "You can never get all the facts from just one newspaper, and unless you have all the facts, you cannot make proper judgements about what is going on"- this statement reflects the need for free access to unbiased information. Not giving people the possibility of political participation and not allowing them to express themselves freely is a significant cause of conflict. On the one hand free, independent and pluralistic media provide a platform for debate and different opinions. On the other hand, media can be misused for propaganda purposes, to incite hatred and spread rumours and therefore artificially create tensions. The transmission of ideas is also not limited to conventional media such as newspapers, TV or radio. Arguably, the traditional media takes primacy in this, however, new technologies, the internet and digital content should also be considered in this context.

Lack of information can, at any stage of a conflict, make people desperate, restless and easy to manipulate. The ability to make informed decisions strengthens societies and fosters economic growth, democratic structures and the positive outlook on the future. For this very reason, the United Nations Millennium Declaration stressed the need "to ensure the freedom of the media to perform their essential role and the right of the public to have access to information".

Journalism does not need justification for its existence. Its service to society is justification in itself. Journalism can not only help to distribute information but also counter hate-speech and create an environment of balanced opinions, an information equilibrium. For the media it can be problematic to find a balance between preventing harm caused by speech and protecting individual expression. Being able to find this balance, however is important especially in conflict situations. Responsible journalism does not just re-publish press releases but is truly concerned with a truthful, balanced and fair account of events. In order to achieve this journalists have to stay clear of judgemental representations and describe reality without embellishment. If democracy is to work properly, society needs access to news and information; analysis of the status quo, debate, practical information and exchange as well as entertainment are needed and provided by the media. The definition of conflict and defining conflict areas is not easy and no two places are alike. Journalists need to know what they can expect on sight in order to define the objectives of their project.

In case of a crisis or a conflict, the international media can attract worldwide attention. The mass media is a pervasive part of daily life especially in industrialised countries and thus able to shine a light on conflicts anywhere in the world. Since most armed conflicts these days have governmental and not territorial reasons; the parties are often concerned with making sure that the majority of people are on "their" side, which bears a lot of potential for misrepresenting facts and trying to seize control over the distribution of information. For this very reason the intervention of unbiased and free global media is important not only for the world public but also for the people directly affected. The number of conflicts, however, that gets international attention is small; therefore local media is vital in this context.

Broadcasting news by using community radios can help reach people in different areas, even with different languages more easily. This way people can be addressed directly and their own personal experiences and lives can be incorporated much better, than with foreign media. The danger of manipulation and inflammation of ethnic tensions, however, cannot be ignored. Another advantage of local media, especially radio is that in border areas it is possible to convey peace messages to passing fighters and refugees alike. Democratic media structures need more than this; it is vital that the use of information within a society is not solemnly passive but that the population gets actively involved in creating content and broadcasting it.

Internal conflicts do not occur spontaneously but tend to have a history. Local media usually have a deeper understanding of the existing political structures, the participants of the conflict as well as the changes preceding the outbreak of violence. The media can therefore not only influence society before the conflict by recognising and properly addressing the issue but also afterwards. Unlike international media covering conflicts, local media are a recognized part of society with the ability to accelerate and magnify fears or reduce them. One should not forget that journalism can play a role in escalating conflicts, which also demonstrates the potential for positive purposes. The media have the power to defuse tensions before they even reach a critical point and keep a critical eye on government, opposition and society. By supplying credible information and reaching a large audience, the media help in managing conflicts and promote democratic principles. In the aftermath of a conflict, reconciliation and societal development can be encouraged as well.

A measure of peace-building can be enhanced peace journalism. Peace journalists try to uncover the causes behind a conflict and true goals of all participants while making sure to humanise all victims of the conflict. The journalists don't try to exploit the loss and suffering but make sure that the reporting is balanced and also demonstrate how easily news can be manipulated. Part of the ethical guidelines for this kind of reporting is to bring out people that use peaceful measures and speak out against war and violence and document the suffering and loss on all sides. Possible solutions and trying to prevent further escalation of the conflict are at the centre of peace journalism as well. A suggested framework used by peace-building media can employ different strategies such as (1) Conflict-sensitive and peace journalism; (2) Peace-promoting entertainment media; (3) Media regulation to prevent incitement of violence, but also (4) Peace-promoting citizen media.

Journalists do not shy away from difficult, sensitive or uncomfortable topics such as human rights abuses. In this context, journalists can be considered the helpers of all human rights defenders for they have committed themselves to ethical and moral standards in reporting as well as to addressing important topics in way that can be productive for everyone involved. Assistance from public opinion is and always has to be the goal of any reporting since without reaching a broad audience that can take action, the effect of the media is limited at best. Therefore non-democratic governments try to harass and persecute journalists in order to keep them in line and prevent them from exposing misconduct and abuse of power. Increasingly this practice can be observed in democratic countries as well and is being heavily criticised. It is noteworthy that despite the fact of democracy being the rule of a majority, a truly democratic framework also demands and ensures that those elected must be accountable. This includes protecting against gender discrimination, protecting the rights of minorities, protecting freedom of speech, and more importantly they do not have the right to justify any transgressions by endorsing new laws.

Media and journalism can be a great assistance in conflict management and peace building. However, the power they have is also limited, as they will never be able to eliminate armed conflicts altogether. The media can be a good tool in a healthy and functioning environment but more is needed than ethical and responsible reporting to ensure lasting peace and safety. The role of the media is twofold: on the one hand, the media report and reflect on pressing issues and can help to question established concepts and ideas. On the other hand, they can be used for propaganda purposes and instead of revealing truths, try to cover things up and by this curtail people's freedom and right to information. Regardless, the potential of the media in conflict and post-conflict situations remains a net positive, and has been sadly underutilized to this point in time.

Media Activities

Media can play an important role in peacebuilding by providing accurate and unbiased information to populations affected by conflicts, and proactively delivering programmes that aim to impact knowledge, attitude and behaviour of the population about different groups and issues related to peacebuilding. Effectively utilizing media in peacebuilding activities requires thorough analysis of the situation, careful planning, and on-going and systematic monitoring and evaluation, as in any other peacebuilding project.

There is a wide variety of actors, including all major donors, international broadcasters and specialised media NGOs, all of whom employ and initiate different approaches and programmes. This kaleidoscope of actors and activities results in a challenge to form a coherent picture. In many countries, the picture becomes further agitated as media projects are run by different organisations and quite often there is no clearing established between their activities. Regarding only the media projects of governments, they are frequently run by different departments or under different programmes.

Media activities can also take the form of objectives, for example the establishment of a free and independent media, and classified as a by-activity aiming at other objectives (anticorruption, strengthening civil society and reviving traditional mediation mechanisms). Therefore, not all the projects with a media component are classified as media projects. Nevertheless, various generalisations can be made about the wide range of activities in the field. They usually comprise one or more of the following areas:

— training (for journalists: professional and issue-based, as well as for media managers),
— media production (news, reports),
— production of specialised programmes (soaps and series),
— support for individual media,
— support for establishing a conducive legal framework (laws, media regulation),
— technical assistance for equipment (printing facilities and transmitters),
— transforming state broadcasters into public service broadcasters,
— promoting coordination and networks among media outlets,
— promoting professional associations,
— security training for journalists,
— legal defence,
— support for audience response systems and media monitoring.

Media Assistance

There are different concepts of media assistance to peacebuilding.

Conflicts Coverage in Western Media

The coverage of conflicts by Western media has an indirect link to peacebuilding as it is a main source of information and opinion building for Western societies, their NGOs and governments. The media have a heavy influence upon the perception of conflicts and thus the ability and readiness to support for peacebuilding initiatives. The reporting of all phases of violent conflicts by Western media has often been criticised as at least inappropriate–if not completely wrong. It has been seen as creating or conveying false images. This is mostly attributed to a lack of professional practice in reporting conflict, which can be seen in the hordes of inexperienced reporters that are sent to crisis regions with hardly any background knowledge.

It is also marked as a usual shortcoming, that Western media only broadcast superficial day-to-day factual news without any strive to highlight background factors or analysing the root causes of the conflict, thus often repeating traditional images and ethnic prejudices of the people involved. Furthermore, the selection of news by Western media focuses on the explosive events of catastrophes and conflict–not on the long slow changes of reconstruction. Good news, such as the progress on reconstruction in post conflict zones, must compete and is often drowned by any catastrophe which might come up during the day.

Some NGOs, political foundations or professional media associations try to open a public debate on the issue of war reporting in Western media. Other initiatives aim at direct improvements. To counter the mere factual reporting and to improve coverage and understanding of conflict issues in the Western world, some organisations and foundations have set up special services.

The media within conflict regions have attracted the attention of donors and NGOs because they have been manipulated to fuel or incite conflicts by broadcasting hate speech and partisan reporting. In general, the role of media for peacebuilding is twofold:

- Professional media by their mere existence can execute a positive influence towards peacebuilding through:
  - providing non-partisan news and reports,
  - informing about different opinions and views (including the views of the "others"),

  - contributing to knowledge (mechanism, people, causes) about politics, local issues and conflictive issues,
  - building well-informed and unbiased opinion,
  - enabling people to take care of and decide on their own issues.
- Professional media are able to contribute additionally towards peacebuilding by addressing issues concerning peace and conflict. This supports
  - improving knowledge of people in peace and conflict relevant issues such as elections, causes of conflict, inter-ethnic understanding, discrimination, truth commissions and war crimes,
  - providing incentives for changing behaviour or attitudes,
  - countering false images or propaganda from biased media,
  - enabling societies to deal with the past and build a common future.

This second role requires the trust of the people in the respective media. Otherwise, it is in danger to be interpreted as poor propaganda and will be either ignored or discredited.

As the usual context of media in peace and conflict is a country or society in violent conflict (latent, ongoing or shortly after the cessation of violence), the role of the media can work along two timeframes: a short- and medium-term perspective, or a long-term perspective. The former refers to initiatives between a few weeks and up to three years, while the latter applies to development sector projects that normally run longer than two or three years. However, there is no exact boundary and a zone of overlapping between these time perspectives.

In the *short- and medium-term* perspective, the role of professional media is mainly to provide non-partisan news, report and analyse context of the conflict and its background factors, gather different views and opinions, focus on specialised peace and conflict issues and prepare the ground for a sound media sector development in the long run.

In the l*ong-term perspective*, the general role of media in democracies comes into focus. This is to establish a sector that provides a free flow of information ensuring that citizens have the opportunity to make responsible informed choices about their future, as well as to provide a watchdog function.

The detailed role media can play in peacebuilding must be determined by the particular conflict setting and the characteristics of the media sector in this society (weak or authoritarian states, different conflict lines, dominance of root or proximate conflict causes, fragmented societies, media control by government or political parties). Under this general umbrella, various activities evolve through different phases.

Activities of Media Assistance

Main activities of media assistance based on various project documents and concept papers. It will aim to provide and review a spectrum of activities and not to produce a list that could be blanketly applied to all situations. The choice of specific activities must be governed by the specific context within which the programme will be applied. This must be determined by a thorough needs analysis and hardcore planning.

Short- and Medium Term Assistance

From the short- and medium-term perspective, media assistance should aim to support peacebuilding activities by:

- providing non-partisan information and balanced news,
- ensuring conditions for receiving and imparting information,
- preventing the incitement of conflict through hate messages,
- assisting victims and refugees,
- creating a platform for all people to voice opinions,
- laying the ground to develop structures for a free and independent media.

The short- and medium perspective is the point where the strict media and peacebuilding focus starts. As a guiding notion, all media activities should be embedded within the overall strategy of peacebuilding, which targets at the root and proximate causes of violence. According to the conflict phase, it is possible to see different needs and detect a variety of possible roles for the media.

Conflict phases

The short- and medium-term approach applies to three conflict phases: pre-conflict, open conflict and post-conflict. Some of the activities described below are general and can occur at all stages of conflict, but in different intensity, some are unique to each phase.

Pre-conflict phase: In a pre-conflict setting (characterised by tensions between rival factions, unrest, weak state and press censorship), most actors agree that the need for greater access to impartial information and human rights information is crucial. Some actors further believe that it is paramount to raise awareness of conflict resolution or transformation mechanisms such as a dialogue processes between the government and the people or re-establishing communication between rival factions. If these needs are met–activities might be very restricted due to the status of the conflict–it might contribute to reducing the intensification of the conflict and prevent violent outbreaks. Media intervention in this phase could provide:

— Research and assessment: Existing news and information sources should be analysed and research efforts directed towards the information needs of the people in conflict areas. Moreover, existing media laws should be reviewed as well as the situation of professional associations.

— Access to non-partisan news: Support is especially needed to provide, or to strengthen, balanced news programming as well as to specialised programming with a focus on human rights, causes of conflict or aimed at promoting mutual understanding, communication and tolerance.

— Media monitoring: In this phase, it might be helpful to establish media monitoring that looks especially at hate messages or other forms of biased reporting and review possible counter measures.

— Training: Training in all aspects (journalism, media research, media law and monitoring) is seen as a support to all these activities.

Open Conflict Phase: In an open conflict situation, the needs and interventions vary according to the intensity of violence and level of conflict. In acute phases (open violence, forced migration, destruction of homes, food insecurity, deterioration, high media regulation), the need for humanitarian information for the vulnerable groups (refugees, IDP) is of the highest priority such as information concerning where and how to get access to shelter, food, water, camps and medicine. As a result, it is crucial to secure information channels by the provision of radios and the investment of transmitters.

The need for balanced reporting, i.e. non-partisan and accurate news, is paramount and, concerning violence inciting messages, might include active hindering or jamming of the broadcasts. In phases of low intensity of violence in the open phase, there might be some additional room for more intense reporting on news stories or peace and conflict orientated programming, for example at the community or local level. This specialised programming includes a variety of different themes, for example support for covering background information on the causes of conflict or examples of traditional reconciliation, and problems of inter-ethnic understanding. Media intervention in this phase should:

— *Continue activities of latent phase*: The activities of the latent phase, such as the research of news and information needs, the media monitoring and the initial support for balanced news, should be continued where possible and appropriate.

— *Attempt to establish non-partisan news and humanitarian information*: Support to local or international media should be provided for dissemination of balanced news and humanitarian information.

— *Provide equipment*: It might be necessary to provide equipment (transmitters, production facilities, radios etc.) as a pre-condition for broadcasting, producing and/or receiving information.

— *Training*: If conditions allow, training in objective reporting, humanitarian reporting and conflictorientated programming should be intensified.

— *Hinder misuse*: Where possible, the hindering or even suppression of the misuse of mass communication for conflict inciting programmes might be appropriate.

— *Support media production*: Support for media production to specialise in peace and conflict-orientated programmes on print media, radio and TV.

Post-conflict (or transition phase): In a post-conflict setting, characterised by implementing peace accords, reconstruction, expanding infrastructure and civil society, relaxing regulation of media, there is the same overall need as in the phase of open conflict. However, the activities can be strongly intensified and focused. As there is a cessation of open violence, there are more opportunities, for example: to systematically establish local media capacity, put higher emphasis on training in conflict areas, support to strengthen the media environment, and build both media pluralism and regulatory framework. In addition to the measures already implemented in the open-conflict phase, the main types of assistance in this post-conflict phase might include:

— *Intensifying support to provision of humanitarian information*: This might comprise the provision of radios, the setting up of transmitters and temporary radio production as well as support to news and other programmes about health, food, activities of relief organisations and humanitarian law.

— *Intensifying support to non-partisan news services and independent reporting*: After the termination of violent conflict, support for non-partisan news services is of high priority. This may take various forms; many prefer to give support to local media, for example with the provision of equipment to start or re-establish production after conflict, or to extend coverage and enhance quality of production. The exchange between local media actors also needs support. If local media cannot fully do this, it might be necessary to fund international broadcasters to bring or to extend news to particular regions.

— *Intensifying training*: Training plays a major role, especially for the development of local media capacity. It covers training in non-partisan reporting, awareness of international law, in humanitarian programming and initial media management.

— *Targeted peacebuilding initiatives*: Specialised programmes and productions can be a useful tool to counter misconceptions, build confidence (radio forums), promoting dialogue (radio drama), facilitate communication (call in listeners), and propose options and solutions to the conflict (report series). Soap operas encouraging inter-ethnic understanding, cross-border communication, and conflict resolution are special tools that are the task of special drama writers than journalists. Training may cover conflictive or contentious issues; there is a wide range of themes, such as elections, constitutional review, land ownership, implementation of peace accord, poverty, inter-ethnic understanding, corruption, minorities and truth commissions.

— *Starting efforts for a free and independent media sector*: This comprises support for regulatory frameworks, to initiate support in building associations or establishing a community media development strategy.

The following summarises the phasing of these possible activities. The considered as a menu of options. What is appropriate to the situation on the ground and what should/can be realised, should be decided by a proper analysis of the:

— conflict setting,
— media situation,
— "fitting" of media activities into the overall strategy for peacebuilding,
— actual needs of the population in the media sector.

Criteria for Suspension: From a donor's perspective, there should be some hard criteria in place to decide under which circumstances or conditions media activities are definitely excluded from the menu of options for external assistance. To my own knowledge, only a few donors have developed these criteria.

Long-term Assistance

The long-term perspective of media assistance applies to the development situation, which starts sometime after the post-conflict phase, when intensity of conflict has come down to levels which allow for reconstruction and continuous development efforts. Since support for strengthening democracies has become a core activity of almost all "development" efforts, objectives for media in the long-term have been defined and mostly agreed upon. These are:

— free flow of information ensures that citizens make responsible, informed choices rather than acting out of ignorance or misinformation,
— information serves a "checking or watchdog function" by ensuring that elected representatives do their job according to democratic rules.

In this ideal view, free, pluralistic and independent media are an intermediate result that serves the final objective of a fully functioning and fledged democracy with a "politically active civil society". Thus media, once directed or overtly controlled by state or government, should become a diverse, open sector that provides different views and has a degree of editorial independence that serves the public interest. The goal is to have a range of various credible voices and a sector that promotes such outlets. This long-term approach can be applied either as a continuation of the media assistance in post-conflict phase or as media assistance within development cooperation in countries where no former violent conflict has taken place.

Areas of Media Activities

There are five areas of media activities in the long-term perspective. Some country programmes undertake a combination of all five areas thereby ensuring a mix of activities with higher probability of having an impact.

For political or other restrictions it is also possible to work only in one or two of the following areas with optimism of impact.

— *Shaping and improving the legal enabling environment*: This approach comprises two elements: first, dealing with the laws and regulations for the media sector, second, other legal restrictions which affect the sensitive issues as the freedom of expression. This option deals with free access to information, government control, licensing procedures for electronic media, media-government relations, regulatory bodies, Codes of Practice, complaints, anti-monopoly-regulations, laws regarding libel, slander, contempt and copyright.

— *Strengthening the media sector and its environment*: This approach aims to promote a working media environment. This is characterised by not only effective media law, but also the existence of media watchdogs, research institutes, think-tanks, advocacy organisations and professional associations, press councils and networks. This includes all efforts to establish common effective training facilities, open to the whole media sector.

— *Removing barriers to access and other obstacles*: Access for information is one of the first requirements for a participative democracy. However, there are many more barriers than legal obstacles. Economic barriers create weak distribution channels, especially outside urban areas; consequently, it is a valid aim to support more efficient distribution systems. Decentralisation of media might be appropriate to reach a wider audience–community radios can be an alternative source of information. Additionally, all measures for improving the economic viability of media further eases access. Improvement of regulations in the advertising market or the enhancement of advertising by for example media monitoring comes into attention.

— *Supporting individual media to be more effective*: This option aims at enabling individual media institutions to provide better output and to become increasingly economically viable. The objective is to promote good quality media output which is relevant and useful to the audience and which allows the expression of a full range of opinions on matters of public concern. This requires well-trained managers as well as professional journalists aware of the needs of their audiences. This area includes support for individual media to clarify their strategies, for choosing the appropriate infrastructure and equipment, providing skills and management training, implementation of audience research systems. Further supporting this, all forms of individual training will contribute largely to the aim of this area.

— *Reform of public service media*: The reform of state broadcasters into public service media can be seen as an area in its own right or as a combination of the efforts within reform laws and supporting individual media.

This long-term approach is clearly aiming at establishing media as a pillar for a functioning democracy. By fulfilling this goal, it will contribute to peacebuilding in itself. However, it should be borne in mind, that free, independent and pluralistic media must remain an ongoing objective that will be a struggle of every day–even in the countries with developed democracies, the ethics of journalism are in danger or they cost money and need to be defended against market forces, pure commercial interests and political intentions. Only a few specialised peacebuilding elements are necessary within this long-term perspective–for example media monitoring, especially in the case of suspicion that the country enters a new "latent" phase. Generally, a fully developed media system should be sufficiently equipped to inform its audience about the contentious issues to be addressed.

Media intervention in short- and medium term phase, especially in the post-conflict phase, has a direct link to the long-term media assistance, which normally runs under "good governance" or "strengthening democracy". Therefore, activities in short-term media assistance to peacebuilding must be coherent with the long-term objectives as the postconflict phase prepares the ground for an efficient media system. For example, the shortterm decisions in legal questions (media law, media regulations) must hold in mind the long-term goal of media pluralism as well as of an economically viable sector.

There might be contradictions between these short- and long-term goals if, for example, there is only one critical voice opposing the government in the actual post-conflict phase. In this situation, it would be better to support one opposition media outlet rather than none at all. However, caution should be exercised in order to prevent a monopoly that is artificially sustained by donor funds. In the case of a former state monopoly accessing major sources of funds for its transformation into a public-service broadcaster, measures must be undertaken with the view that other private media will not be suffocated.

Furthermore, the new publicservice broadcaster needs to be prevented from being taken over by old or new political factions. Concerns similar to this may have convinced some donors to avoid funding single media outlets and to increase investment for media sector support. Researcher on the media situation and intervention in the Balkans, media freedom in many instances cannot be fully installed in one package. In particular situations, content regulation (prevention of incendiary propaganda, zero tolerance to hate speech) must be in the short-term much stricter than in a normal, democratic society. In his view, it also needs careful consideration, whether media should be completely liberalised and left to the market economy in the post-conflict phase or if there should be a set of public institutions. Again, it depends on the concrete conflict analysis and the assessment of the media situation in the respective country what to do to ensure coherence between the short- and long-term activities.

Contentious Issues

As media assistance for peacebuilding is a new field, many issues require further discussion to be clarified.

Role of Journalists

In many activities of media assistance for peacebuilding, journalists play a major role. They are involved in providing or receiving training, conducting enquiries, writing news, analysis and background stories or participating in the design of programmes. There is a common consensus that the "products" of journalists, especially in media assistance within short-term peacebuilding, are generally:

- news and other forms of reports,
- analysis and background information,
- specialised products in peace and conflict issues, such as:
    - print series about elections, or constitutional review,
    - programmes on dealing with the past and war crimes,
    - reports on causes of conflicts (poverty, land distribution, corruption),
    - practical questions like de-mining or de-militarisation.

In practice, there is an ongoing discussion if conventional professional journalism can contribute sufficiently to fulfil the above-mentioned tasks, especially in violent conflict settings, or if it requires alternative roles and approaches. There are mainly two contradictory points of view: professional journalism versus alternative forms of journalism.

Professional journalism

According to received understanding, the role of professional journalists is to:

— provide non-partisan information,
— support opinion building,
— gather different views and opinions,
— provide background information and in-depth analysis.

By increasing the overall knowledge of the consumers, it will enhance them to make decisions about their issues. This should contribute to change their attitudes towards open debates on contentious issues and, consequently, support transforming conflicts into a nonviolent tackling of issues. According to the supporters of professional journalism, this role as outlined above is highly efficient, if fully realised. It should be kept as it is and not be weakened by other commitments than to be "neutral" or "non-partisan" in the sense of gathering the views of all sides, if possible, thus enabling the audience to build their own point of view.

It must be seen, and this has been previously mentioned, that this is an ideal concept–more a kind of a promise than a reality. It is a continuous challenge for journalists; they must fulfil it every day. Sometimes, they do; other times, they do not. Therefore, this concept cannot be seen as a status that has been reached, it is more a process that should be followed daily.

Alternative journalism

The above-described role of professional journalists has been criticised by researchersas well as former professional journalists. According to the critics, it fails in war and conflict situations because of:

— keeping the myth of objectivity,
— maintaining the attitude of not taking sides,
— being neutral in a conflict situation,
— reporting just factual news on the waging of war,
— avoiding to raise the causes of war,

— omitting insights of the victims of war,

— lacking responsibility for the outcome of its reporting.

As an alternative, it is recommended to modify journalism into an approach which the founders call "peace journalism", characterised by its orientation to an intended outcome. Journalists of this type are supposed to report on the background of conflicts, have the perspective of the vulnerable groups, seek "stories which maximise the chance for peacebuilding", and get out "messages crafted to foster peaceful resolution of conflict". Finally, journalism will be "intended outcome programming" designed for transforming attitudes, promoting reconciliation, putting the conflicting sides together for resolution. Others claim additional roles for journalists, namely as facilitators in conflict resolution. They maintain a duty for journalists to use their potential for mediation between conflicting parties.

There is no doubt that the supporters of peace *journalism* and *journalism of attachment* have some valid points in their critique of the coverage conflicts by Western media, especially regarding the selection of news (bad news versus good news), the limitation of space and airtime for background reporting or the sometimes poor and superficial factual reporting. However, the stance as a whole remains somewhat dubiousand questionable.

In short, both stances acknowledge the shortcomings of the practice of professional journalism but differ in how they can be addressed. For professional journalism, these shortcomings are only the "usual" differences between the ideal and reality. This gap should be closed by adapting practice closer to the concept. For alternative journalism, the shortcomings are failures immanent to the system that cannot be cured unless a new form of journalism is adopted–for example outcome oriented peace journalism. Nevertheless, it needs to be clarified if the proclaimed "alternative" forms of journalism can maintain and uphold their claims.

Impact of Media Assistance on Peacebuilding

Contrary to the intensity of the debate on the role of journalist, there is hardly any discussion on the effects or impact of media interventions on the peacebuilding process and conflict.

Models of Media Impact

Currently, a very simple model of media's impact is *implicitly* applied in the sector of media in peace and conflict: a stimulus (message, news) causes an immediate direct effect (hate, violence, understanding). However, it is common knowledge of media research that this simple stimulus-response model does not work sufficiently to predict the results of campaigns/ messages or to explain effects of daily media consumption. Taking into consideration the individual reactions and choices of consumers, more complex models are currently used to deepen knowledge about media's impact. However, they are up to now rarely applied to the field of media in peace and conflict, which might be even more difficult as there are different cultural settings and values.

Only some programmes are supported by social research for example soap operas work with a more complex model. Soap operas create various positive role models for the viewers. However, media project design is frequently conducted on the grounds of the "reverse" assumption alone: the opposite to what is assumed to have worked for inciting hate and conflict is supposed to work in the same way–only with the opposite/positive impact-to foster reconciliation or peace. However, this is at least questionable.

Attitude and behaviour changes, such as a move towards greater tolerance or inter-ethnic understanding, would appear to be more difficult to achieve than spreading a hate message, which in a particular situation might immediately provoke violent acts. It is still not well known, what is required for a sustainable contribution to peacebuilding via media. It seems therefore appropriate to conduct and encourage more research on the whole question of impact (chains and attribution, indicators and measurement) in order to improve design and implementation of media assistance in this field.

Various NGOs have already begun investing more research on these questions, for example the recent programme evaluations by Search for Common Ground in Liberia and in Burundi. The question of impactwas addressed by audience surveys and interviews with key informants. The report confirms an overall impact on peacebuilding, saying that "Studio Ijambo [a major radio programme in Burundi] has contributed to creating a new vocabulary of peaceful coexistence, dialogue and negotiation in the country". However, the report does not provide indicators for measurement and data on the extent of this impact.

It is necessary to be aware of the limited effects of media. In pre- or post-conflict settings, media are not able to change the underlying causes of conflict. The uneven distribution of land, jobs and income might be, for example, an issue of intense reporting, but cannot be altered by the media, only by other means. Nevertheless, media can create adverse effects. Intense reporting can provoke revenge or inciting a new outbreak of violence. This needs careful consideration by editors, broadcasters and donors. Support to media therefore needs to be integrated into a coherent peacebuilding strategy.

Actors and Activities

It would have afforded more time for research to address important questions such as the conceptual differences between various donors and to determine the factors for differentiation. To conduct such a research, it is necessary to undertake a review that clarifies which projects contain media elements, considers their underlying assumptions and hypotheses on impact chains, assesses results and draws conclusions on best practices.

Donors

Governmental donors

United Kingdom–Department for International Development (DfID): The United Kingdom is one of the few donors that places strong emphasis on media development. DfID sees media as a core activity in the field of good governance, and its "Conflict and Humanitarian Affairs" department is trying to develop the subject of media and peacebuilding. For both issues, DfID has produced two leading documents. DfID has participated in many of the well-known projects in media and peacebuilding such as:

— Talking Drums Studio in Liberia (news and soap opera radio production), with Search for Common Ground (SfCG),

— Nashe Maalo in Macedonia (TV series, soap opera style)–also with SfCG,

— Soul City in South Africa (TV, radio and print)–support for independent media,

— BBC Great Lakes Lifeline Service–providing impartial news,

— BBC World Service–Radio New Home, new Life in Afghanistan,

— Operation SPEAR–Albania, Macedonia, Kosovo–provision of humanitarian Information with Media Action International.

A look into the current project list shows that DfID is engaged in a wide range of countries from Sierra Leone to Bangladesh, implementing and funding a broad variety of activities.

— training,
— launching radio stations–impartial news,
— equipment for setting or upgrading stations,
— support for or the transformation into public service broadcasters (Kosovo RTK),
— funding Schools of Journalism, press houses,
— regulatory institutions concerned with media law (licensing),
— special programming towards peace and conflict issues.

Their approach cannot be strictly divided into peace and conflict-related projects and projects for long-term media assistance. An approximate calculation of the total project budget can be placed at £22.5m. (€36.0m.). However, it is not indicated for how many years.

Denmark–FRESTA Programme and DANIDA: Denmark has also a focus on media. The Danish Foreign Ministry has launched the Danish Programme for Peace and Stability (FRESTA). It clearly sees regional collaboration as its key priority. Its fundamental idea is to build civil society networks across national or ethnic boarders. In these networks, people will cooperate because this cross-boundary collaboration is the approach to overcome misunderstandings and ethnically driven enemy images and stereotypes. Through these measures, it aims to promote conflict prevention and democratic development in four segments of civil society: human rights, media, youth and refugees.

At present, FRESTA concentrates on South Eastern Europe. *In the period 1999 to 2003, €8.3m. were dedicated to media projects.* FRESTA funds the Public Broadcasters Network, Network of Local Media Associations and the South East European Network for Professionalisation of the Media (SEENPM; which is co-funded from the Swiss Development Cooperation (SDC)). The SEENPM is engaged in training (election reporting, media management, investigative journalism, reporting diversity, human rights) and the collaboration of regional media and press centres. Cross-cutting activities (refugee radio network, repatriation, human rights) complement the programme. FRESTA implements these programmes with other Danish institutions such as the Danish School of Journalism and the Baltic Media Centre.

In development cooperation (DANIDA), Denmark stresses democratisation and respect for human rights, and their links to peacebuilding: "Denmark's development policy will promote good governance and administrative practices free of corruption as an essential element in the creation of pro-poor growth and in fostering stable societies that possess effective mechanisms for peaceful resolution of conflicts." The development of a free press is considered as a means to achieve these objectives.

Switzerland: Switzerland's media assistance is funded mainly by the Swiss Development Cooperation (SDC), the development cooperation division of the Foreign Ministry, and by the political departments (PA IV) of the same ministry. As media are not a core activity of SDC in the Balkans, media are funded under "conflict prevention" as a main activity. The regional projects are within the framework of the Stability Pact.

An approximate calculation demonstrates that *Switzerland invests €4.2m. (6.4m. CHF) in the current 1 year* period for media assistance. Thereof €3.3m. (4.9m. CHF) comes from SDC, and the remaining €950,000 (1.4m. CHF) comes from PA IV. In comparison to other donor organisations or countries, this amount is already quite substantial for a small country like Switzerland.

Germany: Up to now, Germany's Ministry of Development Cooperation (BMZ) has no media focus, mainly because media projects have been outsourced. This is due to a strategic decision to omit "government sensitive" issues such as media from official development aid. These were undertaken by the political foundations, which are funded by the government, but still have more a non-governmental character. Due to financial restrictions, the foundations have reduced their engagement in media.

On the other hand, the Foreign Ministry has developed some major activities in media. Within the framework of the Stability Pact, Germany is funding 63 projects in South Eastern Europe with a volume of €3.4m. in 2002. There are many different implementing agencies, mostly German radio and TV producers. Activities range from training, provision of equipment, and programme cooperation to workshops and seminars. Officially, there is no special focus or concept for these media initiatives besides "support for development of democracy".

New initiatives will be launched in Afghanistan (€1.1m.) and for the European-Islamic dialogue (€2.3m.). This adds up to €6.7m. (10.1m. CHF) in 2002 for media projects in conflict-related regions.

US Government–USAID: The US Government is funding media activities generally through its Agency for International Development (USAID). Large funding for long-term transition, including media assistance, has been channelled through their regional offices. For conflict-regions, there is the Office for Transition Initiatives (OTI), which belongs to the USAID Bureau for Democracy, Conflict and Humanitarian Assistance. The OTI mission is to assist local partners advance peace and democracy in conflict-prone countries, by providing fast, flexible short-term assistance targeted at key transition needs. The strategy paper "OTI Guide to programme Options in Conflict Prone Settings" of September 2001, outlines major activities:

— expanding democratic political processes (election, civil society, good governance),
— building citizen security (police reform, mine awareness, military),
— promoting reconciliation (human rights processes, conflict management),
— supporting peace negotiations (advisors, peace initiatives).

In this setting, media play a major cross-cutting role in all stages of a conflict–before, during and post-conflict. The media have a two-fold approach:

— *classical news journalism* provides neutral factual information, multiple viewpoints, opinions, thus encouraging people to decide on their own, and keeps the watchdog function to government
— *campaigning* for peace or other important messages of public interest (election, anticorruption)

OTI recommends gaining local media professionals who are willing to work with USAID and to fund broad-scale national media campaigns to accelerate democratic transition. Here is one major difference in protocol to that of other donors. To my knowledge, no other donor provides explicitly strict guidelines what kind of messages should be transferred to the audience and always claims visibility as a priority. Other donors, for example Sweden and the Netherlands, rely upon the local media to find their own way on how to reach their audience and what kind of "messages" fit with the cultural setting.

OTI's country programmes in Croatia, Serbia and Montenegro, Indonesia, East Timor and Kosovo included large media components, for example voter campaign in Croatia, voter education in Indonesia, independent alternative media in Bosnia, Serbia and Montenegro, including provision of technical equipment. In Liberia, OTI was co-funding Star Radio and Talking Drums Studio; in Rwanda, it focuses on giving information on the proceedings of the International Criminal Tribunal for Rwanda. In Angola, OTI funded Voice of America radio programming.

OTI is currently funding activities in Afghanistan (€16.5m. in 2002), East Timor (€10.0m.), Indonesia (€4.0m.), Burundi (€2.0m.), Democratic Republic of Congo (€4.0m.), Zimbabwe (€3.0m.), Macedonia (€7.0m.), Serbia and Montenegro (€10.0m.) and Peru (€7.0m.). There is no breakdown of which proportion of these funds were dedicated to media assistance. In former years, OTI has heavily funded the Balkans. In other countries (not covered by the OTI programme, due to conflict status), assistance to independent media is given by the USAID regional or country offices. For example, strengthening independent media is held as a priority in Kazakhstan, Kyrgyzstan, Tajikistan and Uzbekistan.

Another institution, involved with media assistance is the Centre for Democracy and Governance, which belongs to the USAID–Bureau for Global Programmes. It has a supporting role in designing and implementing democracy strategies. In 1999, it has elaborated a Strategy Paper, "The Role of Media in Democracy: A Strategic Approach", recently is has co-financed the study, "The Enabling Environment for Free and Independent Media" and is working with the World Bank to broaden donor interest in media assistance.

Sweden: Sweden was one of the first countries to give culture (of which media is a part) a special position in governmental development cooperation. In the nineties, Swedish support media has expanded. Already in 1995, the Swedish Development Agency (SIDA) had published a strategy for their media assistance.

It recommends a strong focus on protecting freedom of speech by supporting the reform of legislation, contributing research, making freedom of action possible for journalists and the media, and supporting networks between journalists. Media support is seen as an integral part for the promotion of democracy and human rights. The specific goals are "to support the development journalism in order to ensure that the general public has access to information and the social debate." It is stated clearly that media activities are crucial for good governance. For this objective, SIDA aims to:

— stimulate the growth and vitality of media that are characterised by pluralism, and

— promote the growth and vitality of individual media.

It therefore supports:

— media organisations which work for freedom of speech,

— local media which contribute to diversity and pluralism and which extend popular influence,

— the education of journalists,

— public service activities with a focus on the radio and film media.

SIDA's contribution to media assistance in general has been *approximately €9.3m. (87.0m. SEK) in 2001. This* includes media activities from the Eastern Europe Department and from the Department of Democracy and Human Rights. Sweden supports organisations like the Panos Institute, International Freedom of Expression eXchange (IFEX). A regional focus is the Balkans. A total of €5.4m. are budgeted for media activities the Balkans over a two year period. Includes the funds for the Swedish Helsinki Committee.

To some extent only, media projects were started to be seen as contributing peacebuilding, as SIDA supports some organisations with explicit conflict-related projects (Panos Institute in West Africa, media training in Sierra Leone with IFEX and Canadian Journalists for Free Expression CJFE). For example, the projects with the Institute for War and Peace Reporting are listed under a "conflict management perspective". These media projects add up to €2.0m. and are classified according to the status of the conflict and to the type of intervention in the conflict.

Netherlands: The Foreign Ministry of the Netherlands has also stressed the role of good governance and democracy in their development assistance programmes. Civil society must be allowed to develop. Government must tolerate, if not foster, an enabling environment as part of good governance. Freedom of association is seen as a clear condition. No less important, however, is access to sufficient, independent resources, and channels of communication, unrestricted information, scope for negotiation and independent bodies to settle disputes. In this manner, freedom of expression and development of free and independent media play a vital role.

The Dutch government has given media activities a high ranking position on the agenda for good governance and has fostered many media initiatives. The "Memorandum on the Promotion of Platforms for Independent Broadcasting in Africa", published in March 2002 can be seen as an example for its strategy: On the one hand, it demonstrates a less restrictive (European?) style of approach, which states, "Dutch policy on communication and development is geared to strengthening ownership and demand orientation.

This means that the media organisations in developing countries take responsibility for themselves for programme identification, management and execution. Within the framework of the agreed policy, the actors involved set priorities..." While on the other, it states that the Dutch policy acknowledges and understands the importance of independent media as well as wanting to support the media structure.

The Memorandum states that the Dutch government intends to continue its support for African media initiatives with a new emphasis on strengthening national and regional media platforms. This decision means that the Dutch government will focus its support not on stimulating a single platform but on the development of multiple networks which could ultimately result in an African platform. Their focus can also been deduced from the Memorandum's list of the major problems of media in Africa:

— no responsible media policy,
— restrictive legislation upon the media,
— lack of converting state media into independent broadcasters,
— poor quality of media.

The main points of Dutch media policy in Africa are:

— creating media platforms for consultation between government, public and private media,
— supporting press councils, observatories, regulatory bodies,
— promoting a free media culture.

The Ministry sees a growing role that media can play in contributing to peacebuilding and the prevention of renewed conflict. As the specific role of the media is often less known and not always transparent, the Netherlands has recently convened a conference on the role of the media in conflict prevention and peacebuilding. This focused on a discussion about "Peace Journalism" and the proposal to have worldwide Media Monitoring with the focus on Early Warning in order to detect and to prevent similar cases like Rwanda.

Dutch funds to media assistance have been substantive, although they can only be estimated. In 1995, Dutch media assistance through NGO and bilateral channels has already amounted to €13.0m. (28.0m. hfl.) In 2001, assistance for media in Africa was around €7.0m., according to the Ministry roughly the same amount was given to the Balkans. As the rest of the regions has received only small amounts in media projects, total media assistance is estimated at €15.0m. in 2001.

Multilateral donors

European Union: Conflict-related media projects of the European Union (EU) are funded under the programme "*European Initiative for Democracy and Human Rights*" (EIDHR). Programming and conceptualisation for EIDHR are supervised under the EC's Directorate General for External Relations. Appraisal, implementing, and monitoring of projects is conducted by Europe Aid–a unit for implementing assistance programmes.

EIDHR has several budget lines; the most important segments are "promotion and protection of human rights" (€20.0m. in 2001), "support for democratisation" (€19.4m.) and "prevention of conflict and dealing with the consequences of conflict" (€5.9m.). A special budget line covers the "rehabilitation centres for the victims of torture" inside and outside the EU (€12.0m.). Additionally, there are urgent projects identified by the EC for specific objectives. These "targeted" projects amounted to €36.0m. in 2001. Media projects fall under various segments, mostly "support for democratisation and protection of human rights".

World Bank: In the perspective of the World Bank, the media have just recently started to play a major role. This is due to their contribution to growth and the positive relation between free and independent media and World Bank goals such as market development and institutional change. The World Development Report 2002 stresses that competition between the media, access to public information and broadening the media's reach are essential. The Report compiles the newest data and derives recommendations how to ensure the framework conditions for developing an independent high quality media sector.

From a conflict perspective, the World Bank's efforts have been driven by the concept that reconstruction serves for conflict solving. The Bank's

Conflict Prevention and Reconstruction Unit deals with projects of the Post-Conflict Fund. Various projects were given grants–from transitional support strategies to demilitarisation, employment for displaced women, rehabilitation of the health sector and community development.

UNESCO: Media and communication belong to the core activities of United Nation Educational, Scientific and Cultural Organisation (UNESCO). Besides its political initiatives, UNESCO funds the development of independent and pluralistic media by a special programme; the International Programme for the Development of Communication (IPDC). Since 1980, more than nine hundred projects were funded, among others various news agencies, independent newspapers, community radio stations and multimedia centres, TV channels and public service broadcasters. Various training programmes were established as well as special approaches for women, youth media education and research.

IPDC is funded by voluntary contributions of UN members, and the special fund-in-trust to attract resources from countries that want to support domestic initiatives. It is reported that many donor countries are withdrawing from these multilateral projects. Therefore, funds for UNESCO are becoming scarce. In 2001, IPDC had to declare a moratorium for already approved projects, the moratorium has been lifted recently in April 2002; the budget for 2001 was €2.4m. for projects and assistance secretariat.

IPDC has decided on reforms of its working methods, adopting established priorities of IPDC, professionalising approval, preparation of projects and improving transparency. A new procedure has been announced regarding evaluation of terminated projects by independent consultants. Additionally, UNESCO has created the "Information for all Programme" for funding ICT initiatives. For peace and conflict related issues and conflict-prone regions, UNESCO has created "UNESCO SOS Media", a programme of emergency assistance to help in reconstruction, mainly by expanding access to non-partisan information and promoting diversity during and post-conflict.

The programme started in 1992 in former Yugoslavia. After the 1995 Dayton Accords, UNESCO switched form emergency help to building infrastructure for media and long-term diversity, its emergency operations were then extended to Rwanda and Burundi, and in 1998 to Angola and Indonesia. These activities are wide ranging including: provision of equipment, training, and establishment of TV stations and radio production centres. The total funds of UNESCO SOS Media is €9.2m. (€490,000 came from Switzerland). Numerous international organisations and NGOs have given their support to the UNESCO SOS Media programme.

UNESCO has also fostered cooperation and knowledge sharing among those concerned with media in conflict regions. The UNESCO Round on Media in conflict areas, held on the occasion of World Press Freedom Day 2000, in Geneva in May 2000 has given recommendations for future actions in this field. The list of recommendations refers to situations where the international community intervenes in a conflict or post-conflict situation. The list stresses the fulfilment of clear priority to support the international community, independent local media, both private media or public service media, establishment of the rule of the law, consultation with NGOs, and coordination of donor efforts.

It highlights that any entity set up by an Inter-Governmental Organisation (IGO) should function *ab initio* as an independent public service broadcaster and that IGOs themselves should set an example in respect for the rule of law in their own actions. It recommends to work out a specific strategy for restructuring the media and to develop an agreed handbook with general principles and defining the main strategic choices that must be made in media assistance in conflict regions.

Stability Pact: The Stability Pact, founded in June 1999, is a political declaration of commitment and a framework agreement on international cooperation to develop a shared strategy for stability and growth in South East Europe. However, it is not an international organisation nor does it have its own independent financial resources. In the Stability Pact, more than 40 partner countries (EU, G8, Norway and Switzerland, countries of SEE) and organisations (UN, OSCE, World Bank, IMF, regional initiatives) are committed to foster peace, conflict prevention, democracy and economic prosperity. The EU, including its member states, has a leading role and is the most important donor.

The Stability Pact acts in three Working Tables. Working deals with Democratisation and Human Rights and focuses on four priority areas:

— inter-ethnic dialogue and cross-border cooperation,

— refugee matters,

— media,

— education and youth.

As media is one priority area, a Media Task Force (MTF) was built–a collaborative effort of donors, NGOs and recipient countries. It adopted the Charter for Media Freedom and a Strategy for Media Assistance. By cooperating with media professionals and state authorities (within National Working Groups of seven SEE-countries), MTF works to provide assistance to the development of free, independent, professional and diverse media in SEE. Its activities are determined by the phases of conflict in context, which it has categorised into actual conflict, post-conflict, and rehabilitation phases. Generally, the MTF has four main areas of activity:

— implementing the Charter of Media Freedom by cooperating with State Authorities,

— designing a comprehensive strategy for media assistance to ensure a common focus of donors,

— stimulating targeted support to media development,

— generating carefully selected projects.

In the first funding phase of Stability Pact (March 2000), 33 media projects were funded with *€20.1m.* to run over long-term periods. For the period 2001-2004, a new Strategy for Media Assistance has been adopted. It summarises problems, objectives and areas of action very concisely.

It states that the major problems facing the media in SEE are: political influence, economic dependence, lack of sound journalism training, weak professional structures and an unfinished legislative framework. The document identifies principle objectives:

— a legislative framework,

— relevant institutions are solid, independent and indispensable,

— raised journalistic professionalism,

— balanced coverage of ethnic and religious minorities,

— survival of private media with proven track record and continuation of their work,

— long-term consistent assistance for initiatives that will benefit the media as a whole.

Areas of action are:

— laws and regulation,
— transformation of state to public media,
— support to private and independent media (conditional),
— regional cooperation,
— professionalism (training, universities, institutes, job contracts),
— minorities,
— content (quality),
— archives.

The Strategy Paper and the Action Plans for Bosnia-Herzegovina, Serbia and Croatia contain a thorough analysis of the political situation as well as of the media sector, assess achievements, formulate priorities, detect obstacles and give recommendation for future action. As the Stability Pact has no independent financial resources, all programmes will realise that some donors have already cut or are in the process of withdrawing funds from SEE. This will result in less support, especially from donors like USAID, the World Bank, and Soros Foundation. Not all the media that have been supported, will receive further help. Therefore, there is a process of identifying the quality media that deserve continued support. Much more scrutiny will be placed on projects and on assessing feasibility and viability of individual media.

The Council of Europe, one of the first European institutions, founded in 1949, is an intergovernmental organisation of more than forty countries, working in the area of human rights, culture and social development. Under its Directorate for Human Rights, a Media Division was established. It deals mostly with: legislative reform, implementing laws and training (freedom of expression). In the nineties, the Council has focused its assistance to its priority areas SEE, CIS (Russia, Ukraine, Belarus) and the South Caucasus. Its programmes are implemented with governments or NGOs.

Political foundations play a major role in media assistance. In Europe, the Open Society Foundation is one of the most important.

Open Society Foundation

The Open Society Institutes (OSI) of the Soros Network Foundation has provided aid to independent media in many post-communist countries. Overall sums of their commitment in the media sector are not available, but it is clear that large sums have been spent.

Implementing Agencies

Media assistance is often implemented by the wide variety of specialised media international or national NGOs and professional associations.

International Agencies and NGOs

Institute for War and Peace Reporting (IWPR): The London-based IWPR, founded 1992, is specialised both in intensive reporting on conflict and humanitarian issues, and in journalist training. Through its emphasis on training, it transfers professional skills to countries in conflict and thereby raising the level of quality reporting. The news and reports are published nationally and internationally on the IWPR's website (allowing free downloads) and as a result, it provides Western media with an alternative source of obtaining reports on conflict regions. The training is very strict and focuses on guidelines for styles of writing and editing by international experts.

IWPR also monitors the media in conflict regions thus adding to the political debate. Over the years, it has extended the geographical reach from the Balkans to crisis zones in the former Soviet Union and Central Asia. Currently, it is undertaking projects in Afghanistan, the Balkans, Caucasus and Central Asia. A special focus is their permanent regular reporting on the proceedings of the International Criminal Tribunal for former Yugoslavia (ICTY). The IWPR is staffed by around 20 personnel in London and a further 20 in various regional bureaus. One of the major donors is SIDA and cooperation partners include Media Action International in Afghanistan.

Search for Common Ground (SfCG): The US-based organisation, founded 1982, and its European arm European Center for Common Ground, Brussels, is a conflict resolution NGO. Its "toolbox" has various parts that work with media and SfCG has become one of the leading producers of television and radio programmes for the reduction or prevention of violent conflict.

Baltic Media Centre (BMC): The Baltic Media Centre, founded in 1993, is an independent NGO that supports democratic development and promotes peaceful international cooperation through the active participation of the media. It is funded primarily through the Danish government. It provides training, consultancies and legal advice for radio, TV, production companies and print media. The regional focus has been expanded from the Baltic States to include Russia, South East Europe, Asia and Africa. Their focus is: institution building (associations, networks, transforming state into public broadcasters), raising professionalism (training), supporting media policy (democratic media policy, legislation) and programme cooperation (with all kinds of media, state, commercial, and grassroots).

BMC participates in the FRESTA programme of Danish government and runs the "Good Morning Afghanistan" news service radio in Afghanistan funded by the EU. Its budget for 2001 was €3.8m. The staff is comprised of 18 personnel in Denmark and 20 in the specific regions.

Swiss-based NGOs

Media Action International (MAI): Media Action International, based in Geneva, has evolved out of the International Centre for Humanitarian Reporting (ICHR) and specialises in setting up humanitarian information programmes in conflict- or disaster-prone regions and countries. Media Action International highlights information as a fundamental human right for the recipients. It requires all organisations engaged in humanitarian operations to incorporate an information policy with the affected civilians in order to fulfil their obligation to communicate with the population they are assisting.

MAI criticizes international agencies that are more interested in providing information to improve their profile and visibility rather than imparting information to the population. MAI was one of the first NGOs bringing forward the idea of using media for development as well as for conflict prevention and peacebuilding. MAI has worked intensively in Afghanistan (Radio Education for Afghan Children, with BBC), Kosovo, Albania, Macedonia (youth and humanitarian information programmes, SPEAR), Mozambique (flood victims) and Africa (Lifeline Media).

Medienhilfe: Medienhilfe, founded in 1992 in Zurich as "Medienhilfe Ex-Jugoslawien", is an NGO supporting independent media in the Balkans. These media are seen as important pillars in the fight against authoritarian regimes and as agents for democratic change and interethnic understanding. Medienhilfe has the concept that media should be more than news and information providers. Additionally they should be quasi-NGOs producing specific content, campaigning actively for tolerance and reconciliation. In their current programme, Medienhilfe supports minority media in Kosovo, and local and community media in Macedonia (training, networking, production in conflict prevention). Moreover, practical media monitoring is part of their work.

The Swiss NGO works with the Media Task Force of the Stability Pact and cooperates closely with the International Media Fund, a network that brings together other European media NGOs.

Fondation Hirondelle: Fondation Hirondelle, Lausanne, is specialised in setting up radio programmes in regions of conflict and crisis. Its approach is to provide balanced information to a population in need. Balanced information is seen as a need and as a tool for enabling people to decide on their own issues and to calm tensions. This is to counter the propaganda instruments often used in conflict regions for inciting hatred, creating intolerance and manipulating people. Therefore, the core activity focuses on broadcasting neutral, non-partisan information and credible news.

Cimera

Cimera is a Geneva-based NGO, founded in 1999, working in Central Asia, the Caucasus region and the Balkans. The organisation focuses on civil society, media development, research and analysis. Cimera stresses that its strength lies in their unique combination of projects in media development, cooperation between journalists and politicians, support for civil society development and in-depth analysis and research of the socio-political changes. In their view, media often fail to be an organ for public information and debate in the Balkans and the post-soviet countries. Training and institutional development should raise professional standards and contribute to conflict prevention. Central ongoing projects are:

— Central Asia Media Project,
— Caucasus Media Institute,
— Central Asia Research Network (Media in Kyrgyzstan),
— Media development in Georgia and Armenia.

Others

There are many other important implementers, for example: IREX and Internewsor professional associations such as the International Federation of Journalists, the World Association of Newspapers (WAN), the European

Centre for Journalists (ECJ), also media freedom NGOs, like Reporters Sans Frontiers.

Use of Media for Conflict Prevention

History has shown that the media can incite people toward violence. Hitler used the media to create an entire worldview of hatred for Jews, homosexuals, and other minority groups. Rwanda's radio RTLM urged listeners to pick up machetes and take to the streets to kill what they called 'the cockroaches.' Broadcasters in the Balkans polarized local communities to the point where violence became an acceptable tool for addressing grievances. The media's impact on the escalation of conflict is more widely recognized than the media's impact on peacebuilding.

Yet it is not uncommon to hear experts pronounce that the media's impact on peacebuilding must be significant given its powerful impact on conflict. However, this simple relationship must not be taken for granted and should be critically examined in order to most effectively use the media for conflict prevention and peacebuilding. There are ways the media can assist peacebuilding.

Media's Orientation Toward Conflict

The media shape what we see and hear about conflict. The perspectives of those who run the media shape stories that are covered. Journalists have opinions and beliefs based on their experiences. Media owners have economic interests; they want to sell their stories and programs to a public who will buy their newspapers or watch their programs. Increasing corporate control over media in some countries also plays a role in controlling the types of stories that get covered and the way stories get framed.

Media owners and professionals decide what they think the public or some target audience wants to see and hear. A common journalist principle is this: "If it bleeds, it leads." That means violent conflict will be headline news, not news of cross-cultural dialogue and understanding. The media mostly covers conflict, not peacebuilding. This tendency to cover conflict and violence distorts reality and leads many people to think that conflict is pervasive and peace is abnormal.

Several studies confirm that the impact of the media on conflict is greater than the impact of the media on conflict prevention and peacebuilding. Peace journalism scholar Gadi Wolfsfeld notes there is a "fundamental contradiction between the nature of a peace process and news values, the media often play a destructive role in attempts at making peace." Those who run the media tend to favor four values: immediacy, drama, simplicity and ethnocentrism. These values make it difficult to use the media for peace. The chart below, adapted from Wolfsfeld's work, illustrates the tendency for these values to favor violence rather than peace.The media use the four values identified in the chart to decide what to cover as news, and what makes for entertainment. While many media professionals hold these values, they are likely to be in direct relation to the values of the public at large. The media are, in fact, running a business and as such, need to create a 'product' that will sell to customers who share these values.

It is important for conflict prevention and peacebuilding practitioners to understand these values and the dynamics of media decision-making on covering 'peace' news and entertainment. However, it does not preclude peace practitioners from utilizing the media to promote their own values.

Indeed, the media can play very positive roles in conflict prevention and peacebuilding.

Functions of the Media In Conflict Prevention

The media play a wide range of roles in our lives. Some of these roles are constructive and some are destructive. Recognizing the diversity within media professionals is a first step in critically analyzing how best to use the media to support conflict prevention and peacebuilding.

Media as Information Provider and Interpreter

The media provide people with important information about their environment and respond to more imminent problems. At least in part, people make decisions about whether to dress for warm or cold, choose political leaders to vote for in elections, and judge other groups in society based on the media.The media interpret events beyond our physical realm and help us make sense of them. With the improvement of technologies and the advancement of new media such as the internet, media plays an increasingly more prominent role in our daily communication and entertainment. For example, the Otpor Movement, developed in 1998 by Serbian students, responded to new restrictions on academic and media freedom with a highly unconventional movement called Otpor ('resistance' in Serbian). Otpor developed their own grassroots media campaign to provide information and inspiration to all who resisted the Milosevic government.

Media as Watchdog

The media sometimes acts as a third party 'watchdog' who provide feedback to the public on local problems. Media can bring hidden stories out into the public. Investigative reports can surface public problems. For example, a US journalist uncovered and exposed a veteran's hospital that was dilapidated, rat-infested, and uncaring. This highlighted a problem of how US soldiers are treated before and after their time in the US military.

In Sierra Leone, a video depicting the serious impacts and extent of sexual violence has instigated discussion on the impact of the civil war in that country. The film, titled *Operation Fine Girl: Rape Used as a Weapon of War in Sierra,* was produced by human rights activists with the international non-governmental organization WITNESS. The film demonstrates how media productions can play an important complementary role alongside other post conflict reconciliation processes to promote awareness of critical social issues and bring them into the public arena so they can be addressed.

Media as Gatekeeper

The media can also act as a gatekeeper who sets agendas, filters issues and tries to maintain a balance of views. Media like to portray themselves as 'balanced and fair,' even when they privately seek to promote a particular ideological set of ideas and limit the public's exposure to a wide array of information. In 2006, a cartoonist in Denmark created international conflict with his message about Islam. The global tensions prompted extensive analysis on how and when media professionals should act as a gatekeeper to prevent certain expressions that could be deemed humiliating or offensive to some groups.

Media as Policymaker

The media has influence on policymakers, particularly as they think about how to prevent and respond to violent conflict. The media is also a tool of policymakers to get across their message. Some theorists even claim that CNN has taken over policymaking - at least in humanitarian disaster situations. Images on CNN of genocide, famine, and violence force policymakers to intervene militarily to stop death, even if they do not think it is in the best interest of their country to adopt this policy. In Bosnia, for example, the media played a very important role in motivating the public to press their policymakers to intervene to stop the aggression.

Media as Diplomat

Sometimes the media is used to cover diplomatic initiatives and send messages back and forth between sides of a conflict. While policymakers usually prefer secret negotiations, sometimes there are no direct channels of communication. If one side wants to test reactions to a negotiation proposal, they may send signals and messages to other groups through the media. At times, the news media will invite leaders of opposing groups or nations onto a TV or radio program to talk with each other. The media may help to create bridges among enemies and build confidence needed to open negotiations. For example, an American television show *Nightline* regularly invites two or more people from different sides of a public policy issue to be on the show and dialogue with each other. The host, Ted Koppel, makes a point of trying to find common ground between the two sides.

Media as Peace Promotor

Media events can be used at the beginning of negotiations to build confidence, facilitate negotiations or break diplomatic deadlocks to create a climate conducive to negotiation.

Media events such as press releases, rock concerts, or radio programs can celebrate peace agreements and negotiations. The media events may help to promote and mobilize public support for agreements. For example, in Burundi, Studio Ijambo is attempting to harness the power of radio for constructive purposes. Beginning in 1995, Search for Common Ground set up Studio Ijambo with a team of twenty Hutu and Tutsi journalists to promote dialogue, peace, and reconciliation. Studio Ijambo produces approximately one hundred radio programs per month to create a steady campaign to promote peace.

Media as Bridge Builder

The media can promote positive relationships between groups, particularly in conflicts over national, ethnic, religious identity. The media can lessen polarization between groups in the following ways:

- € *Showing the other in a similar light to self.* Iraqi news media that emphasize how both Shia and Sunni suffer from violence help build a bridge of common empathy.
- € *Depicting people with the same types of problems.* For example, an HBO documentary featured Palestinian and Israeli mothers who share the same grief, both losing children to violence victimized by the conflict.
- € *Sharing similar interests and positions.* For example, a TV show known as 'Heroes from Rwanda' featured stories about people who saved members of the opposite ethnic group from the killings, while often risking their own lives.
- € *Condemning violence.* For example, the Republicans and the Unionists in Omagh, Northern Ireland jointly renounced violent attacks in all newspapers and media in August 1998.

Seeing the common ground between one's own group and another group of people builds empathy. Such thinking leads toward depolarizing and normalizing relations between the groups in conflict.

Effective use of the media to prevent conflict and build peace requires a careful study of the lessons of social marketing to prepare for effective use of the media.

Transformative Goals Of Conflict Prevention And Peacebuilding

The world of media works as a business. People 'buy' their news, entertainment, and any information that they want to receive through a media channel. The field of social marketing blends the vast knowledge of how to use the media to sell a commercial product toward the goal of social movements wanting to sell an idea or a new behavior.

Social marketing campaigns have used the media to sell ideas as products. For example, to community development and health workers, breastfeeding is an idea and a new behavior -a product - to sell. For environmentalists, getting people to stop littering is a behavior - a product - to sell. Groups use the media to sell their ideas, or to get people to adopt a new behavior or stop a former way of behaving.

The field of conflict prevention and peacebuilding has done little to lay out our specific products within a marketing framework. Usually, discussions of using the media aim for some general goal to 'promote peace.' Peace itself is not really a product. It is an idea, but does not necessarily suggest automatically some new specific behavior that the public should adopt. The first step in assessing the wisdom of using the media for conflict prevention and peacebuilding in a region is to determine the specific goals of local conflict prevention and peacebuilding experts that can be 'packaged' as tangible and realistic products to sell.

In general, conflict prevention and peacebuilding programs aim to change attitudes and behaviors away from violence and toward peace. Conflict prevention and peacebuilding respond to violence of all kinds -direct forms of armed violence and structural forms of violence that discriminate against certain ethnic, religious, gender, or economic class groups. A wide range of programs and projects aim to build relationships across the lines of conflict - building a foundation for open communication.

Violence polarizes people - pitting some groups against other groups of people. Peacebuilding seeks to build a bridge between groups of people - de-polarizing people's attitudes and behaviors toward each other. As illustrated in the diagram below, all conflict prevention and peacebuilding aim to be part of this change process.

The goal of conflict prevention and peacebuilding, in general, is to move from polarization to positive relationships. Specific conflict prevention and peacebuilding programs and projects hold more specific goals.

The new behavior you want people to adopt is the 'product' in a social marketing campaign. The new behavior needs to be something that is attractive to and in the interest of the consumer in the target audience. If people do not feel they have a problem or that their situation could be improved, they are unlikely to adopt a new product.

For example, in a peacebuilding project encouraging women in a community to join a women's dialogue group, the 'product' is the dialogue group. A marketing campaign to encourage women to join the dialogue group needs to think about how the product meets the interests of women in that community. Is the product attractive? Is it in women's interests? Media could be used to attract specific target groups to join a dialogue program. Like selling a product, the media would sell the idea of joining the dialogue by highlighting the benefits of joining the dialogue and possibly the costs or risks of not joining in a dialogue.

Conflict prevention and peacebuilding practitioners can best utilize the media if they are clear about their goal (their product) and also know who, specifically, they want to communicate to through the media. Social marketing is never aimed at the 'general public.'A sophisticated and strategic use of the media is more focused on particular target and segment audiences.

For example, if the goal of a social marketing campaign is to stop littering, first research needs to be done to determine who is littering the most. In many cultures, young men are the chief culprits. In this case, young men are the 'target audience.' Successful media campaigns aimed at stopping littering use specific messages like 'littering isn't cool' and target magazines, radio programs and billboards seen by young men.If a peacebuilding organization wants to promote cross-cultural dialogue between ethnic groups, they should think about who, in particular, they would like to join the dialogue. The media can be used successfully only when peacebuilding organizations have done the hard work to narrow down their goals and target audiences. Knowing the specific goals and the audiences required to meet their goal enables peacebuilding professionals to be more sophisticated in their choice of when and where to use the media.

The media can help achieve goals in conflict prevention and peacebuilding when paired with approaches or strategies. The media is not appropriate for all peacebuilding efforts however. Highly-sensitive negotiations, for example, are often best kept quiet without the pressure brought by media seeking to highlight areas of conflict rather than serve to foster a focus on common ground, a problem-solving orientation, and hopefulness required for diplomacy.

Examples of Specific Goals in Conflict Prevention & Peacebuilding Programs

- € A Peacekeeping Mission might aim to improve the relationship between international peacekeepers and local host communities.
- € A Dialogue Project might aim to include key leaders in a community in a dialogue.
- € A Trauma Healing Project might aim to educate a certain number of people in skills for trauma awareness and resilience.
- € A Restorative Justice Project might aim to persuade communities to reintegrate former child soldiers.
- € A Peace Process might aim to encourage participation in and acceptance of a national peace agreement.
- € Peacebuilding products can include physical products (building a

mediation center); services (using a mediation service, taking a peacebuilding training course, or joining a dialogue group); practices (talking to their neighbors of a different religion); or more intangible ideas like creating a culture of peace.

How Does Change Happen?

As the goals illustrate, conflict prevention and peacebuilding aim to invoke several types of changes:

€ *Cognitive Changes.* The ways people think about conflict and other groups of people

€ *Attitudinal Changes.* The attitudes people hold toward each other

€ *Behavioral Changes.* The ways people act with each other

Classic theories of change tell us that people change through compulsion, manipulation, persuasion or a combination of these forces. People are forced or feel *compulsion* to change when threatened with negative impacts such as violence if they do not change. People are *manipulated* to change when they are misled to think that change is good for them. People are *persuaded* to change when they are fully convinced and voluntarily decide to change. Persuasion includes talking, teaching, and media dissemination of new ideas.

Since peacebuilding centers on values of empowerment and self-determination, clearly most peacebuilding efforts aim to persuade rather than force or manipulate people to change. It has been shown that when people's cognition, attitudes, or behaviors change by their own choice, as a result of persuasion, the changes are more likely to be long lasting than if the changes were brought about by force or manipulation.

A growing number of studies have begun constructing the strategy and conditions for positive use of media in conflict prevention and peacebuilding. Those studies recognize the limitations of media effects on people as they have been described in the literature. Some of those conclusions have helped us realize the power and the limitations of media impact on people and the society:

1. The most obvious effect of media is in its ability to increase *cognitive knowledge* by supplying people with information. The media help to set the public agenda and frame the scope of public discussion by providing and limiting the range of ideas from which we can choose.
2. Some well-crafted messages and media formats have been effective

in *modifying and altering attitudes*. The media can prompt us to like or dislike an idea, attitude or behavior.

3. The media *rarely directly affects behaviors*. The media does not work like a hypodermic needle, where something can be injected into the body to make people behave in a desired way. It is unlikely that showing something on TV will propel people to behave in a new way. The media's impact on behavior is more complex and more likely to work on attitudes and opinions that shape behaviors rather than directly affecting people's actions or behaviors.

Because of this important influence, the media are often expected to help further the impact of social movements. In the 1970s and 1980s, the development community incorporated media programs in their work across the world. Practitioners utilized media to assist with some of the most acute issues affecting development - AIDS prevention, poverty elimination, population control, and agricultural development. In addition to the straightforward dissemination of information - media can simply saturate the environment with information in support of a development agency's cause. Development organizations soon started exploring other media formats and techniques in order to increase the effectiveness of its messages. In addition to awareness raising projects through broadcasting and print publications, development agencies also employed entertainment programming and socially oriented marketing through advertisements.

Some peacebuilding professionals have built upon the success of development agencies by employing media in their work. The United Nations uses media to assist with its peacekeeping missions, the UN High Commission on Refugees uses media to mitigate the problems facing refugees in conflict. The Organization for Security Cooperation in Europe (OSCE) uses media to disseminate information on peace agreements and involve people in the electoral process. Non-governmental organizations (NGOs) like Search for Common Ground (SFCG), Foundation Hirondelle, and IMPACS developed their own media productions to address the fundamentals of conflict prevention and peacebuilding. Many other civil society agencies and organization that are not producing their own media programming are organizing their work in such a way so that it can be covered by existing media. It is widely expected that civil society organizations will seek media coverage. It is important to remain optimistic about using media in conflict prevention and peacebuilding while at the same time remaining grounded in the theoretical evidence from the literature about realistic media abilities. New studies began to outline the initial arguments about media's ability to assist the goals of peacebuilding.

Stages pf Change

Another attempt to answer how media can impact peace is offered through the prism of behavioral change theoretical models. Over the last half of the previous century, social scientists described the impact of communication on human behavior. Though they come from different scientific disciplines (e. g. psychology, sociology etc.) they all agree in their description of the model as a process of consecutive steps. All the models of behavioral change agree on the multiple stages necessary for sustainable change to occur.

The earliest attempt to explain behavioral change established a hierarchy of the process: initial *cognition* is followed by *affective response* (like or dislike) and ends with a new behavior or *action.*

Other theorists claim this process is a bit more complicated. They say that first people gain *knowledge* and become aware of some new idea - such as peacebuilding. Then they may or may not become *persuaded* to believe that peacebuilding is a good idea or that it works. Then they *decide* whether they support peacebuilding, as a concept. If they do support it, they may *implement* that support by voting for a politician who promotes peacebuilding values or they may implement their support by donating to peacebuilding organizations. Finally, people revisit their decision to support peacebuilding and *confirm* their belief in its value.

Knowledge Persuasion Decision Implementation Confirmation

Changed behavior is the result of multiple sets of changes in understanding and attitudes toward some new idea. What has been well established in the last 80 years of research the effects of media is that while the direct impact of the media on people's behavior is uncertain, some direct links between the ability of media to sufficiently supply the information and attitudes have been confirmed. Unfortunately, these two kinds of impacts are represented primarily in the first two stages of the behavioral change models. Effects theory supplies the evidence of media's impact mainly on cognition and attitudes.If these stages of behavioral change were generally accepted, the following model of action would need to be considered for using media in conflict prevention and peacebuilding.

The impact of the media decreases as we move from cognition to behavioral change. This is the point when the information has been acquired, the attitude toward it has been established and the audience is ready to make a decision and implement it. Behavioral change is more influenced by environmental factors, such as current events, the escalation of conflict, or the rise of a new leader. Different variables impact the decision to make a behavior change and its implementation, and some act as constraints that can prevent significant positive media effects. For example, a new incidence of violent conflict often drives the audience toward decisions that are not always in accordance with their cognitive value systems. In a typical 'fight, flight, or freeze' reaction to violence, the emotional core of the brain takes over and people revertto acting in automatic or instinctual ways for self-preservation, as detailed further later in this paper. Often, the impact of immediate violence may have a stronger impact on people's behavior than media messages may ever hope to achieve.

Cognitive Change: The Role of Information Programming

The initial stage of behavioral change (knowledge, pre-contemplation/ contemplation, cognition) deals with the supply of information supporting the desired change. A change of behavior at the initial level is instigated. The process of positive change toward peace begins when a new piece of information is made available, safely transferred and acquired by the targeted audience. This change simply cannot occur if peace-oriented information cannot find a way to the audience. In other words, the most persuasive and the best designed media content will remain ineffective if the audience does not have a chance to be exposed to it.

Journalism efficiently supplies information to wide audiences. Therefore, impacting the production of news and journalists' sphere of influence is an important asset to peacebuilding practitioners. The impact of journalism on peace and the responsibility of journalists in conflict prevention and peacebuilding have been passionately debated in the last decade. Two schools of thought have emerged in response to the role of journalism in conflict: standard professional journalism and peace (conflict sensitive) journalism.

On one side is the group of professional journalism proponents who suggest that the news media inherently facilitate conditions that support a peaceful society. To a large degree, professional and ethical journalism, if operated within democratic discourse, contributes to a free exchange of information, informs and educates citizens, thus enabling them to become better equipped with knowledge and participate in the political process. Consequently, citizens under those conditions are in the best position to contribute toward conflict prevention and peacebuilding.

Thus, professional journalists help the peace process by simply being there to facilitate the dialogue between the parties, citizens and the government. One of the best examples of the influence by professional journalists during a peace process is the case of the press in Northern Ireland. Since good journalism has a long history and a strong position in this society, journalists were instrumental in facilitating dialogue between the adversaries. This was done indirectly by releasing political statements and messages through the media, which were received by the other side. Such practices called 'megaphone diplomacy' enable the media to strengthen the dialogue (knowingly and unknowingly) and still maintain professional integrity. Amplifying the voice of different stakeholders in a conflict in a way that fosters analysis of both differences and common ground is an everyday routine of professional journalism.

On the other hand, some journalists believe that standard journalistic practices are not sufficient when news production occurs during conflict. In the mid-nineties, BBC journalist Martin Bell came forth with a warning that the well-intentioned BBC recipe for impartiality and objectivity loses meaning in the circumstances of war. Disappointed with reports emerging from then-besieged Sarajevo which gave the same air-time to both victim and the aggressor, Bell renounced the ideal of absolute objectivity and proposed a counter-thesis of journalism of attachment, or engaged journalism.

At the same Johan Galtung coined the idea of 'peace journalism' which advocates for conflict transformation through constructive discourse. In peace journalism, the only problem is not people. Rather the problem is that people are using violence to address conflicts. Journalism begins then, with understanding different group's objectives and needs within their cultural and historic context. Instead of a careful recitation of losses and damage caused or experienced by each side, peace journalism focuses on shared experiences of suffering. This kind of journalism is openly inclined to peace discourse, and cannot be achieved through the ordinary distribution of information. It requires a proactive approach to the constructs of reporting, and openly admits a bias towards peaceful ways of addressing conflict.

This proactive dissemination of information often requires a delicate information balance. Blatant and overzealous imposition of information may cause an unwanted opposite reaction. The audience does not want to be under the impression that they are being pushed to make a decision without their own input.

This is why the memo leaked by Tom Kelly in 1998 to the British press regarding the McCann Erickson promotion of the Northern Irish peace agreement warns that a blatant push for a certain outcome may not bring positive results:

> While any overt manipulation could be counterproductive, a carefully coordinated timetable of statements from key people will be helpful in giving our message credibility with those they represent. It has the added benefit of providing a fresh face for that message, and ensuring that it is not only government which is seen to be selling the process.

Attitudinal Change: The role of Entertainment Programming and Advertising

Once information is acquired, an audience tends to position itself toward the message. An audience contemplates the value of the message and immediately formulates a positive or a negative response to it. The audience can either be persuaded or remain unconvinced.

Developing a positive relationship with a former enemy due to new knowledge or experience can be accomplished through creation or re-creation of positive attitudes toward a group of people. The media can contribute toward creating positive attitudes. A number of brand new products and service are introduced each year and the process of positive attitude building is carried out successfully through the media in front of our eyes. Marketing and advertising represent an entire industry that specializes in creating attitudes. In campaigning and advertising, the messages are designed to seek out the audience. Campaigns anticipate audience activities and aim to intercept them to deliver the message.

This is where the billboards, posters, leaflets, and also audio, video and print advertisements are used to gain maximum impact. Campaigns that used a combination of these resources have been conducted in peace processes in Ireland, Macedonia, Bosnia and the Great Lakes region of

Africa. For example, social marketing advertising through the media made a significant impact on the success of a peace agreement in Northern Ireland.

Entertainment programming has been known to have the highest appeal to the widest number of audiences. For this reason, in many cases the attractive mass appeal format of radio drama or soap-operas is used to deliver a message about conflict prevention and peacebuilding. Other appealing formats such as music, theater and entertainment in information programming were found to be successful. Search for Common Ground (SFCG) used popular music in Angola and Macedonia, and street theater in Liberia and Macedonia. A music project from Angola successfully exploited the association of the message with popular public personalities, when the most popular pop stars performed the peace song 'A Paz E Que O Povo Chama' (People Are Calling for Peace).

Behavioral Change:The cumulative impact of media and other social institutions

Peace media efforts are most effective if they are integrated into more than a few isolated projects. The impact of conflict is so pervasive that it would be unrealistic to expect a positive impact from a single radio or television project. Peace messages need to be incorporated into the majority of media and would benefit from support by a wider public structure and social institutions.

There is no doubt that conflict prevention and peacebuilding efforts ought to be concerned with media techniques and practices through journalism, entertainment and social marketing advertisements. On the other hand, the success of such media programs depends primarily on the readiness of institutions to end conflict policies. Media do not have the ability to execute the peacebuilding effort on their own. Legal, political, economic and other social institutions must assist in transforming the conflict. In the absence of an integrated effort, media cannot manage structural and cultural violence. The media must be understood as an integral and important segment of peace development. Despite the ability to shape attitudes and opinions in favor of peace, media institutions remain only a segment of a conflict society. The transformation of violent conflict requires an integrated plan of action.

Ideally, the contribution of media to peace development ought to be considered during peace negotiations between the antagonists. Unfortunately, no recent peace agreements (i.e. the Dayton Peace Agreement that ended the Bosnian conflict, the Oslo Peace Agreement between Israelis and Palestinians nor the Good Friday Peace Agreement in Northern Ireland) even mention media as possible contributors to peacebuilding. While the agreements include lengthy descriptions on the transformation of most social institutions, media development is omitted. While media can contribute toward the formation of attitudes, opinions and increased knowledge and awareness by supplying information, the limiting factor is the uncertainty that this positive impact will transfer to behavior or result in action. For this to happen, a number of other variables need to be aligned with the media effort. Because action or behavior is dependent on many outside variables and because these variables contribute to the end result as much as any form of communication initiative, only the true integration of all media genres into a greater peacebuilding strategy can insure a significant move toward a peaceful society. In today's media environment it is not enough to employ just a few uncoordinated messages. The following example from Bosnia explains the need for a cumulative impact and organization of media:

> "During the spring and summer of 1996, the main international powers that were behind the Dayton peace agreement decided to set up an alternative system to the national television stations which was going to be different, much better, more democratic and cover the entire country. This was supposed to erase the negative influence of the national television stations. This is how OBN and radio FERN came into being. This is an excellent idea. What was wrong was that this was the single effort. One isolated project never had a chance to combat the influence of powerful national stations."

Why Do People Change?

Behavioral change is most likely to be achieved through an congruence between the repetition of a peace message via different media channels and an environment which creates space for people to thoughtfully consider change. Scholars claim that people change as a result of a combination of forces. Harvard University scholar Howard Gardner, for example, claims there are seven factors in why people change their minds, attitudes, and behaviors.

1. *Logic and Reason.* People change their minds because they are convinced that it makes sense - there is a logic to the change. For example, many conflict prevention scholars lay out the logic of

preventing violent conflict because it costs less to prevent violence than it does to clean up after violence.

2. *Research.* People change their minds because they are convinced by research that the something is effective. For example, the current drive to prove that conflict prevention and peacebuilding 'work' involves careful quantitative and qualitative research on specific projects, comparing towns where there are peace programs to towns without peace projects to see if the 'peace intervention' has made a difference.
3. *Resonance.* People change their minds because a new idea, attitude or behavior intuitively 'feels right' to them or because they admire someone who persuades them to change. For example, the rock singer Bono has convinced many people that alleviating poverty in Africa is important because people resonate with his charismatic arguments for caring about people.
4. *Representations.* People change their minds when they see a new idea, attitude or behavior represented in multiple ways or contexts. For example, anti-smoking campaigns use many different commercials on radio, T V, and billboards and use different images and words to represent their message aimed at stopping smoking.
5. *Resources and Rewards.* People change their minds when they believe they will be rewarded for adopting a new idea, attitude or behavior. For example, some business leaders have tried to convince others that 'peace is profitable.' Other economists note that key leaders often decide to support war or violence because it is in their economic interest to do so.
6. *Real World Events.* People change their minds because they are influenced by an event that happens, such as an attack, economic depression, hurricane, or an era of peace. For example, the Tsunami that hit Asian countries significantly changed the conflict in Indonesia, creating a context where a peace settlement became possible. In Sri Lanka, however, the Tsunami had an opposite effect as groups accused aid groups of favoring some groups over others.
7. *Resistances.* People decide NOT to change their minds when the resistances to change are stronger than the forces for change. Biologists say that ways of thinking may become physically engraved in the actual texture of the brain. Changing deeply engrained patterns of thinking

may pose too great of a resistance to logic, research, resonance, representations, rewards or real world events. For example, many white Americans changed their mind about African Americans during the U.S. Civil Rights Movement. But those groups with deeply engrained racism such as the Ku Klux Klan, continue to function today. Their patterns of thinking about race are so central to everything else they believe that it is much more difficult to change their minds with real world events portrayed in the media, reason, research or other persuasive methods by charismatic leaders like Martin Luther King, Jr.

Most of the time people change their minds gradually, not in one specific moment or with one revelation. Most people are not aware that they are changing their minds, attitudes or behaviors, so surveys asking people direct questions about whether they have changed their minds are rarely effective. People change their minds usually when the first six elements listed above are fully present and when resistances to change are identified and successfully addressed.

These elements of change are morally-neutral; meaning that people with bad intentions of inciting violence can equally use these principles to that effect. Those working for peace should be well aware, in fact, that the media is more likely to contribute to violence than peace.

People make decisions about whether to adopt some new idea, attitude, or behavior - the 'peacebuilding product' - based on considerations of both benefits and costs. People will ask "What will I get out of this?" And "What is in it for me?" And they will ask "How much will this cost me financially, emotionally, and physically? What will I have to give up to do this new behavior?" Peacebuilding professionals need to think about carefully framing the benefits and addressing the costs of the new behavior that supports conflict prevention and peacebuilding.

For example, if a peacebuilding organization is advertising on billboards and radio programs to ask people to join a dialogue, people in the community would want to know how they might benefit from joining a dialogue group. Will they meet new people, understand the conflict better, develop a solution to their community's problems? And social marketers of a dialogue program will have to think about the costs of joining the dialogue to different segments of the population. Will women need to leave their children at home to attend the dialogue or will there be childcare? Will their husbands be angry? Will they miss time at their workplace?

Strategic use of the media requires careful consideration to all the possible obstacles to change.

Impact of Trauma and Conflict On Cognition

Conflicts are complex - it is usually not possible to narrow down their causes to a few specific triggers. Conflicts are also dynamic, they constantly change. It is not uncommon to see a seemingly minor and isolated event sway a conflict towards violence. In conflict environments, even when the best media projects succeed and civil society performs to the maximum, violence can be hard to avoid. In Howard Gardner's words, the 'resistance' is too great. Efforts to use the media to promote peace in the midst of violent conflict are difficult for a number of reasons.

Conflict and trauma impact the brain and how people think. Understanding the basics of brain biology allows for greater understanding of how and why some forms of communication - including the media - are able to 'penetrate' the brain better than others.

There are three parts to our brains:

€ *The Neocortex*: our rational, thinking brain.

€ *The Limbic System*: the 'emotional brain' and the 'first alert' system that responds to fear.

€ *The Brain Stem*: our older, instinctual brain which controls automatic reactions such as fight, flight or freeze responses.

The neocortex responds well to reason, logic, research, calculating rewards of adopting new behaviors and processing real world events; the facts of peacebuilding. But the limbic system and the brain stem are responsible for how people respond emotionally and intuitively.

In the midst of conflict, people are often responding from their 'emotional brain' rather than the 'rational' brain. Facts and figures - the logic of peacebuilding -may not make an impact. But emotional stories of courageous people undertaking dramatic actions for peace, told through the arts and media, can sometimes make a profound impact on people.

Media audiences are primarily affected by powerful stories told in first-person narratives by people directly involved. Simple stories work the best, since large audiences are usually very diverse and little can be assumed about their shared knowledge or understanding. Good journalism starts out with a personal story, and then links this to some broader social trend. People begin listening and become emotionally engaged in a story first. Then they begin to understand the broader ideas related to the story.

Communication researchers estimate that between sixty to ninety percent of communicated meaning comes from nonverbal cues. People gather information using all the body's senses and communicate both verbally and nonverbally. Words are limiting. When humans feel strong emotions, it is often difficult to express the depth of feeling verbally. When life's events are confusing, complex, and ambiguous, it is challenging to articulate events and relationships through verbal language.

Movies, TV and radio shows and commercials use background music and special lighting to evoke particular emotions. Billboards, films and TV use powerful images to convey important messages. Words are often kept to a minimum - allowing people to use the sights and sounds to make sense of the message.

The cerebral cortex spends the whole day filtering out information - we are all overloaded with facts, figures, and boring details. The doorway to the brain is through the limbic system and brain stem. If we can arouse interest in peace through telling stories that evoke an emotional response, then we are more likely to be able to penetrate through the filters in the neocortex and be heard and understood in a way that transforms the way people think about conflict, and their own empowerment to behave differently in the midst of conflict. The key to communicating about peacebuilding is how we can arouse these other two parts of our brain so that we can gain interest in our work from the third, rational part, the cerebral cortex.

Media and Creating Critical Mass for Peace

Al Qaeda attacks around the world are carried out by small numbers of people, yet they have had a large impact on world events. Similarly, the last fifty years of conflict in Northern Ireland have largely been carried out by a few thousand people on both sides. Consequently, while violence can be caused by a few people, the presence of *peace requires the cooperation of many; a critical mass* of people, groups, institutions, and the media. In other words, it is far easier for a few people to burn down a house. It takes many people to build a house, just as it takes many to build peace. Building a culture of peace requires mass changes in the way people think, their attitudes, and their behaviors.

Malcolm Gladwell's book *The Tipping Point* describes the dynamics of reaching critical mass in each of these areas. Gladwell claims ideas, behaviors and new products move through a population in a similar way to viruses or contagious diseases. A cultural 'meme' is an idea that acts like a virus. *Tipping points* are the levels of critical mass where an idea, attitude or behavior catches on among the public and becomes dominant.

Malcolm claims new ideas, attitudes or behaviors come about when three factors exist. First, 'connectors' or people who interact in many different social networks need to adopt this new idea, attitude or behavior. Second, 'mavens' or information experts need to buy into a new idea, attitude or behavior. Third, charismatic sales agents with powerful negotiation skills need to engage in persuading people to take on a new idea, attitude or behavior.

What does all this have to do with conflict prevention and peacebuilding? The *Reflecting on Peace Project* compared four different approaches for bringing about social change.

1. The 'more-people' approach aims to engage large numbers of people to address an issue. Broad involvement of 'the people' is seen as necessary to change.
2. The 'key-people' approach involves certain important leaders or groups of people who are seen as opinion leaders and able to effect change in a situation.
3. The 'individual-level' approach seeks to change the attitudes, values, perceptions, or circumstances of individuals as an important first step to bringing about real and lasting social change.
4. The 'structural-level' approach more directly aims to change socio-political or institutional structures.

These researchers found that projects focusing on change at the individual level, such as dialogue programs, without translating into action at the structural level, such as policy advocacy, have little discernible effect on addressing the broader political or social issues they seek to change. In addition, the study found that approaches concentrating on including more people, but not necessarily key leaders or groups, did not constructively address social issues. Conversely, the research found that strategies focusing only on key people without including others were equally ineffective. If programs focus on one strategy only, they are unlikely to create social change. Programs that intentionally link individual with structural efforts, or include key people as well as more people are most likely to bring about change.

Given the complex ways these four types of approaches interact to bring about real change, it is easy to see that the media has an important role in reaching many people with a message of structural change. Including the media as one component along with a combination of different forms of peacebuilding strategies seems the most likely path to change.

Some types of peacebuilding projects aim to impact small numbers of people. Mediation and negotiation processes typically involve between 2-20 people to work on specific issues of mutual concern, sometimes to achieve jointly-defined development projects like school or health centers. Dialogue and training workshops often include 20-50 people at a time. These are important forms of peacebuilding, yet many observers note that it is difficult to see a real impact when such small numbers of people are experiencing a transformation in the ways they think and behave in a conflict. In Israel-Palestine, for example, dialogue programs have endured repeated criticism for failing to translate into structural reforms.

However, the amount of behavioral and attitudinal change experienced by people exposed to these forms of peacebuilding projects is likely to be in inverse relation to the number of people reached. For example, a five part dialogue program engaging members of different ethnic groups over a period of weeks or months is likely to make a bigger impact on participants than listening to a one-hour weekly soap opera for five weeks. More research is needed to know if this is true or not, but research on how people learn and change would indicate that processes that more fully involve people experientially (like dialogue) are more likely to make significant changes than the more passive involvement of listening to a radio program.

Bringing about constructive change in a conflict is a challenge. Helping to change people's beliefs, attitudes, and behaviors requires in-depth knowledge about the conditions that enable people to make these changes.

The media's role in contributing to cognitive, attitudinal and behavioral change on a large scale is unique. Conflict prevention and peacebuilding professionals can use the media in harmony with their other programs - if they know when, why, and how to use the media for the most strategic impact in lessoning the polarization between groups. On the other hand, media professionals still have much to learn about why and when their work can contribute to preventing violent conflict and building peace between groups. The media and peace professionals both have their limitations and share an interest in the dynamics of conflict.

Cooperation between agencies, donors, civil society, peacebuilding organizations and media practitioners is essential. There is a need for meetings, seminars and work groups where models and best practices can be shared. Because using media in peacebuilding is a new practice, everyone has a lot to learn from the exchange of experiences. A careful assessment of whether the media is likely to play a positive or negative role in achieving the goals of conflict prevention and peacebuilding requires greater insight into ways the media helps and harms the path toward constructive change. Both peacebuilding and media professionals still have a great deal to learn on this journey.

New Trends in Media and Peacebuilding

There are currently two main trends in the debate of media and peacebuilding: greater attention to media and a stricter examination of media assistance.

First, the issue of media assistance in general and especially in conflict situations is receiving more attention. One sign is that the World Bank has included for the first time a special Media chapter in the World Development Report 2002, with the overall result that free and independent media have a positive effect on other development objectives such as growth and building of democratic institutions.

Another sign is that various international conferences have taken place recently on the issue, one in Paris organised jointly by the World Bank and USAID on the "Global Media Assistance Strategies–role of media in economic and democratic development". Another conference was convened in The Hague, Netherlands, with the topic of "The Role of Media in Conflict Prevention and Peacebuilding". In the former conference, one of the three priority areas for discussion was dedicated to media in conflict situations.

Due to the difficulties in compiling reliable data on the volume of funding for media projects, it cannot be assessed if media assistance in general gets fewer funds or not. On one hand, it seems clear that the Balkans as a region will receive less funding. According to the statements made by interviewees the contributions for media support for this region will be reduced. This is due either to the more democratic development in the region which calls for greater self-reliance–at least this is the view of some donors–or due to donor fatigue with some media outlets.

On the other hand, donor support is to be transferred to other geographical areas (Afghanistan, Central Asia) and, at the moment, the overall result on a global level is not clear. This means that in the media sector of South Eastern Europe there will be more competition among projects, broadcasters and other media for less donor money. As donor support still is the major source of revenue, many newspapers, radio stations and media institutions will face difficulties. This calls for a stricter examination of media projects in order to select the ones for continuous support.

Challenges in Media and Peacebuilding

Considering these recent trends, the media and peacebuilding sector faces the following challenges.

There is a need for quality evaluation of media assistance projects and their impacts, not only urged by the donors but also positively seen by implementers in order to improve ongoing and future media support. However, it is a challenge to conduct professional impact measurement of media projects due to the young state of the field. Only little conceptual work on media's impact has been done, up to now only a few in-depth case studies and evaluations are available.

A review of those studies demonstrates that the sector requires more in-depth research and improved evaluation methodology. Many project reports simply describe quantitative results or outcomes (100 journalists trained, 40 programmes produced) and lack data on audience, as well as qualitative indicators.

It seems necessary to foster impact measurement in strategic projects. This will need more case studies and baseline surveys, as only a few existing projects have implemented activities, which make future impact measuring possible. As one USAID report mentions, baseline surveys *before the project starts* are an indispensable instrument to assess the project's impact. However, this requires additional funds for research and data collection. These efforts could be coordinated within the peacebuilding sector, which actually develops qualitative indicators for impact measurement. As a first step, it seems useful to create indicators for "contribution to peacebuilding" that can be used in questionnaires and interviews. Donors are hopefully ready to spend additional funding and accept additional time for evaluation.

Up to now, only a few efforts had been made to draw lessons from successful media assistance for peacebuilding. There is a need to compile already existing knowledge and to review good and bad practices of different donors and projects. One such review of media activities of inter-governmental organisations in peace operations has been recently published, including the debate and assessment on the legal justifications of both supporting and suppressing certain media activities in a particular conflict situation.

Clarification of Concepts and Approaches

Link to peacebuilding strategy

Often, projects aiming at contributing to peacebuilding require better link or orientation to the overall peacebuilding strategy. They are sometimes targeting only minor issues, not the core problems of the conflict (root and proximate causes). Therefore, a future necessity is to first identify the peacebuilding strategy and then to clarify how the media projects can fit into it. As already mentioned, this needs thorough analysis of the media sector and its problems and opportunities. However, in reality these kind of feasibility studies "are often not conducted at all prior to the launch of a major project and little or no attempt is made by donor governments to conduct a systematic review of a country's media sector", states the Mapping Media Assistance report.

Role of journalists

The actors in the Media and Peacebuilding sector need to *clarify the role they attribute to journalists*. As outlined, this holds consequences for project design in the short-term perspective as well as for the long-term orientation of the media sector. This is equally valid for any additional tasks journalists might or might not take over, for example mediation, facilitation or practical local peacebuilding.

Local and/or International Media?

Most of the actors in the field of media in peace and conflict agree that supporting existing local media is the best way to get access to the population and to foster free and independent media. Nevertheless, if local media do not exist or have not been fully developed in a particular conflict setting, there is a need to identify the alternatives. It can be useful to describe the conditions under which international broadcasters are a "second-best" solution for giving access to non-partisan information for a population in need.

Improving Design and Implementation

Partners selection

The selection of the right partners is a major challenge, especially in countries of conflict. There are no general answers to the crucial questions: Which are the right media to support? Who has the potential of surviving in the long run without donor support? How to decide on partners in a different cultural setting with different models of the role of journalism? How to avoid relying on gatekeepers? It is paramount to have an open exchange on these questions among donors and NGOs to develop common procedures.

However, the analysis and inventory of the media sector, due before the initiation of every major media activity, should at least provide better insight into the local actors and thus help to clarify the larger picture of actors, their interests and goals. From this starting point, it should be easier to create some appropriate selection criteria.

Viability and sustainability

Commercial viability has become a priority for media, as donors aim for sustainability. Up to now, this challenge was met by including training for media business managers and improving marketing skills. This is not enough. Media assistance projects must be integrated, where appropriate, with other development cooperation efforts, like the support for economic recovery– that will hopefully create jobs for journalists and other media professionals which were for example trained through media assistance.

However, it still needs further debate on how far the requirement of commercial viability is indispensable against the background of usually weak economies in post-conflict situations, where media can hardly survive on advertisement revenues alone. Based on the results of this debate, it can be decided, how much subsidies or external institutionalised support is still needed by particular media programmes.

Do no harm

Nevertheless, media projects must be cautious to do no harm. An excessive presence of media NGOs can be counterproductive: Usually high NGO salaries can disrupt the local economy, attract journalists who are otherwise much needed by the local media, or can force promising journalists to leave every week for training in foreign countries. Projects need to avoid this spoiling and hampering of the upcoming local media industry.

References

Bell, Martin. (1998). "The journalism of attachment". In Kieran, M. (ed.) *Media Ethics.* London, UK: Routledge. p. 15-22

Gardner, Howard. (2004). *Changing Minds: The Art and Science of Changing our own and other people's minds*. Massachusetts, USA: Harvard Business School Press.

Gilboa, Eytan. (2002). *Media and Conflict: Framing Issues, Making Policy, Shaping Opinions*. Ardsley, N Y, USA: Transnational Publishers Inc.

Howard, R. Rolt, H. van de Veen, H. Verhoeven. J. (Ed.) (2003). *The Power of the media: A handbook for peacebuilders*. Utrecht, the Netherlands: European Centre for Conflict Prevention.

Loewenberg, Shira and Bent Nørby Bonde (eds.). (2007). *Media in Conflict Prevention and Peace Building Strategies.* Bonn, Germany: DW-Media Services GmbH.

Severin, Werner J. and James W. Tankard. (1991). *Communication theories: Origins, methods, and uses of the mass media.* (3rd ed.). New York, USA: Longman Pub Group.

Wolfsfeld, Gadi. (2004). *Media and the Path to Peace.* New York, USA: Cambridge University Press.

Bibliography

Abercrombie, Nicholas (1996): *Television and Society*. Cambridge: Polity Press

Barnett, C. . Media, democracy and representation: Disembodying the public. In C. Barnett & M. Low (Eds.), *Spaces of Democracy: geographical perspectives on citizenship, participation and representation* (pp. 185–206). London, UK: Sage.

Bell, Martin. (1998). "The journalism of attachment". In Kieran, M. (ed.) *Media Ethics*. London, UK: Routledge. p. 15-22

Beniger, James, (1986). *The Control Revolution: Technological and Economic Origins of the Information Society*, Harvard University Press, Cambridge, Mass. 1986.

Blackman, C. (1998) Convergence between telecommunications and other media: how should regulation adapt? *Telecommunication Policy*, 22:3, 163-170.

Blanchard, Margaret A. (1998). *History of the mass media in the United States: an encyclopedia*. Fitzroy Dearborn.

Bogart, L. . Media and Democracy. In E. E. Dennis & R. W. Snyder (Eds.), *Media & Democracy* (pp. 6-8). USA: Transaction.

Bourgault, L. M., (1995). *Mass Media in Sub-Saharan Africa*, Bloomington, Ind. p. 127.

Carrolll, R, L., et al., (1997). "Consonance in Local Television News Program Content: An Examination of Intermarket Diversity", *Journal of Broadcasting and Electronic Media,* Vol. 41, No. 1, Winter, pp. 132–44.

Centerwall, B.S., (1989). "Exposure to television as a cause of violence," in Comstock G., (ed) *Public Communications as Behavior,* Orlando, FL: Academic Press, Inc.

Cruz, J. & Justin Lewis (1994): *Viewing, Reading, Listening: Audiences and Cultural Reception.* Boulder, CO: Westview

David Grayson. (2007). *Business-Led Corporate Responsibility Coalitions: Learning from the example of Business in the Community*. CSR Initiative of the Kennedy School of Government, Harvard.

EU Commission Green Paper. (2001). *Promoting a European Framework for Corporate Social Responsibility*, COM.

Flew, T. . Democracy, participation and convergent media: case studies in contemporary online news journalism in Australia. *Communication, Politics & Culture,* 42(2), pp. 87-115